MW01093662

Touching the Elephant

Values the World's Religions Share and How They Can Transform Us

Nancy J. Thompson

Nancy J. Thompson

Touching the Elephant

Values the World's Religions Share
and How They Can Transform Us

Edited by Cosimo Giovine
Artwork by Xiaochun Li
Graphic & Cover Design by Mindy Reznik

Zio Apollo Press
San Diego, CA

Touching the Elephant

Zio Apollo Press

Trade paperback edition/September 2019
All rights reserved.
Copyright © 2019 by Nancy J. Thompson
Library of Congress Card Catalog Number: 2019947994
ISBN-10: 1-7331955-0-5
ISBN-13: 978-1-7331955-0-8
Printed in the United States of America.
No part of this book may be reproduced or transmitted in any form
or by any means, electronic or mechanical, including photocopying,
recording, or by any information storage and retrieval system,
without permission in writing from the publisher.

"I believe that what Jesus and Mohammed and Buddha and all the rest said was right. It's just that the translations have gone wrong."

—*John Lennon*

ACKNOWLEDGEMENTS

I'm indebted to many through writing this book. First, my publisher Cosimo Giovine made the book possible. He made valuable suggestions, kept me on task, and asked all the right questions. Writer and publishing expert Retha Powers read the draft, offered important advice, and worked to help me find a home for it. Thank you to the New York Writers Workshop, who helped me perfect the pitch (and pitch it).

I could not have written the book without great teachers. Thank you to Yangsi Rinpoche from Maitripa College and to Maitripa's guests, most especially Dr. John Dunne from Emory University and Dr. Thubten Jinpa from McGill and Stanford; Geshe Kalsang Damdul, with whom I took my vows; Rabbi Howard Cohen from Congregation Shirat Hayam in Massachusetts; Dr. Stephen Carver of George Fox University who also taught Judaic Studies at Portland State University; the late Father Kevin Fogarty from Mount Melleray Abbey in Waterford, Ireland (my deepest regret is that he passed before I could give him the book); Rabbi Michael Cahana from Beth Israel Congregation in Portland, Oregon. Thank you to Congregation Beth El; the various Jehovah's Witnesses in Portland, Oregon who found many hours to talk and debate with me; and those who have engaged in religious conversation with me around the world. Thank you to Huston Smith and Karen Armstrong, whose writing has taught me and made me a better teacher. I bow in thanks to Zen Master Thay, Thich Nhat Hanh and to His Holiness Tenzin Gyatso, the Fourteenth Dalai Lama, for sharing the Dharma: their teaching on compassion sustains and guides me.

To my many religion and spirituality students over the years at NVU-Johnson and Community College of Vermont, thank you all so very much for asking, for thinking, for listening, and for caring. You are my heart.

Thank you to my daughter and son, Xiao Chun and Jeson Li, for believing in me and believing the book would succeed. Thank you to the many other friends and acquaintances who expressed support and pushed me to the finish line in various ways, especially Michael Street, Carolyn Rogers, and Carolyn Caggiano, who all offered important advice for revision. Your belief in the message has sustained me through all the ups and downs.

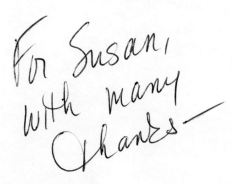

_With love to Xiao Chun and Jeson, who keep me on the path,
and to all those travelling on or seeking a path._

Table of Contents

Introduction

In the beginning of 2017, the Doomsday Clock moved its hands half a minute forward, to two and a half minutes until midnight – global catastrophe – and the Bulletin of the Atomic Scientists stated, "Wise public officials should act immediately, guiding humanity away from the brink. If they do not, wise citizens must step forward and lead the way."

Lately, many people think the world is going crazy. Right wing nationalism, racism, and xenophobia are tipping elections and targeting citizens and non-citizen workers with hate and violence. Syria's war disemboweled the country and created a hemorrhage of refugees with nowhere to go; around the world, they have been turned away because they are Arab and Muslim. The world is once again concerned about the risk of nuclear war; in January 2018, Hawaiians panicked, believing that a nuclear missile was headed their way (it was not), and their fear was justifiable given rhetoric from North Korea's leader, Kim Jong Un, that "a nuclear button is always on my desk" and the United States president's reply that America's nuclear capability is "much bigger and more powerful." Such threats coupled with the possibility of Iran once again ramping up its plutonium enrichment program and the possibility of material falling into the hands of terrorists with desire and capability to make a so-called "dirty bomb" means that to some experts, the threat of nuclear devastation being unleashed today is "greater than it was during the Cold War."[1]

Additionally, if we read or listen to the news and preachers and politicians on the topics of God and religion, we might feel as if *we're* going crazy, and for good reason: we hear that America is a Christian country (which it isn't), but that religion is responsible for all the evils in the world. We read that God loves us, but God hates us. We are told that God and religion are stories made up by people to control other people, but angels guard and protect us. We are taught by some that all religions are equal paths to God, and by others that there is only one true religion.

What should people think? What *do* people think?

First, many people don't believe in God. Atheism is at perhaps a historic high. Some sociologists think that there may be as many as half a *billion* self-identified atheists in the world. Even for those who do profess a belief in God, church membership and denominational identification has been decreasing in many parts of the world.

Some reject anything to do with religion because they see it as superstition in a modern age of reason. Many reject religions because they see them as responsible for much of the violence in the world. Like the religious scholar and writer Karen Armstrong, who debunked that notion comprehensively in her book *Fields of Blood*, I think that view oversimplifies matters. However, students of history see that wars have been fought over religion, and people read that terrorists still continue to commit terrible violence under a banner of religion, and it is common knowledge that various cults have traumatized and killed people or incited them to suicide in the name of their religions. Jim Jones and the People's Temple immediately comes to mind, along with David Koresh at Waco, Marshall Hepplewhite (Do) and the Heaven's Gate cult, and others. Can we see correlations between religion and violence? At least on the surface, yes, even when much of that violence is ultimately political or pathological.

On the other hand, many people *do* believe in God. Many people believe in religion and identify as religious. Religious ideas are ancient. Many religions have perished from the earth, but others have endured all over the world for thousands of years. If religions were utterly without redemption, purely controlling, evil and violent, oppressive and misery-making, why haven't they died out completely, especially as democracy and science and reason have spread? What do they offer people? Why has religion persisted in places that have tried to obliterate it, even when the people who practiced it were persecuted for their beliefs? Further, why haven't reason and science eradicated the social problems – crime, poverty, war, violence?

Let's complicate things even more. How is it possible that people who may not believe in God have strong religious beliefs? That they do is more common than many people might at first realize.

I'm starting with a lot of questions because throughout this book I try to answer them. My goal in writing this book is to bridge two realms: the sacred and the secular. I don't want to convert readers. I am not going to tell readers that they should or must believe in God. I am not going to urge anyone to hurry down to the local church, temple, mosque, or synagogue. Rather, I want to help readers understand an important idea, regardless of whether they believe in God or not. The idea is that the world's diverse religious texts have certain themes and values in common. These themes and values are stressed for practical reasons that matter to us as individuals and societies. The values can mesh to make a beneficial difference in our lives, families, and communities. People do not need to "get religion" to benefit from them.

The philosopher Emile Durkheim, who connected the ideas of society and religion, wrote that religion "has given birth to all that is essential in society" because "the idea of society is the soul of religion."[2] To Durkheim, religion was a tribal affair, one that was not at its heart supernatural. Instead, Durkheim said that religion depends on a separation between the spheres of the sacred and the profane, the profane being our mundane, conventional reality. In our everyday realities, people all have similar basic wants and needs, no matter who they are or where they live. We all need shelter. We all hope to avoid injury. We all want happiness. One of the real benefits that we can gain from looking at where the world's major religions intersect is the realization of what we have in common and what, as Durkheim said, is "essential in society." To do that, we need to become aware of the sacred.

If we think about it, what's most essential in society is that we can live together in harmony. At its heart, that's what society is: orderly community. If we are honest with ourselves, though, we can see that many of our societies today are ill. They are plagued not only by poverty and often preventable illness but with violence of various sorts, such as racial and ethnic violence, youth violence, domestic violence, elder abuse, police violence, and sexual violence, not to mention war, riots, and violence associated with various kinds of criminal and political mischief. The World Health Organization, in fact, calls violence a "global public health problem" and points out that although such violence is pervasive in the world, it can be prevented, and it can be turned around in places where it has already taken root.[3]

Violence correlates in part to social isolation. More and more, we see people who isolate themselves and their families. Some become survivalists who plan for what they believe is the coming apocalypse and who believe they can survive by protecting only themselves, by withdrawing from the world, by learning basic survival skills. To turn society around from self-destruction and other-destruction, however, we must believe we can; we cannot be apathetic. To do so, we must care for more than ourselves.

To care for others, and to care for ourselves, we can and should cultivate eight specific traits that the world's major religions all prize. These traits can create abundant transformative good that can heal our angers and hatreds, build healthier lives, strengthen our families, improve our communities, and even mend the world. They can help us rise to the challenge of the atomic scientists and become those wise citizens who can step forward and lead the way.

Rescuing the World

In the summer of 2018, the world watched helplessly as enormous resources were marshalled in Thailand to rescue twelve school-age boys – the Wild Boar soccer team – and their 25-year old coach. They had been trapped on a ledge in a flooded cave, more than a mile from the cave's entrance, for over a week when searchers found them. Over another week would pass before all were rescued by teams of divers. The rescue was dangerous; one diver died trying to get oxygen to the group.

On social media, two trends became apparent. One was prayers for the group's safety. The other was recriminations. In fact, it was easy for me to imagine how the scene would have played out in America. Parents would have immediately hired lawyers. Civil charges would be filed against the coach for trauma, reckless endangerment, and negligence; just a few months earlier, in May 2018, an appellate court reconsidered a lawsuit against a baseball coach charged with being reckless and negligent just for asking a player to slide[4]. If a coach brought a sports team into a cave in America and got the players trapped, television stations would be broadcasting fury along with fear.

In contrast, in Thailand, parents sent messages of support and forgiveness. Parents waited together at the cave until all the boys were out; as precious as each boy is, all were precious. A woman whose fields were flooded when water was pumped out of the cave opted not to apply for government compensation, even though she is not a wealthy person.

Despite the fears of parents, their values were clear: compassion. Forgiveness. Generosity. Effort: the rescue effort was massive, and some with no stake at all in it did what they could to help, even if it was bringing food or praying. Despite how frantic so many must have felt, order prevailed. In fact, order saved the lives of all thirteen.

In contrast, as I sat up the night before the last five were rescued, I was horrified by a story about an incident in California that happened at the same time as the Thai rescue. A 92-year-old Mexican man, who was in California visiting his family as he has done each summer for years, was beaten with a concrete brick by a group of people who shouted at him to go back to Mexico. He sustained fractures to his face and ribs.

What kinds of values did his assailants have? What made them feel emboldened to do such a thing?

Some would look at that assault and the expressions of hate and violence in the world and dismiss it as "human nature" or with the pronouncement that "God is dead" and this is the proof. I don't believe God is dead, although perhaps God is also not "alive," at least not in any conventional sense. I do believe that we can benefit if we stop arguing about what God is and whether God is and whose idea of God is the "right" idea of God. We can benefit if we stop insisting that people *should* believe in God. We can benefit if we focus instead on the shared spiritual values that shape human society. We can benefit if we will admit that there *are* beliefs and actions that can beneficially bind human society together and work to cultivate them.

We can see examples in the world around us. What makes a place "happy"? Despite what we might think, it's not endless money, rampant materialism, and loads of fame. An article in *National Geographic*'s travel website focused on some of the countries rated as happiest in the U.N.'s *World Happiness Report*. It concluded that "All possess a winning formula of good governance, strong sense of community, respect for fellow citizens, and general high quality of life."[5] Among the countries highlighted in the article, Iceland values integrity; Australia values respect for people's dignity; New Zealand values effort to protect the environment; tolerance and kindness are Dutch values.

I use the word "values," and I want to define it, because the word is too often used in vague ways today (such as the common "family values," which could conceivably mean anything from watching television together to insisting on abstinence to using corporal punishment on children who disobey). In sociology, values are a culture's shared beliefs about what is beneficial/desirable and harmful/undesirable. For example, early Christianity valued martyrdom. Early Judaism valued justice and law. Sometimes values endure, and sometimes they change; Christianity, for example, no longer places such a premium on martyrdom that people are encouraged to seek it.

Today, at least eight values prized by all the world's religions and that have endured in the world's religions help us to live happily together. Our ability to live together in societies has enabled human survival and spread since the earliest appearance of humankind. Without being able to join forces and cooperate, our species most likely would have perished quickly from the earth. Human babies are helpless for years. Threats to babies and adults alike were numerous even after civilization developed, not to mention before. Until they invented weapons, humans had few defenses against predators such as bears and saber tooth tigers. Joining together helped our human ancestors to increase their defenses and to spread risk.

The problem is that humans and their societies are inclined to self-advancement, and humans have proven to be quite willing to sacrifice fellow humans to achieve it. The history of humanity is the history of sacrifice and murder. The oldest known human sacrifice in Africa, found in Sudan, dates back 5,500 years,[6] and the theorized murder of Otzi the Iceman likewise dates back over 5,000 years. Groups routinely kill members of other groups, even today. Society can thus both protect us and threaten us.

The obvious secular answer to this paradox of our helping and hurting each other is that the rule of law helps humans live together. That's true in part, but it's not the whole story. The United States provides an illustration. The country has laws against homicide and assault, but the CDC still reports over 15,000 homicides in a year plus 1.4 million emergency room visits for assault.[7]At the end of 2012, the country reeled from just one such homicidal assault that killed 20 small children and eight adults at Sandy Hook Elementary School in Newtown, Connecticut, despite laws against murder and trespass. Law did nothing to save those lives. Nor did laws victims from death and injury in the 2013 Boston Marathon bombing, a 2015 mass shooting at Inland Regional Center in San Bernardino, California, a 2016 mass murder at Pulse nightclub in Orlando, Florida, or from the many other senseless acts of violence that are either reported or ignored in the news each day.

Some people might not want to think about values from religions because they believe that religion, too, contributes to violence. The world's religions give people a group identity, and those group identities can become so fixed and so dogmatic that they lead to conflict where and when they collide. For example, Islamic fundamentalist entities as ISIS and the Islamic State have enacted terrible violence. In 2017 and 2018, the world even witnessed supposedly non-violent Buddhists persecuting Rohingya Muslims, to the extent that the persecution might qualify as genocide.[8] Violence can indeed be spurred by religions, but it also transcends religion.

The fact is that much of what humans do—both good and bad—is born of ideology. We follow political leaders, military leaders, and social leaders because we believe in abstract ideals like economic systems (such as capitalism), political systems (such as democracy), and social concepts (such as liberty and the pursuit of happiness). Humans have shown themselves to be willing to kill and be killed for abstract concepts, both secular and religious. Blind, unquestioning, unthinking adherence to anything is dangerous. For example, faith in political systems and economic systems can bring great wealth and freedoms, but can also cause great catastrophes: totalitarianism, war, and even famine.

The same is true of religious ideals. Blind adherence to religious beliefs can have dangers, but we are perfectly capable of considering and using ideas and values from those religions without being married to the entire system that accompanies them. The world's religions offer us ideals that will benefit ourselves and our societies if we put them into practice, but that doesn't mean we must "become" one religion or another to benefit from them. We just have to focus on what "right" is and do it. As actor Viola Davis insisted at the women's march in Los Angeles in 2018, "time needs to be helped by every single moment doing right."

THE ELEPHANT

This book takes its title from a parable in which six men set off to see an elephant, although all the men are blind. When they find the elephant, the first man feels the elephant's side. He determines that the elephant is like a wall. The second explores the tusk, which prompts his belief that the elephant is like a spear. The third, grasping the trunk, is convinced that the elephant is like a snake. The fourth gropes until he feels the elephant's knee, at which he pronounces the elephant to be like a tree. The fifth examines only the elephant's ear, so he decides that an elephant is like a fan. Finally, the sixth happens upon the tail and declares that the rest, who are now arguing, are all wrong. The elephant is like a rope, he insists, and he joins the argument. The irony is that all six men are correct, yet they are all wrong. Each is limited by his insistence that what he feels is all there is.

I've talked to many people about the idea of the Infinite. What I've learned is that you can put a dozen people in a room, ask them all about their concept of it, and get twelve different ideas about what that is. If the Infinite can be symbolized as an elephant, maybe our problem is not that we "feel" just one part of the elephant, like the men in the parable did. Instead, maybe the problem is that we see a whole elephant, but we imagine nothing more than the elephant we know. If I conceptualize the Infinite as a bearded man in a white robe, and another person conceptualizes the Infinite as emptiness or as enlightenment, we might have difficulty understanding each other. We may be unwilling to look beyond what we think we know. Our challenge, then, is to imagine what others imagine, to feel what others feel, and to see what others see. Doing so allows us to consider the commonalities amongst the world's sacred texts.

There's a reason to care what the texts have in common, even if we don't believe in any religion. The texts are from diverse cultures in various parts of the world. They span lengthy time periods. Each text had its own purpose. The cultures that gave birth to them had little in common. The main ideas in them are often unrelated. For example, nothing in the sacred texts of Judaism suggests that Jesus is the Messiah. Nothing in the New Testament refers to the Dao. Hinduism believes in a personal soul, but Buddhism doesn't. However, despite how different these texts are, their common values directly relate to the concerns that all humans share. The commonalities can help us understand our human existence. This is crucial, because if human existence is utterly meaningless, then anything goes. That "anything" can get ugly. Focusing only on what separates us can also get ugly, as wars, genocides, racism and prejudice, slavery, and other destructive behaviors have shown the world.

In contrast, the ideas that are treasured in common by the world's spiritual texts have the potential to bring us together rather than separating us. The different texts and their stories are a cacophony of many voices, a kind of Babel. Deep beneath their surface is quiet yet steadfast truth that has the power to transform our lives, our families, and our societies.

WHY CHANGE?

Throughout this book, I compare spiritual texts from Judaism, Christianity, Islam, Hinduism, Buddhism, Jainism, Sikhism, Daoism and Confucianism to show the values they share. At least three important sources of resistance can arise when examining and comparing spiritual texts. One source of resistance is that the texts are all just a bunch of superstitious rubbish that come from "pre-scientific" times, and that they are nothing more than the attempts of early peoples to make sense of the universe and their place in it. Such a stance is really limited. It assumes that there is absolutely no wisdom to be found in the texts purely because they are ancient, mythological, and spiritual. That stance overlooks the usefulness of the texts in providing guidance for groups of people and the staying power of the texts. Clearly, plenty of old texts have been abandoned. Most people today, for example, don't argue over the Code of Hammurabi or the ancient Egyptian Pyramid Texts. What in *these* texts makes them endure? What purpose do they serve? Those questions are worth exploring.

Another source of resistance, as mentioned earlier in the chapter, is that people may find it difficult to look beyond their own spiritual or religious concepts. If I believe in something called the Dao but not in something called God, and you believe in something called God but not the Dao, then I will be inclined to dismiss what your text says because I don't believe in the authority of it. Likewise, you will dismiss what my text says because you believe that yours is the authoritative one.

The third source of resistance focuses on God. Many people perceive the Infinite as God. However, even within any one religion (say, Christianity or Judaism or Islam), believers have differing and often competing images of God. God might be seen as a warrior, as a father, as compassionate, as a tyrant, as a miracle worker, as unknowable, and so on. Some readers might dismiss the values found in texts such as the Bible or the Qur'an *not* because the values are faulty, but because they see God as cruel or authoritarian or capricious. They might also reject the ideas simply because they don't believe in God.

Despite all that, it's important to talk about God. Talking about God helps us understand how other people think and act in the world. One can be an atheist and study theology: that's no contradiction. Oxford's Dr. William Wood, a University Lecturer in Philosophical Theology explained why in an article in *The Atlantic*: "theology is the closest thing we have at the moment to the kind of general study of all aspects of human culture.[9]" When we study each other, we better understand each other. At a time when we too often don't understand each other – witness the rise of hate crimes in the United States and the rise of violence around the world – better understanding each other has tangible benefits. In fact, examining the world's spiritual texts encourages us to be aware of an important constant: our shared humanity.

To think that people around the globe are intrinsically different from each other because of where they live is a mistake.

Yes, cultures have their own social customs and norms. Yes, they may practice indigenous rituals and religions. However, beneath the layers of social identity, all people have commonalities. In the 1940s, Abraham Maslow proposed his famous theory of the hierarchy of needs. The basic needs of all people everywhere are physiological, Maslow argued. To survive we must have food and water. We must be able to maintain homeostasis. We must be able to breathe. We must be able to have sex because reproduction is an essential drive of all living beings. Before we can be concerned about anything else, those most basic needs must be met. Once they are met, the next level of needs that all people try to satisfy is security. The drive to be secure and safe—to know that no one will creep into where we sleep at night and steal our treasures or bop us over the head or flee with our children—prompts us to create order and to strive for control. Security comes from social relationships and order.

We cannot begin to think about higher needs, such as friendships, romances, families, the need for self-esteem, or the drive to reach our own individual fullest potential, unless those first two basic levels of physical and security needs are met. All over the world, whether rich or poor, whether a country dweller or an urbanite, whether an indigenous person or a migrant, we have the same basic needs for survival and safety. The world's spiritual texts reflect those needs. Although many ideas in the texts are specific to the cultures that gave birth to them – Indian, Chinese, Middle Eastern, and so on —we can find many ideas in these texts of how humans can ensure their security, safety, and basic survival. We learn too about love, fealty, how emotions can affect us, duty, and more.

In examining the texts, one other caution is useful. We should beware of delusions. Delusions are all around us and within us,

and it's important for us to be aware of them because they so easily
lead us to distort information. To be deluded is not to be psychotic
or naïve. Delusions are simply mistaken ideas that arise from a
whole host of factors. How we were raised by our parents, the work
experiences we have had, how we have been treated at the hands of
others, the advertising inducements and judgments we are fed, and
the subtle and not-so-subtle messages of the media all are examples
of factors that contribute to delusions. Many women in America,
for example, do not consider how the pictures that confront
them daily of happy, smiling size zero women on billboards, in
newspaper and magazine ads, and on television programs are
fabricated. Therefore, they labor under the delusion that they must
be a size zero to be beautiful. When delusions are projected onto
text, we can misunderstand it. We can, for example, become angry
at the surface message of a story, and thus not dig for the deeper
meaning, the more complex understanding of the text. That can be
a real stumbling point for those who have been taught to read texts
such as the Bible literally.

Recognizing our delusions and getting past our resistance to
consider what the texts share has important benefits. These ideas
can help us change our own lives and improve the lives of others.

The central idea of this book is that the wisdom that the world's
spiritual texts share can help us improve ourselves, our families,
our communities, and the world. Such a position assumes that our
families, societies, and the world have problems that need to be
addressed. I believe that's true. To understand why we should want
to create change, it's useful to examine where we are.

"Where we are," of course, varies from country to country.
In the United States, certain problems rise to the top of citizens'
concerns. For example, people are dissatisfied with the healthcare
system. Many are still uninsured, and access to healthcare is not

equitable. Many citizens are concerned about race relations; in recent years, police killings of African American males have made headline news and sparked riots and protests.[10] Wealth inequality is a global concern; in early 2015, Oxfam released a report that indicated that the wealthiest one percent of the world's population would control half the world's total wealth by 2016.[11] This inequality is evident in the United States, where families at the top of the net worth ladder have seventy times more wealth than those at the bottom.[12] The World Economic Forum included concerns about government, the economy, unemployment, and income disparity in its *Global Risks 2014* report along with food and water crises and "profound political and social instability."[13]Certainly, those concerns bore fruit in various parts of the world in 2014 as Ebola threatened western African nations, ISIS cut a swath of violence and terror across parts of the Middle East, and California staggered under a historic drought.

Signs of unease and distress can also be found on a more local and personal level. For example, heroin and opioid use has been increasing amongst Americans. Over the twelve-year period from 1991 to 2013, the number of opioid prescriptions almost tripled and the United States became the world's almost sole consumer of opioids such as Oxycodone. Over the seven-year period from 2005 to 2012, the number of heroin users in the United States rose by 176%.[14] In January of 2017, *The New York Times* reported that the addiction rate was continuing to increase: in 2015, the *Times* reported, deaths from heroin overdose had surpassed gun homicide deaths for the first time in American history, destroying the lives of 33,000 users.[15] Drug addiction is not the only problem. The Centers for Disease Control reported that suicide rates in America in 2014 were the highest they had been for the past 25 years.[16] In the second half of 2014, the *Washington Post* reported on the CDC's National

Intimate Partner and Sexual Violence Survey, which indicated that over 30% of American women have been battered by partners and almost 20% have been raped.[17] The voices of many women who have experienced sexual violence are now being heard in the #MeToo and Time's Up movements.

Sexual violence is not limited to America. It happens around the globe. So does extremism. In America, a white nationalist movement has experienced a resurgence, and it has quickly resulted in violence and death. In fact, the Anti-Defamation League reports that in 2017, "white supremacists were 'directly responsible' for 18 out of 34 United States extremist-related deaths"; in contrast, only nine deaths that year were attributed to Muslim extremists.[18]

Around the globe, people are suffering too from environmental mayhem. The United States, presumably a major contributor to global climate change, has pulled out of the Paris Agreement. Weather is becoming more extreme in the United States, but it is also changing around the globe, impacting the agricultural output, flood patterns, storm patterns and survival of people from the Arctic to coastal areas.

Not all of our suffering is as dire as poverty, hurricanes, rape, war, and other pains. Often, we are just unhappy. We are lonely. Our relationships fail. We measure ourselves against the successes of others, and we think we are coming up short. We work longer and harder. We become more stressed. We become convinced that we are competing in a "dog eat dog" world, and we snap up whatever opportunities we perceive, whether they are "poisoned meat" or good for us and regardless of whether we are snarling at others. We may immerse ourselves in various vices: prostitution, alcohol binging, gambling. We may suffer from illness. We may immerse ourselves online, oblivious to the findings that being online tends to make us unhappier.[19] We buy too much or try to create new income streams; we get into debt. Debt increases our stress. The cycle continues.

Because we are under so much stress, we might not think about how we can help each other. We might make the wrong kinds of effort. We might become selfish, angry, addicted, prejudiced, self-protective, and our families, partners, and friends might suffer. We might do things we regret. We may lash out at others; we might even try to intentionally hurt others to gain whatever we think we will gain.

One indicator of how disconnected we are can be found on news blogs and websites that allow readers to make comments. Frequently, the unkindness and mean-spiritedness of comments are shocking. People wish death to people they've never met. They bully strangers who have had losses and experienced deaths. They clamor for executions of people not even convicted of crimes and damn them to hell. The worst, "trolls," have been associated with a variety of psychological issues including sadism.[20] The deep unhappiness, envy, fears, and narcissism that is often expressed in such comments should concern us; they indicate a violent kind of mob thinking.

The good news is that the world's spiritual texts help us learn how to change. We can make ourselves healthier and happier, and we can make our societies healthier and happier. We can see in the news how determined people armed with weapons can make enormous changes in the world. My goal with this book is to show how determined people armed with knowledge and compassion can also make changes. What the world's religious texts have in common is that knowledge and compassion. The following chapters explore eight values religions around the world share, and how they can help transform us. It starts with effort, including our own effort to want to learn how and why we can transform ourselves.

Effort

When I was young, I loved Batman more than Superman. Superman had it easy. He had been born with superpowers. He could see into buildings with his x-ray vision and hear conversations from far away with his super hearing. He could outrun trains with his superspeed or pick them up and hurl them into space with his super strength. He could fly. The only thing that could stop Superman was Kryptonite, and it's not as if Earth had mines full of Kryptonite.

The other superheroes all had their superpowers too, powers such as Hulk's massive strength or Wonder Woman's abilities to fly and talk with animals. However, most superheroes were not fully human. They were all heroes because they were "other."

Batman, though, was my hero because he had no superpowers. Batman could bleed. He could be broken. He was driven by familiar emotions. He may have had a speedy armored Batmobile and lots of bat gadgets, but Batman was fully human. Batman was going to live or die by his own wits and his own efforts, and all that (along with his cool costume) is what made him more special to me than any of the other superheroes.

In a sense, the Infinite is Superman. What else can we call something that can be all places and all times at once and that is eternal and infinite, predating time itself? What else can Jews, Christians and Muslims call a Being who can create the entire universe and everything in it in six days? What else can we call Enlightenment or the Dao? No matter how much technology we develop and no matter how much we extend our lives, humans generally do not have the powers of omniscience, omnipotence, and omnipresence.

Our lack of those powers doesn't mean that we are meant to be slackers, though. When we look at the world's sacred texts, a point becomes clear: we are meant to be Batman. Batman trained. He pushed himself through emotional and physical pain. He cultivated strength and ingenuity and used them to survive because Batman put himself on the line again and again. Routinely, he faced death at the hands of villains but willingly engaged through his determination to save Gotham City. We are meant to put forth similar effort, to face the death of our limitations, to best the villains of self-doubt and anger and complacency that keep us from achieving what might seem impossible. The effort that we are meant to put forth is mighty. It's not an "Oh well, I tried" effort. Through effort, we are meant to push ourselves to the max because it is the only way that we can achieve our fullest potential. Through effort, we save ourselves, our communities, and perhaps our world. Through effort we accomplish what we would otherwise believe could not be done, and in doing what we believe we cannot do and exerting what seems like superhuman effort, we bring ourselves closer to the Infinite.

BIBLICAL SUPERHEROES

Imagine Noah who saw the rainbow, a man who was righteous in his own time. Was he perfect? No. In fact, compared to Abraham, Noah might have been a bit of a slacker. Rashi, the renowned biblical commentator who lived and wrote in 11th century France, says that had Noah "lived in the generation of Abraham, he would have been considered as nothing." For his own time, though, Noah made monumental effort. During the time that he lived, Noah "walked with God."[21] That was good, because God had plans for Noah. "Build an ark," God said, but not just any ark. God wanted an ark that was three stories tall and more than 400 feet long and over 70 feet wide—longer than an American pro football field and approaching half as wide as one—built of a particular kind of wood and finished both inside and outside with pitch. Noah did not pull out his brand name chainsaw and his big box store power tools, hire up a crew of unionized factory workers, and whip out that ark in a few weeks. Noah had no electricity and no gas. Noah cut down the trees by hand, and then he had to strip the trees and slice them and plane them. He pegged the wood together, and then he boiled down the pitch and applied it, all by hand.

Consider that it took Dutchman Johan Huibers three years, from 2008 to 2011, to build his almost 3,000 ton life-size replica of the ark. That was with modern tools and more than a million and a half dollars. We don't know how many biblical years it took Noah to build the ark, given the tools he had at the time and his singlehanded labor. That construction effort took blood, sweat, muscle, resources, and anxiety. The effort surely affected his family because his family members would have been the ones responsible for taking care of Noah's business and lands while Noah was building the ark. God didn't say to Noah, "When you get off work at five o'clock, put in an hour or two a night from Monday to Friday, and see if you can get in an eight-hour day on the weekend." God said, "build the ark," and given the enormity of the task and the impending consequences—do it or drown—we can bet safely that Noah probably built during every waking moment of every day.

As many years and as much effort as it took Noah to build the ark, that was not enough. God also commanded that Noah should find, gather up, and bring onto the ark two of every creature alive.[22] Likewise, Noah should gather up every kind of food that people and animals ate so that Noah, his family, and the animals could all be nourished through the coming flood. Granted, Noah was not the first world explorer, and there's no evidence that he set off from the Arctic to the Antarctic to gather up some polar bears and a pair of penguins. Noah's world was smaller than that, but the task was still monumental. Imagine, for example, if you had to go to every supermarket, farm stand, butcher, fishmonger, organic grocer, bakery, dairy, pet store, and beekeeper in your state and bring home some of everything edible that each one carried, enough to sustain you and your family and a zoo full of animals (two of every animal in the state) for months. How much effort might that take?

Clearly, God asked a lot of Noah. However, as Rashi noted, He asked even more of Abraham. Abraham was one hundred biblical years old when God delivered on His promise to deliver Abraham a son through his wife, Sarai. Then, when the son, Isaac, was a young man, God told Abraham, "'Take now thy son, thine only son, whom thou lovest, even Isaac, and get thee into the land of Moriah; and offer him there for a burnt-offering upon one of the mountains."[23]Abraham did not question or protest. He packed up the knife, the fire, the wood, and his son and headed for the mountain to do as he was told. As he was about to plunge the knife into his son's chest—can we even imagine the anguish and tumult inside Abraham, the pounding of his heart, the way that his muscles must have involuntarily resisted the task, the cold sweat running off his face and out of the palm of the hand that held the knife, or what his son must have thought as he lay bound on the sacrificial pyre, looking into his father's determined face?—an angel of God stopped Abraham's hand. The time had come to stop human sacrifice. That he was willing to make an almost superhuman effort to murder his son and only heir was enough. No wonder Rashi found the labors of Noah lacking compared to the efforts of Abraham.

The stories of Noah and Abraham suggest that we are meant to exert effort to our outermost bounds, perhaps even beyond what we think we are capable of. In that effort, we snap the bonds of our preconceptions and put ourselves to service for something bigger than ourselves.

It is true that in the Torah, the first five books of the Hebrew Bible that would later become the greater part of the Christian Old Testament, God asks for obedience from the tribe who would become the Jewish people. That is one way of seeing both the above stories. God asks for more than just obedience, though. God stresses that people need to *work* at doing the right thing.

In the Torah, God hands down not ten laws, but law after law after law. God gave the Hebrews 613 mitzvot (rules), such as laws regarding taxes, laws regarding charity, laws regarding familial relations, laws regarding property, and so on. God also gave the Hebrews rules about Himself. Believers – members of the tribe— must know that God is real, love Him, fear Him, keep His name holy, and imitate Him.[24] What could it possibly mean for humans to imitate God, the perfect and the omnipotent? To imitate God seems impossible, especially because God makes very clear to humankind in the Torah that we are not gods. However, God wants humans to make that kind of superhuman effort because it's the only way by which we can recognize our own Infinite-nature.

The Torah also tells us that when the effort falls short, consequences follow. In Numbers, for example, God has His patience tried by the Israelites over and over again. He has led the people out of their bondage in Egypt. He has fed them with manna. He has traveled with them in a pillar of smoke. He has appeared before multitudes so that they may believe in Him. He has provided for them again and again, and He has led them to the very doorstep of the land of Canaan that He has promised to them, but at every step of the way He is besieged by the continual fears and complaints of the Israelites, who are simply unable to submit to Him.

The story reaches a climax when God tells Moses to send out some of the tribe to scout the land of Canaan. The men go, and they see that the land is fertile and bountiful. No matter. When they come back with their report and Caleb suggests that they take over the land as God wants them to do, the men figuratively throw up their hands, take a step back, and say the equivalent of, "Oh, no. Can't do that." They were too afraid. Productive land helps to build strong people, as the history of agriculture and civilization has shown us, and they had seen the strength of the people living in Canaan.

To overthrow a people and overtake their land took as much effort back in biblical times as it does now, perhaps more. The Israelites had no benefit of fighter jets, tanks, or artillery. Whether or not the ancient Israelites really overthrew Canaanites doesn't matter. No archeological evidence has been found yet that they did. Nor are the stories of Torah meant to be literal truths. Rather, the point of the story is that the land could be won by the Israelites only through effort and faith that God was in their corner. That effort and faith was too taxing, and the men shied away from that effort. It was easier to lie and say that the land was full of dangerous giants.25 Instead, they incited a rebellion, convincing the people that the Canaanites would kill them and steal their children as bounty if they attacked. Moses and Aaron saw the shirking and fear for what it was, and they pleaded with the Israelites to no avail. In fact, the only effort the Israelites talked about putting forth was to discuss stoning Moses and Aaron to death. As a result, God finally got fed up.

Although He forgave the Israelites their lack of faithfulness and resulting lack of effort, His judgment against them was chilling. God had promised this land to a people that He brought out of slavery and turned into travelers, but now He rescinded His promise. Only two, Caleb and Joshua, would enter the Promised Land. Everyone else would struggle outside it for the next forty years. They became lifelong exiles. In God's Promised Land, there was no room for those who would not take up the struggle and make the strong effort needed to maintain faith, conquer their fears, and submit to the Divine will.

Laziness is easy and tempting. Effort makes us sweat; it's painful. However, it's fulfilling. It can break old traditions, save us from catastrophe, build a people and move us to a better place. The stories make clear that we are meant to exert effort.

BUDDHISM'S RIGHT EFFORT

At first, compared to the stories of Torah, Buddhism's sense of effort might look like...nothing. It might look like people sitting silently on the floor. Don't be fooled that it is nothing, though. Here's an example: in the spacious Jokhang meditation hall of Maitripa College in Portland, Oregon, not quite a dozen students, including me, sat cross-legged on maroon and saffron cushions on the smoothly polished bamboo floor facing both the teacher and an array of almost life-size gilded statues housed in a glass case that shine against a celestial blue background. We students were taking a class in Buddhist thought shifting and were working on memorizing and discussing the eight verses on transforming the mind. Transforming the mind means getting past the idea of a fixed and solid self, a self that we see and feel. It means realizing that what we think is our "self" is changing all the time; cells are being born and cells are dying. We grow. We shrink. Our ideas and emotions change. According to Buddhism, we are no more fixed than the wind is, but we act as if we are as solid as granite boulders. To understand that we are not what we think takes tremendous effort.

Our instructor, Rachel Ryer, had us pair off to discuss the fourth teaching, which might seem absurd. The forth teaching says "Whenever I see beings who are wicked in nature and overwhelmed by violent negative actions and suffering I will hold such rare ones dear, as if I had found a precious treasure."[26] Ryer had us consider a question: from a Buddhist perspective, what is a practical response to someone who is committing a violent act?

People might think that the response would be heroism: to tackle the person, to stop the person, to shoot the person if need be. What isn't immediately obvious is that the right response might not look like much, yet it takes an enormous effort. For example, a student asked, "Would it be possible to drop kick the person if it was done from the right intention?" "It could be," Ryer responded, as long as the person wasn't fooling herself. Anger isn't a right intention.

She then relayed to the class a story from the Jataka tales, which are stories from India from the 4th century BCE. This tale tells of the previous lives of the Buddha. In one of those lives, Ryer explained, when he was not yet the Buddha but was a bodhisattva, the Buddha was the captain of a ship that had five hundred sailors. His training was so strong and his wisdom so advanced that he could perceive that one of the five hundred had the intention to kill all the rest of the crew and had set the idea along the path to fruition. The sailor had both the plan and the means to do the killing. Out of concern and true wisdom, the captain killed the sailor. He knew that he was bringing negative karma onto himself for killing the villain, but he also knew that he had prevented that man from accumulating the much greater negative karma of killing five hundred innocents. By this act the Buddha violated the most fundamental precept of Buddhism: not killing. To kill took tremendous mental and emotional effort, as much as it would have taken Abraham to kill his beloved son.

"It's not just controlling the outer manifestations of our emotions," Ryer explained to the group. "It's using the arising of these emotions to get at the root of our delusions, which are all caused by grasping at the idea of a self that is not real." After all, Buddhism asks, what is the self? Is it our physical being? If so, then the self I was at age seventeen with slim hips, long hair, a narrow waist, and firm skin is surely not the shorter haired and somewhat podgier self with wrinkles who looks back at me today. If the self is our ideas, then how many of us have precisely the same ideas as we had in childhood or in our teenage years? Personally, I am glad some of my own ideas have changed for the better since then, but if our ideas have changed, then have "we" changed, too? What effort must I make to determine who and what I really am?

The group reconsidered the third teaching: "Vigilant, the moment a delusion appears in my mind, endangering myself and others, I shall confront and avert it without delay."[27]A middle-aged woman with long dark hair who was sitting on a chair in the back of the room raised her hand. "It seems as if mindfulness is something that we are supposed to do every second," she said in a slightly shocked and disbelieving tone.

Ryer fixed the group with a serious and steady look. "It is," she said. "Mindfulness is the most difficult task we will face in our lives. It is not for the faint of heart. To be mindful means to be working all the time." To have cultivated true bodhicitta — the desire for enlightenment to benefit all sentient beings — means that a person would have vanquished all delusions so that she would know what is right for herself at every moment, and she would also know what is right for every other person everywhere, simultaneously.

As she spoke those words, two images flashed through my mind at once. One was of perfect freedom born of the clearest omniscience. The other was of the crushing labor of Atlas, bearing the entire sky upon his shoulders, forever keeping separated the earth and the celestial sphere. The effort required to cultivate true compassion seems that impossible to me: the verses tell me to consider myself the lowest of all, to think of people who harm me when I trust them as my holy teachers, and to bear unavoidable abuse and insults by offering the victory to the one who has insulted me, all without becoming a doormat. Yet the Buddha tells us that it can be done and has been done, with the result of perfect, brilliant enlightenment.

The Buddha's own story is one that tells us this. Legend has it that he was born into a royal family, a prince who had the best of everything. He was protected from any sights or sounds that might sadden his charmed existence. Then one day he escaped from the palace grounds with the help of an aide. What he saw shocked him. Around him in the streets of India lay beggars, people covered with the filth of the streets in which they slept, people covered with sores, people dying. The prince was shocked. He had never seen suffering before this, and once he saw this suffering that all people experience, he could not get that pain out of his mind. Therefore, the Buddha left his perfect life and his family, including his wife and young son, and went out into the world to become an ascetic. In those days in India, that's what people did if they were searching for answers that they believed lie beyond what we can see and measure in this world.

The life of renunciation, of fasting, and of begging that serves to focus on the life of the spirit is still common today to a variety of religious monastic traditions from Jainism to Christianity. Finally, the prince sat beneath a bodhi tree, weak from hunger and tired from his years of searching. There, he decided, he would sit until he either died or gained the answers he sought. Through temptations, delusions and demons he sat, until finally he reached enlightenment and discovered how humans could be liberated from their suffering. Through his valiant effort, he discovered the Four Noble Truths of Buddhism: suffering exists, suffering has a cause, suffering has an end, and there is a way to end the suffering. Further, he discovered the Eightfold Path by which humans could achieve their own liberation. His enormous efforts brought him face-to-face with the real possibility of his own death. Regardless of that threat, he persevered, and his efforts have since shown millions how to open their eyes and wake out of their own living "deaths" of unawareness.

I have a bit of a dark side, though, as many of us do. I judge others. I judge my kids when I think they are not working hard enough at school. I judge people where I worship – or rather the lack of them – when they do not show up. I judge people at work and often believe they are judging me. It's easy to think that others are not doing what they "need" to do, until I step back and realize that I am deciding for others what their effort should be and is. Truthfully, I have no idea how hard my kids may be working. I don't know what might weigh on them every moment. I don't know what obligations may keep others from worship or participating at work. In truth, I am not omniscient, and my judgments of others show exactly how lacking in clarity I really am.

Effort is one of the steps of the Eightfold Path that is at the heart of Buddhism. Just as the stories of Noah, Abraham, Moses, and others in the Old Testament suggest, effort itself isn't enough. *Right* effort is needed. From the Buddhist perspective, right effort for any situation has four separate components. One is to prevent afflictions and delusions, such as anger, hatreds, impatience, and so on, from arising. This doesn't mean to just choke them back so that they manifest in some other way. Rather, it means becoming more and more aware of what gives birth to those reactions and slowly, over time, extinguishing the root causes.

A father, for example, may feel angry when his son brings home a failing grade on a report card. Right effort isn't as simple as the father thinking, "This makes me mad, but I won't yell." Nor is the goal that the dad should smile graciously to mask his anger when the son brings home the report card and say, "I'm sure you did the best you could." Right effort means that Dad must get to the root of why he feels angry when his son brings home the failing grade. Does Dad feel disrespected? Does he feel fearful? The feelings that cause the dad's reactions have arisen from the dad's mind, and the goal is for Dad to see that his anger is not going to transform the grade and probably will not create a deep change in the son's behavior, either.

This goes hand in hand with the second task of right effort, which is to extinguish the undesirable qualities that have already arisen. Perhaps one has racial prejudices. Perhaps one judges others based on appearance or lack of wealth. Perhaps one feels stuck in a gloomy rut. Why? Right effort, in Buddhism, prompts a person to see that the root cause of the thoughts that create misery for ourselves and unhappiness for others around us arise inside each of us. We treat them as though they are real.

Pulitzer Prize-winning journalist Jose Antonio Vargas provides an example. In the summer of 2011, Vargas revealed in an astounding first person article for the *New York Times Sunday Magazine* that he was an undocumented immigrant, having arrived in the United States when he was twelve years old with a fake green card.[28] He did not know until he was old enough to drive and tried to get a license that his green card was fake. Vargas wrote about the many years that passed as he lived in fear, feeling miserable even in the face of winning the Pulitzer as part of a *Washington*

Post reporting team, because of the constant threat of being found out and deported. That threat and fear could have consumed his life. Instead, he finally chose to face it head on and see it for what it was, including writing about it, even though American law meant that he could be deported back to the Philippines for at least ten years and perhaps even for life. Being deported could have been utterly disastrous for his thriving journalistic career.

To write an article like that takes tremendous courage and tremendous effort. Vargas' identity was on the line. Vargas had clearly made the right effort. However, it was equally clear that some of those readers who responded to his article were not making right effort to understand. Their responses were angry and full of prejudice. Those responders suggested that undocumented aliens were responsible for the poverty that besets millions of Americans, even though there is absolutely no evidence that this is true. What causes such emotions to arise? Right effort in Buddhism prompts the person experiencing the emotion to probe those origins.

Those tasks are hard enough, but right effort requires two more tasks. One is to cultivate wholesome qualities that haven't yet arisen in ourselves. In other words, maybe I am not especially generous. Maybe I don't have a wealth of loving kindness. My job, according to right effort, is to look for and take opportunities to help develop those qualities in myself. Becoming a mom, for example, meant that I needed to learn how to love and care for a small human being. That didn't come naturally to me. I had been born to parents who didn't understand how to show true loving kindness to a baby, especially one that they hadn't planned and didn't really want. Some parents never learn these skills, which is why society has abused and neglected children. For me, learning to be a reasonably good mom has been very hard work, and what convinces me that I am putting forth the right effort is that I keep trying to get better at it, cultivating qualities that I know I don't have.

I also want to improve the good qualities that I know I do have, qualities such as patience, and that is the last requirement of right effort: not being content with the "goodness" of what we already do well, but striving to make those traits even stronger. Truly, as Ryer said, such efforts are not for the fainthearted, and they are not just for this lifetime. In Buddhist thought, they are for future lifetimes and the benefit of all beings, just as the efforts of Abraham and Moses were not solely for themselves, but for future generations. In everyday reality, those "future lifetimes" might be the health and happiness of our children and grandchildren, and the future generations of those we affect. In Buddhism, only by exerting our own efforts can we enter the "Promised Land" of enlightenment.

THE HINDU WARRIOR'S BATTLE

"There are three branches of the law," the Upanishads say. One branch is performing sacrifice, studying, and giving to charity. Another one is austerity. The third is to live with a teacher as a Brahmacharin, a male who seeks Brahman as a student.[29] The effort and self-denial that these tasks require bring to mind the story of a man who was a profound teacher and interpreter of both Hinduism and Islam. The man, Sai Baba of Shirdi, arrived as a teenager in British-governed Maharashtra in the mid-1850s. By the early 1900s, pilgrims were coming to visit him. His teachings transcended religious dogma. For Sai Baba, the one Truth was God, the One God, who permeates everything at all times. Sai Baba believed that coming to realize the unity of God and one's oneness with God was the human goal. He taught the Hindu concept that all that happens to a person in his or her present lifetime and in future lifetimes is a result of karma, and everything the person does creates karma. He was a man revered by Hindu saints, yet he taught Muslims as well as Hindus, and he encouraged each to follow his own religion and each to live a full life rather than to renounce family and community ties.

The Forum for Hindu Awakening retells a story of Sai Baba and his views about effort. In the story, Sai Baba plays with a handful of coins, jingling them repeatedly in his palms and looking at them, one by one. After about an hour of watching his master repeat the action, one of his disciples finally asks what he is doing. Sai Baba begins by pointing out that most flowers that bloom on fruit trees never bear fruit to ripeness. He then explains, "In the same manner, thousands of devotees are coming to me. Are they all maturing into good devotees? Many drop off halfway on the path. Some come for study. Many seek wealth while many others come in connection with success in their jobs, marriages, or other such personal desires. There is some defect or the other in each of them." Those who drop away haven't come purely for the sake of God, Sai Baba points out.

Then he explains why he is looking at the coins: to see their faults. Seeing the faults in the coins keeps him mindful to look for the faults in his devotees. Perfection is the goal, and they can't achieve it if all they care about is what the material world can offer them, Sai Baba asserts. It is not possible to attain God when one is concerned only with the everyday world. He points out, "How can you reach your destination if you get into a train that is going in some other direction than your destination? They want God, but they don't make efforts to realize God. Among the many that come, it is only one in a thousand who really makes the efforts to realize God!"[30] We could say the same about our lives even if we are not seeking God; if we don't make the effort to save our marriages and relationships, to become educated, to tackle disaster, to become healthy, to succeed at our work or to achieve our potential, how can we possibly succeed?

In *The Bhagavad Gita*, the extended conversation between
Arjuna and Krishna makes the same point. Although Arjuna, the
warrior of the Pandava clan, was bound by duty and class to battle
his kinsmen the Kauravas for the return of his clan's kingdom, he
didn't want to do it. He didn't believe that any good could come
of his battling and slaying his relations. Beset by sadness, Arjuna
considered leaving the battlefield, but God in the form of Krishna
came to convince him to stay. To convince Arjuna, Krishna makes
clear the importance of effort, explaining that a person can only
reach God through his own efforts. He tells Arjuna,

> The man of discipline whose self is contented with
> knowledge and experience, who is unmoved, who has
> restrained his senses, and to whom a clump of dirt, a stone,
> and gold are alike, is said to be spiritually disciplined. And
> he is esteemed highest who thinks alike about well-wishers,
> friends, and enemies, and those who are indifferent, and
> those who take both sides, and those who are objects
> of hatred, and relatives, as well as about the good and
> the sinful.
>
> Discipline is not his, Arjuna, who eats too much, nor his
> who eats not at all; discipline is not his who is addicted to
> too much sleep, nor his who is always awake.
>
> That spiritual discipline which destroys all suffering is
> his, who takes necessary food and exercise, who toils
> moderately in all necessary works, and who sleeps and
> wakes at the proper time…. Thus constantly devoting his
> self to abstraction, a man of discipline, freed from sin,
> easily obtains that supreme happiness—contact with the
> Brahman. He who has devoted his self to abstraction, by
> discipline, looking alike on everything, sees the self-abiding

in all beings, and all beings in the self. To him who sees Me
in everything, and everything in Me, I am never lost, and
he is not lost to Me. The man of discipline who worships
me abiding in all beings, holding that all is one, lives in
Me, however he may be living.[31]

In the story, Arjuna at first is unconvinced by his conversations
with Krishna. He continues to resist the idea that he must slay
his cousins. In fact, he asks Krishna why he should go to war if
devotion is better than work. Krishna, with great kindness, tells the
warrior that we must perform action that is required of us, because
"He who in this world does not contribute to the turning of this
wheel is living a sinful life and indulging his senses, and, Arjuna,
he lives his life in vain."[32] As they continue to talk, and as Krishna
continues to show Arjuna the nature of true reality, Arjuna slowly
comes to see the importance of his doing his duty, despite the pain
that it will bring him.

A thought still concerns him, though: what happens if he
doesn't make enough effort? Is faith enough, Arjuna wonders?[33]
Krishna explains to him the same idea that the Torah shows
through the story of Moses: such a person who tries but falls
short will not be condemned to eternal damnation. Nonetheless,
neither will such a person achieve the ultimate goal in Hinduism:
liberation. Such a person will not rise above the mundane world
and its limitations. "No-one who performs good deeds comes to an
evil end," Krishna tells Arjuna, but that person will continue the
cycle of rebirth, again and again, until she makes enough effort to
achieve perfection.[34]

Hindus, like Buddhists, may incorporate sitting meditation
as part of their practice. When I read Krishna's words, I think of
my own abysmal efforts to sit. Just sit. Empty the mind. It sounds
so simple. Yet I fail at it again and again. It seems so difficult,

so uncomfortable, so static. I have too many questions. Am I meditating correctly? Is there a correct way to meditate? Why can't I generate the feeling I am trying to generate? Am I doing something wrong? Is something wrong with me? Am I really a hell being and just don't know it? Then comes the big one: is trying to reach enlightenment hopeless? A childlike thought pops into my mind. "Am I there yet?" I sympathize with Arjuna. For the Hindu, as for Moses, the Promised Land will not be achieved without the most perfect effort.

Yet I don't want to exert that effort. Why? It's uncomfortable. On the simplest of levels, who would not rather sit on a comfortable sofa than on a hard cushion? Who would not rather watch Netflix than the parade of afflictive and scattered thoughts in one's own mind? Tuning out is so pleasant. On a more serious note, who would not rather avoid facing the reality that a relationship is unhealthy, that a child might be on drugs, that the time to leave a job has long passed, that our health might be compromised: all the uncomfortable truths that poke us and prod us and that we convince ourselves are just idle worries to be pushed aside? What we really need is strength and purpose, a diamond blade to cut through our own misguided B.S., and the courage to act. Ultimately, we are all warriors of life. Many of us talk about the many lives we have lived in this lifetime. To reach perfection, a place where we can stop striving to be better, we cannot shirk the effort.

STRIVING FOR THE IMPOSSIBLE

The year that I was born, Jains opened a bird hospital in Delhi. Jainism is one of the world's oldest religions. Some say it is even older than Hinduism. The guiding principle of all Jains is non-violence toward humans, other living beings, plants, and the

world. They eat no animals, will not work as slaughterers, and
shun certain root vegetables such as onions because pulling them
from the earth might injure small insects. Pious Jains routinely
wear a thin mask over the nose and mouth to avoid accidentally
inhaling and thus killing small flying bugs. The bird hospital, which
houses thousands of birds, is just one of sanctuaries all over India
that Jains run for animals. They believe that all living creatures in
the world deserve to live out their lives naturally, and they work
diligently toward that end. Their efforts in the bird sanctuary have
tangible results: approximately 75% of the birds admitted to the
hospital recover. Those who die are cremated with respect.[35]

Effort and discipline are as much a part of the Jain religion
as any other religion. Some might argue the effort is even more,
because Jain asceticism doesn't guarantee any kind of desired
outcome. In fact, some see the religion as very pessimistic.
Mahavira, the founder of Jainism, said, 'Endowed with conduct
and discipline, who practices control of self, Who throws out all
his bondage, He attains the eternal place."[36] Later in the same
sutra, Mahavira says, "No conduct is possible without knowledge,
without conduct, there's no liberation, and without liberation, no
deliverance."[37]Perhaps only a hero such as Mahavira is likely to
achieve liberation in this lifetime. That's because of the Jain view of
karma. Jains imagine karma as physical particles. Those physical
particles stick to people's souls. Any kind of negative karma,
such as through thoughtless deeds that create any kind of harm,
especially to others, is very heavy. The heaviness of the karma keeps
the soul from ascending upward to achieve enlightenment and
liberation. The only hope to achieve liberation is to purge the soul
of its negative karma.

Sometimes that effort toward liberation may be shocking to
Westerners. A Jain near the end of life due to terminal disease or

old age, for example, may undertake the ritual of sallekhana.[38] Sallekhana is death by fasting, chosen with full intent and overseen by a monk. It is not considered suicide. Suicide is viewed as a rash and violent decision. Sallekhana, on the other hand, is prolonged and meditative. It is, to a Jain, a kind of perfection, as eating nothing means no violence to any living thing. Thus, it offers a devout Jain karmic purification.

Sallekhana is not easy. Think about going for a day without food. I have done it during the Jewish High Holy Days, and I know the gnawing feeling in my stomach, the feeling of lightheadedness, the sense of anxiety and irritability. I cannot imagine experiencing those sensations for days and weeks, even a month, until death finally fills the emptiness within. Americans live in a culture in which even violent criminals are put to death relatively quickly and with a focus on the least pain possible. To choose to die inch by inch, ounce by ounce, takes an effort that many non-Jains cannot fathom. However, for a Jain, the body is the jailer of the soul. Purifying the negative karmic particles "stuck" to body and soul, even through starvation, is worth the prize: liberation from cyclic existence and oneness with the Infinite.

JIHAD, THE STRUGGLE

Today, perhaps no religion on Earth is more feared, more fearsome, more complicated, and more misunderstood than Islam. In "The Children of Israel," Sura 17 of the Qur'an, Allah says, "Surely this Qur'an guides to that which is most upright and gives good news to the believers who do good that they shall have a great reward."[39] Allah lays down a variety of laws in the chapter: not to kill one's children because of fear of poverty; not to kill anyone unjustly; to practice fairness and honesty; to abstain from sex; and to serve Allah. To do all this, effort is necessary. Allah says,

"...whoever desires the hereafter and strives for it as he ought to strive and he is a believer; (as for) these, their striving shall surely be accepted."[40]

One of my favorite stories about the Islamic concept of effort is this:

> This is the story of the giant ship engine that failed. The ship's owners tried one expert after another, but none of them could figure out how to fix the engine. Then they brought in an old man who had been fixing ships since he was a youngster. He carried a large bag of tools with him, and when he arrived, he immediately went to work. He inspected the engine very carefully, from top to bottom.
>
> Two of the ship's owners were there, watching this man, hoping he would know what to do. After looking things over, the old man searched into his bag and pulled out a small hammer. He gently tapped something. & instantly, the engine lurched into life & got started.
>
> He carefully put his hammer away. The engine was fixed! A week later, the owners received a bill from the old man for £10,000.
>
> 'What?!' the owners exclaimed. 'He hardly did anything!' So they wrote the old man a note saying, "Please send us an itemised bill."
>
> The man sent a bill that read:
>
> Tapping with a hammer...£2.00
> Knowing where to tap...£9,998.00
>
> Total £10,000

Moral of The Story:
Effort itself is important, but knowing where to make
an effort in your life, 'Makes all the difference.' So
often we see people striving, working and making effort
tirelessly, often for years only for them to later on realize
that they were all misplaced and how they wish they had
spent the time and effort on something more fruitful."[41]

At a time when so many in the world believe that the efforts
of Muslims are directed at terrorizing and killing non-Muslims
and Muslims alike, it bears reflection that terrorism and wanton
murder are not espoused in the most holy text of Islam. Whether
or not some radicals and fundamentalists on the fringe of Islam
are interpreting the words of God that way is beside the point. The
idea of effort in mainstream Islam is doing good and doing the right
thing, not doing evil.

That brings us to the concept of jihad. Westerners think that
jihad means holy war. It doesn't help that Westerners see videos of
radical Muslims perpetrating unspeakable violence and claiming
that it is justified by their faith. Jihad, though, means struggle
and effort, and Muhammad saw the most important jihad as the
struggle of the self over the self. "The best jihad is the one who
strives against his own self for Allah," Muhammad said. Personal
jihad is the struggle to purify oneself from evil, just as a Christian
may purify herself of evil by doing penance or a Hindu may purify
himself by doing puja, or a Jain may purify herself through fasting.

Jihad is also about making the effort to do right action. In
2011, the Oregon Islamic Academy graduated its first class. One of
its graduates was Amira Fattom. Amira and other teenagers from
OIA went to Japan in their senior year to help in the city of Sendai,
which had been brutalized by a tsunami earlier in the year. "Our
teachers showed us how to put how we feel into action, by actually

going there and helping people," Amira said at the graduation banquet. "We furnished temporary homes. We helped set up a base so families can work their way back up."[42] Amira is just one of millions of mainstream Muslims who understand that effort to both overcome one's own tendencies toward sin and to reach out to help others is the cornerstone of their faith.

Let's be clear: people can make wrong kinds of effort. Both terrorist attacks and the many mass shootings in America show us that. The many people in jail for a variety of violent crimes, many of which were complex in their planning, tell us that. Making right effort means thinking about more than ourselves. It means seeing others as having the same feelings and needs and desires as ourselves. It means seeing others as brethren rather than as targets or strangers to be feared.

Sometimes, all our effort goes into defending an identity that we have built for ourselves. We put our effort into shutting others out. I often see those kinds of posts on social media: many who post express opinions that others are not worthwhile, and many who post think others have disappointed them. If others have disappointed us, perhaps we need to look at what we wanted and expected from them. If we think others are not worthwhile, perhaps we need to consider why we cannot see the good in them and to consider whether we would want others to see us that way. Cherishing others is very hard work. The first step is to think of ourselves as baby chicks and to crack ourselves out of our own shell. Then we need to really explore the new world in which we find ourselves. That world is likely to be very frightening. We may harbor hatred for others. We may see others as enemies. Effort means looking past that to abandon our prejudices, including our prejudices about ourselves.

THE BENEFITS OF EFFORT

To be a decent human being takes effort. "Decent" is a
judgment, but most reasonable persons would agree that individuals
who plunder the homes of others, rob people on the streets, rape
and assault others, abuse children and animals, and kill wantonly
are not acting decently. In fact, harming others is not terribly
difficult. It does not take special effort to point a gun at someone
during a robbery and pull a trigger. It may take some expertise
to break a window or jimmy a lock to burgle a house, but it
doesn't take soul searching. Many criminals admit they acted out
of impulse. So do many others who have done wrong things that
they later regret. To do the right thing can be hard. A 2013 poll
of Wall Street workers helps to illustrate this. Almost half of those
surveyed had firsthand knowledge of wrongdoing. Almost a quarter
said they would engage in insider trading to make $10 million if
they could get away with it. Twenty-nine percent believed that
financial professionals may *need* to act unethically or illegally in
order to succeed, and 28% believed that in the financial services
industry, the interests of the client do not come first.[43] The smaller
the perceived chance of consequences and the bigger the perceived
payoff, the more likely people are to act in ways that hurt others,
which is how society ends up with criminals such as Bernie Madoff,
who scammed his investors out of $65 million in the biggest Ponzi
scheme in American history. As Madoff made more and more
money, the temptation to keep doing so must have been enormous.
In a sense, continuing the crime would have been easier than
stopping it. In contrast, determining the right thing to do and doing
it can be very difficult.

Effort has real benefits in the conventional world. A study
in the *British Journal of Psychology* analyzed the relationship
between effort and anxiety in golfers. The surprising finding was

that the more effort golfers perceived that they exerted, the more their anxiety was lessened.[44] Lower anxiety resulted in improved performance. The benefits of effort aren't limited to athletics. Effort also matters in school in surprising ways. Research has shown that professors whose classes are perceived to be hard and to require more effort receive better evaluations from students than professors whose classes are perceived to be easy, so long as the effort the professor expects is appropriate to the task.[45] In other words, the "easy" professor is not seen by students as the better professor; students understand the value of hard work.

It's true that working harder and working more doesn't automatically guarantee a better outcome or product. We all know stories of students, workers, spouses and friends who have worked hard at something and either failed altogether or didn't improve the product or situation. All the same, extraordinary effort is needed to produce extraordinary results. The story of professor and number theorist Andrew Wiles is an example.

Wiles was obsessed with solving a puzzle famous in the world of mathematics known as Fermat's Last Theorem. The theorem was that the equation $x^n+y^n=z^n$ had no whole number solutions when n was greater than 2. For over 300 years, no mathematician had been able to prove that this was true or untrue. Wiles took up the challenge in 1987 after learning that the theorem could be proved or disproved in relation to a theorem on elliptical curves called the Taniyama-Shimura conjecture. Elliptical curves were one of his areas of expertise. For most of six years, he worked on the problem alone and in secret. He related that his marriage had been spent on working on the problem and that he told his wife early on that the only things he had time for were their family and the problem. The problem consumed his time, but he finally confided his efforts to a colleague at Princeton. The two double-checked Wiles' work over months, and Wiles finally presented his proof at a conference in June 1993. Immediately, he was thrust onto a world stage. It seemed that he had done the impossible.

Then trouble struck. The proof needed to be verified by other mathematicians. In their verification, his peers discovered an error in the proof. At first, Wiles thought the proof would be easily fixed. It wasn't. Weeks dragged into months. For over a year he struggled to fix the proof with the aid of a former student. However, it wouldn't yield. The stakes were tremendous. He hadn't released the manuscript to the math world in the meantime for fear that someone else might be able to fix the error. Whoever fixed the error would get the glory for solving the problem. His years of solitary obsession and struggle would be for nothing. Finally, in September 1994, he was ready to give up. He felt beaten by the problem and was ready to release the manuscript. He couldn't resolve to do that, though, without going back to the problem one last time. By then exhausted, isolated, beset by the storm brewing around him of mathematicians demanding to see the entire manuscript, no doubt feeling the pressure of his immediate fame now intertwined with his academic career—would it reflect badly on Princeton if he could not deliver on his boast? —he returned to the puzzle. This time, he saw the answer that had eluded him so long.[46] His effort paid off. An "impossible" problem was finally solved.

Sometimes the effort is about more than one person and fame. Sometimes extraordinary effort is needed just to sustain existence. In 2014, that was the case in western Africa. The reason was Ebola. The virus that was first discovered in central Africa in the mid-1970s erupted in a virulent form in western Africa early that year. Genetics analysis shows that the outbreak started at the end of 2013 from one person, a two-year-old who died of the disease. Soon most of the child's immediate family was dead. Within three

months, three western African countries were under siege from the
virus. By the end of the year, *Time* magazine would name Ebola
fighters its "Person of the Year."

The stories from Ebola's front lines were sobering. Dr.
Philip Ireland, an Ebola doctor who contracted the disease and
miraculously survived it, said, "Ebola is very scary. You have to
have courage." In the same interview, he described the efforts
to contain the disease and to keep people alive as "... fighting a
war."[47] Those struggling against Ebola made heroic efforts. They
knew they could die. They knew the odds were stacked against
them. There was no guaranteed treatment that would ensure their
survival if they caught the disease, and according to the World
Health Organization (WHO) the fatality rate averages 50%. One
of every two people who contracts the virus will die.[48] The same
organization predicted that western Africa would eventually
experience more than 20,000 cases. Some rural medical facilities in
affected countries were primarily places for people to die; they had
undeveloped infrastructure and few ambulances. Still, medics and
volunteers fought on and turned the tide. Without the collective and
selfless efforts of those fighting Ebola, entire communities would
have run the risk of disappearing in bloody death. Instead, progress
contained the virus and kept citizens alive.

A big effort might not even look that big from the outside. Still,
it might have momentous results. For example, because I committed
myself to effort, two strangers' lives were changed, hopefully for
the better. It was hard to make the decision to adopt a child as a
single parent and hard to earn the money to go through with the
adoption. It was desperately hard to get on a plane to China by
myself and fly thousands of miles away. I knew becoming a parent
would change me. I would need to become more responsible, less of
a free spirit. Despite my fear I made the effort.

They did, too. Think of the emotional and psychological effort my children—first a nine-year-old, then a twelve-year-old—must have made to get onto a plane with someone they had known for only a few days and fly those thousands of miles *away* from everyone and everything they knew. My daughter left children in the orphanage whom she knew as her brothers and sisters. She left the mango tree where she used to climb to pick sweet, fresh fruit, and she left the predictability of her life in the orphanage. Even her language and diet changed. My son left behind the excitement and ease of getting around in Nanjing City. He left the woman he thought of as his older sister, and he left the woman he knew as his "grandma" who had taken him into the old folks' home that she managed and who had babied him from shortly after his birth. What sense of fear and emotional pain must those kids have overcome to go away with me and to trust me enough over the years to become my daughter and my son, to become new people?

Part of our effort meant learning to respect each other and our backgrounds. We come from different cultures. We like different foods. We have different beliefs. My kids are atheists. I am a Buddhist who worships at a synagogue. I do not want to force them to be me. They know better than to try to force me to be them.

To understand and accept and honor our differences takes real effort. We are surrounded by these stories of effort, from the very famous to the hardly known. Sakena Yacoobi's efforts to start forbidden education programs in Pakistan and Afghanistan now benefit hundreds of thousands of women and girls. Whit Alexander strove to help lift people out of poverty in Africa through developing a business based on rechargeable Burro batteries. Rescue workers have dug out and labored with people in Thailand, China, the Philippines, Indonesia, New Orleans, Haiti, and Puerto Rico. There are so many around us who have accomplished what others cannot imagine attempting because they have respected the needs of others, no matter that the others might not be "like them."

Sometimes effort helps only us, and that can be enough. "My job is to see your weaknesses and drive them out," tai chi master Gregory Fong tells his tai chi and kung fu classes. I was one of his tai chi students. I was in pain many times. Despite the pain, I did what he told me to do, even as I sometimes cursed him under my breath. My own story is not miraculous, although my energy and my body have both strengthened tremendously. I saw small miracles in his class, though. People with diabetes made dramatic improvements in their blood sugar levels. People overcame crippling conditions like lupus. People watched their blood pressure drop to normal levels. Work works. It's not magic. Even the Mayo Clinic acknowledges that physical exertion helps people to lose weight, improve their health, feel happier, and have more energy because of muscle and connective tissue getting more oxygen and nourishment.[49] The only problem is that each of us has to overcome our own tendency to laziness. It is easy and often pleasant to think "I can't" or "Nothing can be done," or "This is just the way it is" or "That's unfortunate." Blinding ourselves to our potential to change can seem comfortable. To do the real work makes us like Batman: pained but trained. We become strong and adept. Sometimes we might even put our lives on the line in order to make a difference, though our risks might not always be quite that dramatic.

While such effort makes us human superheroes, it makes us closer to the Infinite, too. Reaching for a sense of the Infinite takes strenuous effort. It takes real work. That's what all the spiritual texts tell us. Making effort means that we are willing to have a vision of what can be accomplished. We are willing to have faith and bring something into being where before there was a void. We are willing to see and trust in the best of human nature rather than the worst. We're also willing to trust that there is a reason bigger than us.

I can think of two times in my life when I have come close to making adequate effort to reach a spiritual Ideal. One was kneeling in a confessional in a Trappist monastery long after I had renounced Catholicism. With a shaking voice I confessed my sins. The sins I had carried within myself for years were profound, and I asked for forgiveness, fully believing that I did not deserve it. I expected to be lambasted. I expected to be told that atonement was impossible. Instead, the kindness in the monk's voice as he offered me absolution shattered what little composure I'd had when I'd entered the confessional. To confess those sins aloud to another fallible human being, one whom I fully expected to scorn, berate, and disdain me, took fortitude. I had to relinquish my ego and my pride. In my mind and in my heart, I had to truly accept myself as the lowest of all, and that was backbreaking. So was facing that I had committed the sins I confessed. The true effort was in admitting the wrongness of them to myself. It was confronting my wrong actions and the evil in me and admitting that I could have acted differently but didn't. Because of my wrong actions, others had been hurt. For a person with a conscience, that is a troubling realization, but I needed to both admit and confess my wrongdoing to ensure that I would learn from it and become a better person.

The second time I made such an effort, I killed a mouse. Laugh if you will. In Buddhism, killing another living being is prohibited. I was in the house of a friend who had a mouse infestation, and she had set out glue traps. She had never seen what glue traps do to small living beings. A mouse was screaming piteously, pulling himself to bits on the trap. There was no way of freeing him without killing him. Whether rightly or wrongly, I believed that the most beneficial thing I could do for the mouse was to end its suffering. I picked up a rock and crushed its skull, and every fiber of my hands and arms resisted that act. I sometimes wonder if I would do the same thing today now that I have a better understanding of what suffering really is and how universal it is. I've learned in the ensuing years that it would now take me as much effort to resist killing the mouse and putting it out of its earthly misery as it took me then to kill it. As a spiritual seeker, I don't know which action is "better." I'm still working to find that perfection, just as so many of us are.

Most of us won't cure Ebola. Most of us won't solve perplexing mathematical problems. Most of us won't even shoulder a burden as warriors and join the military. There's no shame in any of that. We all have our own struggles, and we can engage mightily in them. Maybe we will leave an abusive relationship. The National Domestic Violence Hotline notes that on average it takes a person suffering domestic abuse seven times to leave for good, providing she or he is not killed in the meantime. Think of how hard it can be to find our own self-worth, to believe in it, and to act on it, knowing that we put ourselves at risk in doing so. Maybe we will make the medical or mental health appointment that has been terrifying us. Maybe we can get the clarity that even if the news is a dire disease, we can start to plan for the next steps we must take on our life journey, whether that is a cure, healing, or preparing for what comes next. Maybe we will challenge someone's racist ideas. Maybe we will conquer our fears of being shunned or disliked or laughed at to stand up for vulnerable people, and maybe we can refuse to see others as fundamentally different from us. Maybe we can expand our families and give others a chance at a life filled with love and security. Maybe we can love our own family members. Maybe we can help a homeless person find housing. Maybe we can sit and meditate until our anger quiets. Every one of us has the power to work harder, to do the uncomfortable.

To reach beyond our limits requires more from us than we think we can do. Without hard exercise, we cannot grow a strong muscle. Without strong effort, we cannot grow a strong good heart, a strong spirit, and a strong sense of connection.

Compassion

When a synagogue official named Jairus fell at the feet of
Jesus and asked Jesus to heal his dying daughter, Jesus went off
with the man. Jesus' fame had grown, and He could go nowhere
without attracting great crowds, as He did that day. As Jairus
and Jesus walked together, a woman pressed forward through
the crowd. For years, she had been plagued with hemorrhages.
Doctors had not been able to help her. If the story were written
today, she would probably be diagnosed with endometriosis. The
story relates that the woman "suffered greatly at the hands of many
doctors,"[50]meaning she had been painfully poked and prodded. She
was probably anemic. In that time, she would not have gotten the
treatment that many women, including me, have had for the same
affliction: a hysterectomy. That procedure wasn't performed for
the first time until 1843, when it was undertaken in England rather
than the dry and dusty streets of Galilee.[51] In other words, her
situation was hopeless. She may have been infertile, adding to her
problems. Who would want to stay married to an infertile woman
in that place and that time? Even now, fertile women are seen as
more desirable than infertile women.[52]

This nameless woman had heard about Jesus, and she had a
faith in him that was so extraordinary that she thought, "If I but
touch His clothes, I shall be cured."[53]So she came up behind him
and she touched his cloak.[54] When I try to imagine that moment,
all that comes to mind are bad kung fu movies in which the good-
guy master suddenly loses all his power. Jesus knew He had been
touched. He could feel whatever happened to him when she touched
him. There He was, setting off to cure Jairus' daughter who lay
near death when whoosh, his power dissipated. Maybe he felt afraid
of the weakness. At the very least he might have felt perturbed

because he stopped and scanned the crowd to see who had touched him and drained him of his healing powers.

He didn't have to look far. The woman, terrified and shaking, fell to the ground in front of Jesus and confessed that she was the one He was looking for. The moment she had touched him she felt herself healed. Perhaps she stammered as she told him her story. There she groveled in the dust before Jesus, who was a renowned Jewish man. In all likelihood, she was ritually unclean when she touched Jesus; endometriosis doesn't confine menstrual periods to neat 28-day periods interrupted by just four or five days of bleeding. At frequently unpredictable times, blood can issue forth in a gush so profound that she may have passed clots the size of her fist when she wasn't spotting at odd intervals. Her bleeding would have made her unclean. Unclean women weren't supposed to touch men.

There is a popular saying in Buddhism: anyone can be compassionate when sitting on a cushion. Jesus wasn't on a cushion. He was caught in a crowd, and there isn't much evidence that He adored crowds. Jesus didn't seem to have rock star fantasies. Caring for afflicted and dying people must have been hard work, especially since so many – then as now – expected to be cured of the incurable. Jesus did challenge some taboos, such as the table fellowship rules of the Pharisees, but He had also been clear that the law was the law. By touching him, the woman had violated law. In return, Jesus could have been angry and vengeful. He could have sent her off to suffer the rest of her days on Earth in blood, pain, and misery.

However, He didn't. Perhaps He told her to get up as He said to her, "Daughter, your faith has saved you. Go in peace and be cured of your affliction."[55] If He was faced with the temptation to act like a pompous jerk, He didn't show it, at least not in the Gospel stories. What He showed instead was compassion.

Jesus demanded compassion from others as well. A story from
the Gospel of John illustrates that. John (or a later writer; there is
some evidence that the story was added after the original text of the
gospel had been written) narrates the story that begins when Jesus,
after a night at the Mount of Olives, returned to the temple early in
the morning. Waiting for him was a group of scribes and Pharisees.
The Pharisees were like the lawyers of their time. For the Pharisees,
the Law of Moses was everything. God was personal although
distant: God had delivered Israel from slavery and He needed to
be praised through people keeping God's law. The Pharisees, who
became the eventual writers of the Mishnah, asserted that as long
as people are ungodly, God's anger is upon the world. In their
view, the death of the wicked was a benefit to the world, because
otherwise God was going to smite people, and as the stories in
the Torah tell us, God's acts of retribution were terrible in their
consequences. Stories abound of suffering and death, plagues, and
exile. Therefore, righteousness was everything to the Pharisees.
They believed that people *must* be righteous. Then along came
Jesus. Jesus knew the Law of Moses very well, but He perceived an
even higher law, that of Love: not carnal love, not romantic love,
but compassionate love.

Clearly, the Pharisees were not entirely sure what to make of
Jesus. John tells this next story as if what happened next was a
setup, as if the Pharisees were trying to test Jesus and were hoping
to find him guilty of some transgression, but by this point Jesus
was known to have entered the homes of sinners and eaten dinner
with them. He was known to have performed a variety of miracles.
People knew about him, even if they were skeptical about him. Even
his own family had said He was crazy. Therefore, what would have
been the point of a test? On the other hand, discourse and even
dispute over interpretations of the law were and are an essential

part of Jewish tradition. Perhaps it was less to test than to debate when the Pharisees brought to the middle of the temple area a woman who had been caught in the act of adultery.

We can assume that eyewitnesses accused her. How quickly had she been caught and brought to the temple? Had she had time to clothe herself, or did she stand before the assembled men, now her judges, embarrassed by her nakedness as well as by her wrongdoing? From John's account, it is impossible to know if the Pharisees who brought her forth did so roughly or dispassionately. We don't know whether they felt any sense of anticipation or contempt. We do know that the Pharisees wanted to hear the opinion of Jesus, whom they may have viewed as an eccentric judge. "In the law, Moses commanded us to stone such women," the Pharisees said to him. "So what do you say?"[56]

Jesus smartly said nothing. Instead He bent over and started to write in the dirt with his finger. It's impossible to say what the Pharisees thought as they watched this. Was He drawing charms? Doodling? Ignoring them? Finally, after a long moment He answered them: "Let the one among you who is without sin be the first to throw a stone at her."[57] To sin was to break the law, Jesus might as well have said, and those who had broken the law had no right to sit in judgment against others who had done the same. Tellingly, no stone was thrown.

Did those men somehow instantly become compassionate? Maybe not. Maybe their hands had been itching to dig the pit and to thrust the woman into it, to pick up the heavy stones and hear them thud into her flesh with satisfaction, as has happened in recent times in Islamic State controlled areas.[58] Then again, maybe the seeds of true compassion were planted that day. Perhaps, for a fleeting instant those men came to understand that whatever weakness landed the woman in the arms of a forbidden man, they shared that weakness. Maybe they realized suddenly that whatever judgment they believed awaited them from God awaited them all. Possibly they finally understood that their job on this earth was to be compassionate toward each other, as Jesus so many times tried to show those who followed him.

WAVES OF COMPASSION: ISLAM AND SUFISM

On December 26, 2004, the day after Christians around the world had celebrated the birth of their Lord, Banda Aceh in Indonesia was flattened. Buildings were shredded and cars thrown like Matchbox toys in Phuket and Patong Beach in Thailand, and European tourists were feared buried in mass graves. Although most of the dead were Indonesian and Sri Lankan, people from all over the world perished when the India and Burma tectonic plates ruptured by twenty meters, unleashing a force equivalent to 23,000 Hiroshima bombs.[59] The resulting fifteen to thirty-foot-high walls of water smashed into Indonesia and Thailand at 200 miles per hour. Less than two months of relief efforts later, the death count had reached over 225,000, a staggering number that seemed biblical in its excess. To many in the world, this was simply the latest chapter in a story that was already thousands of years old. Its predecessor had been seen in the story in which God used the Red Sea to annihilate the Egyptian army.

"Why did God choose to do this to all those poor people?" Mohan Siromani, an Indian oil worker who lives part time in Abu Dhabi, asked me in an email. "What is the reason for this?" Some people, such as Muslim cleric Mohammed Faizeen, seemed to know the answer to Mohan's question. "Allah signed His name," Faizeen said. "He sent it as punishment. This comes from ignoring His laws."[60] His words make clear Faizeen's belief in an authoritarian God.

In the 21st century, perhaps no topic is more contentious and misunderstood as whether God expects Muslims to be compassionate. This is an era in which we have seen photos and videos of Westerners being beheaded by Muslim extremists. It is the post-9/11 era, and Americans are determined not to forget that 3,000 of their country's citizens perished simply because they went to work on a morning when several Muslim men who were utterly lacking in compassion had enacted their plot to strike terror into the hearts of Americans and other Westerners. The message of those men was that if such devastation could happen in America, it could happen anywhere. It has. Indonesia, China, Russia, France, England and more have lost scores to terrorism. There is nothing compassionate about such acts; they are the antithesis of compassionate. They are unilaterally and wantonly cruel.

Frequently, political commentators seem to want people to think that this is the true nature of Islam and that it is warlike, barbaric, and aggressive, especially in a time when groups such as the Islamic State, Boko Haram, al-Qaeda, and others wage aggressive war that shocks Middle Eastern and global citizens alike. That stance is useful for making people feel afraid. It's effective when people don't further educate themselves. The responses I get when I ask in class, "What three things surprise you as you learn about Islam?" are telling. "I didn't know that Islam respects Jesus," one person will invariably say. "I didn't know that Islam was founded by Abraham, just like Judaism and Christianity," another will express. Someone will comment, "I never knew that Islam tried to give Arab women more equality and make their lives better." Always, at least person will offer, "I never understood that Islam has an emphasis on compassion."

Many non-Muslim people believe that Allah must be merciless, and it's true that God in the Qur'an is not a being to be trifled with. All throughout the Qur'an, though, God is addressed "In the name of God, the Compassionate, the Merciful." Would the Compassionate, Merciful God want humans to act like vicious thugs, or would it be more logical to think that the Compassionate, Merciful God wants people to act in His image, compassionately and mercifully?

"In Islam, compassion is one of the main goals we strive for," Amirah Fattom, the student at Oregon Islamic Academy who went to Japan to help the Japanese people rebuild, asserts.[61] I think back to my days studying at Portland State University, when I became friends with Firyal Isa, a Palestinian Muslim woman in my Middle Eastern history class. Most of Firyal's family lived in Ramallah, a Muslim and Christian city on Israel's West Bank that was one of the hubs of the first Intifada in the 1980s, during which the Israeli Defense Force sprayed people with tear gas and imposed restrictions on their travel, their education, and their livelihood. Firyal's voice would shake when she would talk about the 1982 massacre at Sabra and Chatila, the refugee camps for Palestinians in Lebanon, in which as many as 3,000 Palestinians were killed by Lebanese Christian Phalangists at the behest of Ariel Sharon. Eyewitnesses at the time reported the streets being littered with corpses of children and adults alike. Firyal had lost family in that massacre.

Then Firyal would buy me a Coke. I remember once when I protested. "You bought last time," I said. "I'll buy this time." It was the only time I knew her to divide us into "you" and "we," meaning "Americans" and "Palestinians." "*You* have to keep track of everything, like a balance sheet, who owes who," she erupted. "*We* do not think that way. We give, because to see that someone would like something and to give it without being asked is the right thing to do."

For Firyal, the fast for the month of Ramadan was a chance
to practice compassion every day. To spend every day for a month
feeling hunger during the day made her and her family more
cognizant of the suffering of others, especially the poor who so
often struggle to eat, and grateful for all they had, which they
expressed after sundown when they would gather to break the fast
with an array of delicious foods. In this way, they could be mindful
of the hardships of others, be mindful of their own abundance,
and be mindful of God's assertion to work to lessen the gap
between those who have and those who have not, because all are
equally precious.

In Islam, caring for others is a virtue. "Let not those of virtue
among you and wealth swear not to give to their relatives and
the needy and the emigrants for the cause of Allah, and let them
pardon and overlook," God says in the Qur'an.[62] "Would you not
like that Allah should forgive you?" In other words, God says in
that book that we should treat others as we would want Him to
treat us. What radicals in any religion refuse to consider is that
not one of them, if asked, would want to be beheaded, mutilated,
tortured, dismembered, or blown up by God.

Mainstream Islam understands and practices compassion.
Egyptian president Mohamed Morsi showed an example of that
in April 2013 when violence against Coptic Christians erupted in
Egypt. Hundreds of Christians took refuge in the Coptic cathedral
in Cairo as they were beset by a Muslim mob who wanted their
blood. President Morsi could have ignored the situation. If he
had, certainly hundreds would have died. Instead he showed both
compassion and leadership by ordering guards to the cathedral
and insisting that it was the state's responsibility to protect
those inside.[63]

From that very practical expression of Islam to more mystical expressions, compassion stems from a God more benevolent than the authoritarian God that Mohammed Faizeen imagined. For example, the Sufi mystic Muhammad Raheem Bawa Muhaiyaddeen believed that God and all of Islam itself was full of compassion. Muhaiyaddeen believed that even the tiniest bits of all the atoms swirling in the universe contained God and His energy, and the mystic insisted that "If we reflect on this, anyone who calls himself Islam will never harm anyone." His words are the antithesis of the terrible actions carried out today by extremist Muslims against mainstream Muslims as well as against other targets: "To all who say they believe in God, please realize with your faith that God hears every word you say.... Realizing this, speak only what is truth and act only with God's qualities of love, compassion, justice, patience, and the realization that each life is as important as your own. This is the true message within the Qur'an."[64] Muhaiyaddeen's view of Islamic compassion is one that resonates throughout other spiritual texts.

CURRENTS OF COMPASSION: CONFUCIUS, THE DAO, AND HINDU

Compassion is not feeling sorry for others. It's not giving others a free pass. Often, we believe that compassion for others means that we lose or give up something ourselves. That is not true. Compassion is to feel with someone; it is to understand on the deepest level what motivates someone and how someone feels. Compassion is empathy, and the major religions and ethical systems of the world agree about the importance of compassion. In the *Analects*, for example, Ci Gong asks Confucius, "'Is there one word which may serve as a rule of practice for all one's life?' The Master said, 'Is not reciprocity such a word? What you do not want done to

yourself, do not do to others.'"[65] Confucius' point has everything in
common with Rabbi Hillel's directive in the Talmud. Rabbi Hillel
declared, "What is hateful to yourself, do not do to your fellow
man. That is the whole Torah; the rest is just commentary." Rabbi
Hillel's own point comes straight from Leviticus, where God sums
up admonitions not to bear hatred in one's heart, not to do wrong
to others, and not to seek vengeance with the directive, "Thou shalt
love thy neighbor as thyself."[66] The Gospel of Mark (12:31) tells us
Jesus agreed. Many miles and centuries apart, Confucius, Leviticus,
and Jesus equally stressed compassion.

Compassion is stressed in the *Dao De Jing*, too. The twenty-
third chapter tells us, "There is such a thing as aligning one's
actions with the Way. If you accord with the Way, you become
one with it. If you accord with virtue, you become one with it." In
other words, our task is to feel with and act with, to abandon our
ego-centered view that sees all from our own limited perspectives.
We see it in the twenty-seventh chapter as well, where the sage tells
us, "...the sage is always skillful in elevating people. Therefore she
does not discard anything." The compassionate person doesn't
look for only the best, the text explains, because to choose only
what appears to be the best is the act of those who want to elevate
only themselves. As a result, they will eventually fall. The clearest
expression, though, is in the sixty-seventh chapter. There, the sage
tells us,

> I have three treasures that I hold and cherish. The first
> is compassion, the second is frugality, [and] the third
> is not daring to put myself ahead of everybody. Having
> compassion, I can be brave. Having frugality, I can be
> generous. Not daring to put myself ahead of everybody I
> can take the time to perfect my abilities. Now, if I am brave
> without compassion, generous without frugality, or go to

the fore without putting my own concerns last, I might as
well be dead. If you wage war with compassion, you will
win. If you protect yourself with compassion, you will be
impervious. Heaven will take care of you, protecting you
with compassion.

Through selflessness, the text tells us, we are able to perfect
ourselves,[67] and selflessness can be accomplished only if we can
imagine ourselves as the other. Our imagination must be vivid
and accurate. We need to feel as the other feels, see as the other
sees, and move past our own immediate feelings and reactions to
imagine the effects of what we do unto others.

What many commonly call the Golden Rule is found in
Hinduism, too. As Krishna tries to persuade Arjuna to do his duty
in the *Bhagavad Gita*, he alludes to it. "An enlightened person
looks at a learned and humble Brahmana, an outcast, even a cow,
an elephant, or a dog with an equal eye," he tells Arjuna. "Such a
person has realized Brahman (God) because Brahman is flawless
and impartial."[68]In other words, in the heart of God as well as in
the cosmic scheme of things, Krishna says, our cats, the neighbor's
schnauzer, the goldfish that used to live in the backyard pond, the
raccoons that ate the goldfish and destroyed the pond plants in
their ravenous glee, perhaps even the pond plants, the old man who
scours through the glass on trash day for any returnable deposit
bottles, the spider that bit my daughter, my daughter, and myself
are all perfectly equal. No one with fame, fortune or power—the
president of the World Bank, the president of the United States, the
Pope, Lady Gaga, Steven Spielberg, Harvey Weinstein—is more or
less precious than any of us, even the little biting spider. To see all
living beings equally and to understand that we are not essentially
different from them is the heart of compassion. Can I easily abuse
or abandon a dog, for example, if I realize that the dog feels pain,

just as I do, and that the dog is not subordinate to me; that in fact, the dog and I are equal beings?

This is not Hinduism's only expression of the value of compassion. The *Bhagavad Gita* is part of a longer epic, the *Mahabharata*. In Book 13 of the epic, the Vedic deity Brihaspati tells Yudhishthira, who is leader of the Pandava clan and the eldest brother of Arjuna,

> I shall tell thee what constitutes the highest good of a human being. That man who practices the religion of universal compassion achieves his highest good.... He who, from motives of his own happiness, slays other harmless creatures with the rod of chastisement, never attains to happiness, in the next world. That man who regards all creatures as his own self, and behaves towards them as towards his own self, laying aside the rod of chastisement and completely subjugating his wrath, succeeds in attaining to happiness.... One should never do that to another which one regards as injurious to one's own self.[69]

Every day, many Hindus perform acts of compassion, but the story of one now-famous woman helps to showcase this spiritual ideal. Amma, sometimes called "the hugging saint," began her life in a Kerala village as a girl named Sudhamani Idamannel. By the time the young Sudhamani was nine years old, she was finished with school and was responsible for the more important tasks of helping the family, for she had been born into a family that was not high caste and not wealthy. A curious irony of the world seems to be that some of those who have struggled the most, whether against prejudice, poverty, or abuse, seem to take a certain delight when those kinds of misfortunes befall others, especially those who are perceived as having more than they do. Sudhamani's attitudes in her childhood and her teenaged experiences displayed none of that delight. Instead, when she collected scraps from neighbors to feed her family's livestock, she would give items in return, even though her family punished her for giving away what little they had. More importantly, she listened to people and cried at their problems and reached out to them. It didn't matter to her that by touching men as well as women she was breaking cultural taboos.

Now she is known as Mata Amritanandamayi, or, more simply, Amma, and she is a force for compassion in the world. "She is simply the essence, the embodiment, of compassion," said one spiritual seeker when Amma came to California. [70] To Amma, the world is suffering not just from a lack of necessities for so many in need; it is suffering from "a lack of love and compassion."[71] Her acts of compassion include far more than hugs. She is responsible for projects that include housing for the poor and homeless, medical care for the poor, hospices, support for destitute women, tree planting efforts, schools and classes in India from elementary through graduate level that emphasize spiritual development as well as technical knowledge, and soup kitchens, including in the United States.

The why of her actions is simple. Amma doesn't believe that compassionate action makes us better than others or gives us a "good check mark" in any book of God. Rather, by loving each other, we love God. We become Godlike. As Amma once said to a reporter, "When a bee hovers over a garden of varied flowers, what it beholds is not the difference between the flowers but the honey within them." In the same way, she said, she "sees the same Supreme Self in each and every one."[72] True compassion is thus seeing the Infinite in each other and seeing the sameness in me and thee.

By imagining the sameness and suffering of others, we can work to relieve it. The website of the Hindu volunteer organization Bochasanwasi Akshar Purushottam Sanstha (BAPS) notes that it works to help society through a focus on selflessness. After the devastating earthquake in Gujarat in 2001 that killed more than 20,000 people and left more than a million without homes,[73]the spiritual director of BAPS, Pramukh Swami Maharaj, said, "... whatever has to happen, happens. The good and the painful all are a part of life, and we should accept both with equanimity. When people are facing difficulties and sorrows, our Indian tradition is to offer them solace. We feel that by serving the human beings we serve the Lord Himself."[74] Hinduism doesn't teach us to blame God or people's actions for the tsunami or other disasters: the earthquake, the fire, the train wreck. When the waters come, though, our compassion for others is a boat by which we can perfect ourselves. By focusing ourselves on protecting and helping others, we can protect our own sense of connection and good heart. We can learn to give up our prejudices and hatreds.

A STREAM OF COMPASSION: BUDDHISM

The Buddha put the idea of reciprocity and compassion yet another way. In the fifth chapter of the Sanskrit collection the *Udana*, the "Discourse About the King," King Pasenadi and Queen Mallika go around in a conversation in which both confess the limitations of their love. Queen Mallika loves no one more than herself, and King Pasenadi loves no one more than himself. King Pasenadi relates the conversation to the Buddha, who was staying at the time in a monastery in Jeta's Wood. Upon hearing the story, the Buddha uttered, "There is surely no one found who is loved more than oneself. In the same way others each love themselves, therefore one who cares for himself should not harm another."[75]What does

that mean? Why should we not harm others if we love ourselves
best? Simply because true compassion means realizing that there
is no boundary between ourselves and others. To harm others
means harming ourselves, the spiritual part of ourselves as well
as, perhaps, the living, breathing part of ourselves that may
suffer revenge at the hands of the person we harm. So many of
our experiences, both real and imagined, are full of such stories
of vengeance.

Fortunately, though, our collective wisdom is also filled with
tales of compassion, often exemplified by self-sacrifice. Another
Jataka story tells such a tale. According to the story, before the
Buddha became enlightened he was the teacher of other seekers.
One day as he and a disciple made their way through the forest, the
not-yet-Buddha came across a tigress with her cubs. In one version
of the story, she was so starved that her milk had dried up and the
cubs would be dead from starvation by nightfall. In another, the
tigress was so famished that she was on the verge of killing her
own cubs and eating them. The Buddha-to-be sent off his disciple
on a distraction of an errand so that he would not be distressed by
what was about to happen, for in the depths of his compassion, the
not-yet-Buddha understood that there was no boundary between
himself and the tigress. As soon as the disciple had gone, the man
who would in another lifetime become the Buddha offered his own
body to the tigress, who devoured it and shared it with her cubs.
Thus he saved three lives with his own.[76]

Compassion is the heart of Buddhism. Compassion is the
driving force that compels those on the Mahayana path of
Buddhism to return to cyclic existence even if they have achieved
Buddhism's ultimate goal of liberation from that cycle—nirvana—
in order to work to help benefit all sentient beings. "To abstain
from all evil, the practice of good, and the thorough purification

of one's mind: this is the teaching of the Buddhas," the Buddha himself said.[77] In yet another iteration of the Golden Rule he also asserted, "All fear violence, life is dear to all. Seeing the similarity to oneself, one should not use violence or have it used...Don't speak harshly to anyone. If you do people will speak to you in the same way. Harsh words are painful and their retaliation will hurt you."[78] Today, news stories show us that truth every day.

Hateful and harmful speech and actions are difficult to curb, especially when compassion is ignored. One example is the war that went on for decades in Vietnam. That war was brought to mind three months after an earthquake and tsunami ravaged the northeastern part of Japan in 2011. At that time, the renowned Vietnamese Zen master Thich Nhat Hanh published a letter as a meditation for those who had suffered and were still suffering from the cataclysmic event that ruptured families as well as nuclear power plants and swept away hope as well as homes, farm buildings, vehicles, and the thousand small things that decorate everyday life. He wrote, "Let us tell our friends there, those who survived the catastrophe, that we are with them, we suffer with them, and we need their courage and their perseverance to maintain our hope." He went on to tell how "close to despair" he had felt during the war in Vietnam. Five times, Thay and Buddhist social workers had rebuilt the village of Tra Loc, located near the demilitarized zone between North and South Vietnam. The effort of rebuilding, and the compassion that motivated the rebuilding, kept him and other Buddhist Vietnamese from despair. The war seemed unending to the young people with him; how could the fighting be resolved? The idea seemed impossible as it raged on for years. Thay, however, buoyed their spirits by reminding them that the Buddha had taught that everything is impermanent. The war could not go on forever. Neither would the suffering of the Japanese people.

At the end of the letter, Thay reminded suffering Japanese citizens of the commonality of human experience, telling them, "Dear brothers and sisters, please do not lose hope. We are aware that you are doing your best. Not only for you, but for your children, for your people, and also for us. We also need hope. Your courage and your compassion will help us retain our humanity and our hope. The situation is really difficult. But the world is with you. We are with you. The tsunami hit us all." [79] Not just adversity binds us. Overcoming it does, too.

Thay is now ninety years old and has lived in exile from his country for more than four decades. Rather than give in to the despair of his experiences in Vietnam as a young monk, he helped to develop the idea of "engaged Buddhism," acting compassionately in the world. He also founded the Buddhist monastic and lay sangha Plum Village in France, has worked diligently for peace, has helped to rescue boat people, has established Zen practice centers in North America, and has written scores of books in prose and poetry. Although he suffered a severe stroke in late 2014, he continues to live with his sangha and continues to practice compassion and loving kindness.

I came to know of Thich Nhat Hanh through another Vietnamese man, Nguyen Vodinh. I met Nguyen when he was a community college student in the 1980s and attempting to get his associate's degree. To do so, he had to pass college level English composition classes. Nguyen had come to the United States in his mid-forties after getting out of a Vietnamese re-education camp. He had found himself on the wrong side of Communism after Vietnam fell, and his life in the camp was physically painful and humiliating. Additionally, he was hammered with attempted political indoctrination. Nguyen had been a math teacher prior to the fall of Vietnam. He had a master's degree. Now he was a janitor at the Albany Medical Center in upstate New York and was starting over, struggling for everything that he had and trying to support his wife and young son in their tiny apartment.

I don't think I've ever known a student who worked as hard as Nguyen did. His goal was to excel. Day after day I would sit with him and go through his essays with him, pointing out how to fix punctuation and correctly structure sentences. Even more than his hard work, though, what I remember best about Nguyen was the day that I asked students to write for a few minutes in class about what they would do if they won the lottery. When they were done, I asked for a few volunteers to read their brief essays out loud. Several guys in the class read about the beer parties they would throw, the fast cars they would buy, and the beautiful women they would attract. One female read about the shopping spree she would look forward to. Then Nguyen raised his hand. The room fell silent as we worked to listen through his accent. If he won the lottery, he said, he would not keep any of the money because he would not have earned it honestly. Instead, he would give it away to different charitable organizations to help people. When he was done, students applauded. At the end of that semester, I came back to my office one day to find an anonymous beautifully wrapped gift on my desk: a copy of Thich Nhat Hanh's *Peace is Every Step*. I have no doubt who brought it to me.

Master Thich Nhat Hanh is not the only famous exile in the world to be teaching compassion. So does His Holiness Tenzin Gyatso, the Fourteenth Dalai Lama. At this point, I have read so many books and articles about what the monks, nuns, and ordinary people of Tibet have endured under Chinese occupation that I sometimes feel numb. Through all the similar stories brought to him, including by those who have endured the most terrible punishments such as beatings, forced disrobing, electrical shocks to genitals, use of iron tongs, and so on, His Holiness has not advocated violence in return. He does not delight in hearing about misfortunes that have befallen Chinese people. Rather, he has consistently advocated compassion. He has wept at the stories of those who have come to him out of imprisonment and through perilous escapes, but he has not called for vengeance. That is because, to the Dalai Lama, "the purpose of life is to be happy."[80] Happiness, in his view, is achieved through compassion.

His Holiness explains that all experience can be divided into physical and mental. As he puts it, for many people happiness and the lack of it are not about physical existence because, "If the body is content, we virtually ignore it."[81] Instead, it is our mind that plagues us. Most of the people who celebrated on hearing of the killing of Osama bin Laden, for example, had not been personally harmed by him. The joy and hatred on the faces of many of those celebrating made clear that they were not thinking of bin Laden as a human being. They were being ruled by emotions that imagined that he had hurt them personally when he engineered the World Trade Center attacks in 2001. They were unaware that death was not a cause for true happiness.

In contrast, the Dalai Lama stresses how compassion can help us free ourselves from such cycles of violence, anger, and hatred, because we are the ones who perpetrate such destructive acts in the world. They cannot come into being without our doing them, and before we do them we must first think and feel them. "From my own limited experience I have found that the greatest degree of inner tranquility comes from the development of love and compassion," he writes. "The more we care for the happiness of others, the greater our own sense of well-being becomes.... This helps remove whatever fears or insecurities we may have and gives us the strength to cope with any obstacles we encounter. It is the ultimate source of success in life. As long as we live in this world we are bound to encounter problems. If, at such times, we lose hope and become discouraged, we diminish our ability to face difficulties. If, on the other hand, we remember that it is not just ourselves but everyone who has to undergo suffering, this more realistic perspective will increase our determination and capacity to overcome troubles."[82] In Buddhism, compassion is the highest good. By practicing compassion we improve earthly existence for ourselves as well as for those around us.

Compassion isn't limited to just recognizing other beings and their experiences. In fact, the feeling that we generate for others might be just our own fear or own experience of suffering. The feeling may appear to be cherishing another being, but it might be self-cherishing. In *Practicing the Path*, Yangsi Rinpoche defines two additional types of compassion: 1) the type that sees that all phenomena are impermanent and 2) the non-conceptual compassion that sees the nature of reality: emptiness.[83] Yangsi Rinpoche defines the type that sees that all phenomena are impermanent as a deeper compassion that stems from our gradual realization that all beings, all actions, all circumstances, and everything that we perceive, are impermanent.[84] On the one hand, it might be easy to think that "if all is impermanent, then what need is there for compassion? The circumstances will inevitably change, eventually for the better." However, this is wrong thinking. In Buddhist thinking, this second form of compassion comes from meditation and the wish to liberate beings from impermanence because cyclic existence causes them suffering and harm.

His Holiness the Dalai Lama notes that true compassion, including this type, can be developed only with "patience and time" and through "constant and conscious effort."[85] Compassion becomes the clear stream that carries away obstacles, that nourishes and sustains, and that flows with great power. Seeing the nature of reality as emptiness enables Buddhist practitioners to generate boundless compassion by realizing that causes and effects create repercussions over many lifetimes. Compassion thus transcends the here and now to recognize the suffering of all beings in all times.

THE BENEFITS OF COMPASSION

Compassion connects us, whether we see our compassionate acts as a reflection of God or not. Sometimes we need to take compassion into the ruins. The Christian Reformed World Relief Committee (CRWRC), for example, helped provide aid in the form of food, water, shelter, medical care, and education to almost 20,000 people in Indonesia after the tsunami there in an effort that lasted a full year. Several years later CRWRC aid worker Ida Kaastra Mutoigo wrote about the many ways in which the organization reached out to others, including helping fisherman to procure new boats, building a house for a woman who was widowed and lost 17 other members of her family in the disaster, and providing advice for a woman who was starting a small bakery business with the hopes of earning enough money to educate her children, including a daughter who wanted to become a physician.[86] "The point of hope and compassion overcoming despair cannot be overemphasized," Mutoigo wrote.[87]

The story of Gloria Thiessen and Cindy Wittmier offers another example. Thiessen had polycystic kidney disease, a genetic disorder in which the kidneys slowly fill with cysts. It's a painful condition that can cause the kidneys to eventually fail, putting the person's life in danger, which is what happened to Thiessen. Dialysis helped to keep her alive, but the only possibility for truly saving her was a kidney transplant. That's when her longtime friend Wittmier stepped in. Because she knew that it can take years for a kidney donor to be matched with a patient—years that Thiessen would not survive—Wittmier volunteered one of her own kidneys for her friend's surgery. Wittmier's perspective was "God gave us two kidneys. We only need one. The other we can donate."[88] In comparison to self-cherishing beliefs, which would be expressed in a sentiment such as "I will gladly donate a kidney after I am dead, but not when I am alive, because something may happen to one and I will need the other one," Wittmier's statement is steeped in true compassion. In 2017, pop star Selena Gomez's best friend Francia Raisa did the same for her, and similar stories abound, such as the New Hampshire police lieutenant, Steve Tenney, who donated part of his liver to save baby Sloan St. James, who was in last stage liver failure from the biliary atresia she was born with.[89]

Compassion has health benefits other than providing transplants, and it can save society money. Medical professionals have pointed out that people are living longer lifespans. As a result, they tend to die of chronic and degenerative diseases. Conventional medicine isn't going to save their lives, but compassion can benefit their quality of life. The more disconnected patients feel, the more depressed they can feel. The more depressed they feel, the more they use health care services. Having someone simply listen to them and care about what they are experiencing lessens depression and reliance on health care.[90] Compassion also drives charity, and that can bring reciprocal and tangible rewards such as tax credits, publicity, increased sales, and similar benefits.

Two additional brief stories show the power of compassion. The first is the story of Dalia Landau, who emigrated to Israel with her Jewish family when she was just a baby. She grew up to love her home and the lemon tree in its yard. When she was almost 20, an

Arab man named Bashir al-Khayri and his two cousins came to
the house, and it was only then that she learned that they had been
forcibly evicted from the house so that it could be given to Jewish
settlers. Later, Bashir's father, who had built the house, came to
visit, and carried away with him some of the lemons from the tree
that he had planted. He treasured the fruits as if they were purest
gold. When Dalia inherited the house, she approached Bashir, who
suggested that it be used as a place to serve Arab children. Both
were able to see past their own sufferings and their own life losses
to create a compassionate bridge for peace and understanding.[91]

   The second story took place in Schenectady, New York, just
after the 9/11 attack. Because of the death threats that were flying
like shrapnel around the Capital District, the Muslim Annur School
closed for a week. When it reopened, the answering machine was
filled with messages, creating a sense of panic amongst the staff
who expected to be subjected to anonymous threats and abuse.
Instead, the messages included one from a synagogue that called
to offer its support and a church that called to offer to send men
to help guard the school if needed. Every call was a message of
support.[92] This is what compassion prompts us to do: to step back
from the edge at which we are most likely to strike out with fury
and bleakness and hopelessness and fear in our hearts and to see
clearly with cherishing hearts the sacred in the mundane world.
The sacred texts of the world urge us to compassion because
without that quality, we and the world in which we live are in grave
danger. Without compassion, we are like cancer cells that attack
other healthy cells and organs in the body until all is ruined and the
living organism succumbs to mindless destruction.

FORGIVENESS: THE SURGE OF COMPASSION

It seems impossible to conclude any discussion of compassion without considering forgiveness. Forgiveness takes tremendous effort. If we have not been injured in some way, we have nothing to forgive, and any quick look at our modern society shows that our usual reaction to being hurt is to want revenge. Born of that desire for revenge, people often want to strike back and cause even more damage than what they have been caused. The desire for revenge leads to blood feuds between families. It leads to spurned lovers lashing out in dramatically shocking and often violent ways, as Richard Remes did to Patricia LeFranc when she ended their relationship in 2009, spraying her in the face with sulphuric acid and thus condemning her to more than eighty surgeries, blindness in one eye, deafness in an ear, an amputated finger, and massive scarring all over her face that has resulted in continual psychological trauma to her.[93] It leads to sustained gang warfare of the kind that erupted on my street one night at 3:00 a.m., terrifying me and my neighbors. The next morning, local police collected over twenty slugs from trees, telephone poles, and the street.

Forgiveness is the antithesis of revenge. It's born of compassion and of the ability to remove the mental separation between ourselves and the person who has injured us. Compassion enables us to see the humanity of the person rather than the label that we so often want to ascribe: "Enemy." It's easy to think that forgiveness is for fools and weaklings, especially when we are in pain and when we burn with sorrow and indignation. However, forgiveness allows us to lay down our own psychological burden. It doesn't mean that we don't care about what the person did. How could LeFranc, for example, not care about what Remes did to her, when fused and melted skin would look back at her from mirrors for the rest of her life and when children taunted her on the streets, calling her a monster? Instead, forgiveness allows for the power of redemption. It means that we will not allow ourselves to be dominated and driven by hatred for the person who has done the damage, a person we might not even know.

Two stories of forgiveness stand out to me. One is the story of Azim Khamisa. Khamisa came from a family that practiced Sufism. He had emigrated to the United States from Kenya and had pursued a career in banking. His would seem to be a typical American success story until the day in 1995 when he received the phone call that perhaps no parent can truly comprehend: his son, Tariq, was dead. He had been murdered. Khamisa's son had been delivering a pizza, nothing more. Gang members had intercepted him and demanded that he hand it over to them. He refused, and a shot tore into him, bleeding his life into the streets of San Diego.[94]

The killer was a fourteen-year-old male, Tony Hicks. Hicks didn't know Tariq. It's easy to imagine the public outcry against Hicks, the blood lust demanding both justice and vengeance. It is easy to imagine Azim Khamisa joining that outcry, perhaps wishing his son's killer to be killed.

That is not what happened. Instead, Khamisa forgave Hicks. Khamisa didn't stop being in pain. To the contrary, Khamisa says that he "grieved hard" for over three years.[95]However, Khamisa quickly realized that if he carried hatred toward Hicks he would be continuing the cycle of violence. There would be no respite. To forgive was to step outside that cycle and to thwart its impulse to do more damage.

Instead, Khamisa founded a foundation in his son's name, and he reached out to Hick's grandfather and guardian, Ples Felix, who was devastated by what his grandson had done. Together, the two men went into schools to spread a message of non-violence and to encourage youth to think about the ramifications of their actions. Khamisa says that he and Felix "...share a common purpose. We believe that in every crime there is an opportunity to improve society by learning how to prevent that crime from happening again. Tariq was a victim of Tony, but Tony was a victim of American society—and society is a mirror image of each and every one of us. What gives me hope is the fact that when Ples and I give talks in school, you can see the metamorphosis as the kids are moved by our story." He explains his motivation this way: "You do forgiveness for yourself, because it moves you on. The fact that it can also heal the perpetrator is the icing on the cake."[96]

Khamisa's story moves me and shames me because it reminds me of my reaction to a breakup with a person I loved deeply. In addition to losing this love, I also lost my home, my dog, my cats, and much of the material life I had built up over the years. I remember saying at the time, "I can never forgive him. He will never be welcome at my table ever again." I had this reaction for the most mundane of pains. I was willing to harbor hatred just because someone had fallen out of love with me. To what can I attribute that sentiment but to my own ego? Did it make me feel any better to harbor my grudges for as long as I did? Did it undo the damage? Did it do anything other than alienate friends and acquaintances who finally grew tired of listening to my self-righteous litany?

Eventually I came to my senses and was able to forgive my ex-partner. In doing so, I was freed of the weight that I had carried for years after we split up. Compassion led me to forgiveness, just as it led Khamisa to it. So did effort. Had I hurt others? Yes, and I needed to acknowledge that to myself. Had my ex acted out of fear? In some ways yes, and who in this world is exempt from fear? Was he unhappy at the time that he wanted out of our relationship? Yes, and who wishes to be unhappy? If I cannot wish unhappiness on myself, then what right did I have to demand it from him and

to damn him if he wasn't willing to embrace it? However, even
though I can now look back on that time and feel embarrassed
at my thoughts and behavior, I confess that the idea of forgiving
someone who might harm my children leaves me breathless. When
I think of such a thing, I become very still. It's as if everything
around me stops while I contemplate something that seems almost
unfathomable to me. How difficult such a thing would be, were it
ever to be demanded of me.

Gandhi knew about the difficulty of forgiveness and of its
power. He said in an interview that "One cannot forgive too
much. The weak can never forgive. Forgiveness is the attribute of
the strong."[97] Such forgiveness is essential. The great theologian
and ethicist Reinhold Niebuhr wrote that "Nothing that is worth
doing can be achieved in our lifetime; therefore we must be
saved by hope. Nothing which is true or beautiful or good makes
complete sense in any immediate context of history; therefore we
must be saved by faith. Nothing we do, however virtuous, can be
accomplished alone; therefore we are saved by love. No virtuous act
is quite as virtuous from the standpoint of our friend or foe as it is
from our standpoint. Therefore we must be saved by the final form
of love, which is forgiveness."[98] Forgiveness is that enormous and
that powerful.

The idea of forgiveness as a form of love leads to the second
story. To be fair, the people in this story, Robi Damelin and Ali
Abu Awwad, would be unlikely to say that theirs is a story of
forgiveness. Rather, they would be more likely to say that it is a
story of using pain constructively. Damelin is Israeli. Abu Awwad
is Palestinian. Both have been devastated by senseless murder.
Damelin's son, David, was shot dead when a Palestinian sniper
looked down the sights of his gun, saw David in his crosshairs,
and pulled the trigger, knowing nothing about him other than that

he was an Israeli. He was the enemy. Abu Awwad lost his brother, Yusuf, to a bullet fired into his skull by an Israeli soldier at the entrance into his own village. He too was the enemy.

For decades now, hatreds have been entrenched between many Israelis and Palestinians. The hatreds stem in part from just such unfathomable losses and such wellsprings of grief. Violence seems almost a given and something impossible to end. In the autumn of 2012 Hamas incited conflict in Gaza and started lobbing missiles. By November 2012, Hamas's leader had claimed victory and swore to fight on to take over Israel "inch by inch." In response, Israel's Prime Minister Benjamin Netanyahu responded that Israelis had "again been exposed to the true face of our enemies. They have no intention of compromising with us. They want to destroy our country."[99] The adversarial stance was all but guaranteed to produce more death, more bloodshed, more riven families, and more anguished funerals of mothers, brothers, fathers, and children on both sides. Even now, years later, it is impossible to know whether lasting peace will ever be achieved.

Given this context, how can Damelin and Abu Awwad possibly be friends? They are, though. Both are members of a group of bereaved individuals called The Parents' Circle. In an interview in the American Public Media program *On Being,* both speak to the power of what can only be called compassion to break the cycle of violence. In the interview, Abu Awwad speaks of the tremendous pain that he felt on losing his brother, then explains, "I don't want just to deal with my pain. I also want to use it because this is the soul of nonviolence." He explains the very real ramifications, pointing out that "...if I'm reacting by violence, I'm giving the occupation the excuse and the reason to make the wall more high and to put more checkpoints and to be right by killing us. So I decide, and my mother and my family, everybody, to be involved

and to join the Parents Circle." Abu Awwad explained that as a
result of joining the Parents Circle and working toward forgiveness,
he discovered that the root of the violence between Israelis and
Palestinians was fear: fear of daily suffering, fear related to
occupation, fear of the Other. No miracles occurred as a result of
these steps, but healing and forgiveness did, and they are a first step
to rapprochement. As Abu Awwad says, "...life doesn't become
better, but it became possible."

To find peace—to *make* peace, as both Damelin and Abu
Awwad put it—is a hard task. Abu Awwad explains," to be honest,
it's very difficult. Nobody want[s] to be honest. Everybody want[s]
to be right, and this is the problem." He's correct. We cannot
forgive if we must insist on looking down at others, at being in
the right.

Damelin follows up on this idea in the interview, asserting that
"...if you ask me about religion, there's something about "sorry"
which, for me, is very religious if you mean it. Because I've actually
recognized the power of apologies...." Together, Damelin and
Abu Awwad travel the world, presenting their views, and working
toward reconciliation by getting people to recognize the power that
they have to break free of the destructive cycles in whose grasp
they may have spun for generations. Damelin explains, "what we
really want to do is to make people understand that they have the
potential to change things within themselves, and they don't have
to be politicians to be able to do that."[100] Any of us, with the right
motivation can break free of cycles of hatreds, prejudices, and
violence through forgiveness.

I understand that Damelin and Abu Abbas might say that their
actions and their beliefs are not about forgiveness. Still, forgiving
is not about excusing. It doesn't assume that anything is magically
okay. In a real way, acts that damage us are never in the past;

we live with the pain and we live with the loss every day, and forgiveness doesn't change that. What it restores to us is not what we have lost but what we could so easily lose: ourselves.

To see the other in ourselves and ourselves in the other; to move past taking sides and seeking vengeance; to extinguish the flame of hatred that is eager to consume us; perhaps nothing requires greater exertion, and compassion is the fuel that makes such exertion possible. Perhaps any one of you has read a story about a murder, rape, or other violent crime, and has posted a comment in response suggesting that the perpetrator should die, be tortured, or be locked away from all contact and forgot about. Imagine instead feeling grief for the person that he or she created such suffering in his own life and the life of others. Imagine feeling grief for people so consumed by hatred, jealously, addiction, or other afflictive conditions that they would perpetrate such violence. Imagine the anger you might feel if someone at your workplace takes credit for good and important work that you have done, then imagine how the person seeking credit must be suffering from fear, insecurity, perhaps self-loathing, lack of confidence, doubt, or any painful emotion, or thinking that you too may have experienced and suffered from at a different time. In acknowledging those shortcomings that you may have shared, could you move past your desire for vengeance to find a constructive solution?

For a model, imagine the dying moment in which Jesus, with such boundless forgiveness, beseeched God to forgive those who had scourged and mocked and crucified and pierced Him, flaying him to ribbons of bleeding and agonized flesh, "for they know not what they do."[101] Such a statement can be born only of the most incredible strength, clear-sightedness, and compassion. Even if the story is not literal, it reminds us that willingly or not, with understanding or not, we *will* hurt each other. Vengeance will not break that cycle. Compassion can.

Generosity

My ex-boyfriend once said to me in jest, "What's mine is mine, and what's yours is mine, too." Unfortunately, that seems to have been the attitude of much of the world throughout history. Such attitudes gave rise to imperialism in the late 1800s, the idea that more powerful countries were entitled to the resources of less powerful countries and nations and had the right to dominate those places from afar. In many places, the belief in those attitudes still seems to persist. When the United States became engaged in war in Iraq in 2003, for example, the criticism leveled at the United States was that it wanted control of Iraq's oil fields.

The drive to acquire what may rightfully belong to others doesn't limit itself to national governments. Many view the worldwide economic recession that hit hard in 2008 and beyond as a function of greed on a variety of levels. Wall Street bankers became demonized for what seemed to many like predatory practices, and Russell Wassendorf, Sr. became yet another example of greed gone berserk when he admitted in 2012 to having stolen over $200 million from his investment clients in order to keep his business afloat. He joined the ranks of white collar criminals such as Allen Stanford and Thomas Petters, who between them defrauded people of over $11 *billion*. No doubt some of the investors were working class individuals who had scrimped together the savings that they entrusted to those who took advantage of them. When the game became exposed, they lost everything. I know how they felt. During my breakup with my ex-boyfriend, what had been mine became my ex-boyfriend's when I gave up to him the home I had built. I may not have been technically defrauded, but I felt cheated.

Often, we learn selfishness and acquisitiveness as children. We hear children on the playground or at day care shouting "That's mine!" as another one wails, "I want that!" While it would be nice to think that we grow out of that tendency, adults have had physical fights in stores over items such as dolls that they want to buy at holiday time for their children. Getting the best bargains for themselves is so important to Black Friday shoppers that brawls break out almost every year now. In 2008, a mob of Long Island Wal-Mart shoppers was so insistent on having what they wanted on Black Friday that they smashed open the doors of the Valley Stream store and trampled a worker to death.[102] We see it; we want it. We are told in ad after ad in the West that we deserve it, whatever *it* may be.

In an age when so many are enamored of the idea of a gospel of wealth and acquisition, of getting what we think we deserve, it may seem like heresy to suggest that we are meant to *give* freely and willingly. When we look at the spiritual texts of the world, though, that's exactly what we learn. The texts prompt us to be generous. Generosity strengthens the bonds between us. We are tempted to overlook those bonds because of differences in skin color, language, culture, and even religion. By practicing generosity, however, we better understand the worth of everyone and all that surrounds us in the world, and all that lies beyond it. Generosity doesn't just stem from compassion; practicing it can help us cultivate compassion. By giving, we have the potential to offer new life to others. We become bigger than ourselves; we become like the dynamic embodiment of God in the Sistine Chapel painting who generously breathed life into Adam.

ZAKAT

Willfully taking from others can create enmity, but giving can
forge bonds of peace and goodwill. Spiritual texts teach us that
we are not just to give. Rather, we are to give willingly, without
keeping track of what we give. Islam, for example, has the concept
of the *zakat* or *zakah*, or a tax for charity. Everyone who can give
is expected to give, and what is given is meant to be distributed
to those in need. The *zakat* is not seen just as something good to
do. Rather, it is a duty. A Muslim gives because he or she believes
that God wills it, and the second chapter of the Qur'an validates
the belief. In that chapter, Allah says, "The example of those who
spend their wealth in the way of Allah is like a seed of grain which
grows seven spikes; in each spike is a hundred grains.... Oh you
who have believed, do not invalidate your charities with reminders
or injuries. If you disclose your charitable expenditures, they are
good; but if you conceal them and give to the poor, it is better for
you...Indeed, those who believe and do righteous deeds and give
zakah will have their reward with the Lord."[103] A hadith, or saying
of the Prophet Muhammad also praises generosity, asserting that
"Generosity is near to Allah, near to Paradise, near to the people,
and far from the Hellfire.... An ignorant generous person is more
beloved to Allah the Exalted than a stingy scholar."[104] By selflessly
improving the lives of others, we acknowledge our common worth.

The Muslim belief that God cares about *zakat* is influenced
by Arab history. At the time of Muhammad, much of the Arabian
peninsula was a harsh place to live. Lack of rainfall made water
a precious commodity. Agriculture followed water and developed
near springs. Because there was little water, there was little
agriculture. Where there was water, cities and towns sprang up,
but living conditions were often harsh. They were no less harsh
in the desert, where people were nomadic. Raiding was common,

and eking out an existence was normal. Life was tribal. The tribe, most often bonded by kinship, provided protection and a means of avenging wrongdoing, although the youngest and weakest members of a tribe often were exploited or ignored by older or stronger members. Survival was for those who could afford to survive.

Protecting what little one had was one means of survival. Taking from others who were unable to protect what they had was another. Intertribal fighting was common. Life was often treacherous. To this world, Allah spoke through his Prophet, Muhammad, and what Allah wanted was nothing short of miraculous from this world: Allah wanted submission. Allah wanted not the submission of some, but the submission of all. After a very wobbly start marked by warfare, Islam would become the great unifying force of the peninsula, and a majestic and learned empire was built through Islam that swept across Africa and into Europe.

That could not have happened without generosity. Islam would have been less likely to succeed if individuals had been focused solely on amassing wealth and power for themselves at the expense of others because it is human nature to resent exploitation.

We can see evidence of this idea in our own time. In some Middle Eastern countries, *zakat* is collected and distributed by the central government. The amount collected depends on how much the wealthy are willing to give. Where there is wealth, there can be temptation to amass it for oneself. Amassing wealth for oneself can result in just the meanest of offerings for the poor. In some places in the world, many are poor. It can be tempting to think that the poor are lesser beings, social failures, and that they should be content with what they are allotted, that they should be grateful for a crust of bread while the wealthy dine on banquets around them. Such thinking is a kind of injustice, and to underestimate the poor, to

think that they don't notice inequity and that they are too weak to
do anything about it even if they do notice, can invite rebellion.

In the Arab Spring of 2011, such rebellion happened. Ordinary
people, many of whom were poor, rose up throughout the Middle
East against various forms of despotism, including financial
oppression. In Egypt, the Facebook generation ousted Egypt's
president, Hosni Mubarak, and then prosecuted him and his
family. One reason for their action was a call for greater democracy
in Egypt, but another reason was the inequitable distribution of
wealth that had left many young men all over the country too
poor even to marry. Suddenly, government after government was
challenged in the Arab world, and bloodshed became common as
people fought for the basic standards of living that they believed
had been denied to them from greed.

Their struggle was mighty, because those with power do not
relinquish it easily, as the war in Syria has taught us. It hadn't
mattered that the Qur'an had warned against the combination of
influence, authority, and conspicuous consumption. When Allah
referred to the people who use their wealth ostentatiously for
dominance and power, He said, "His example is like that of a
large, smooth stone upon which is dust and is hit by a downpour
that leaves it bare. They are unable to keep anything of what they
earned.... And for the wrongdoers there are no helpers."[105] Now,
those in power in the Arab Spring learned the truth of these words
the hard way. They fought mightily to cling to their power, but in
some cases, such as in Egypt and Tunisia, they lost it altogether,
in part because of a longstanding lack of generosity to the
common person.

What comes next for the Middle East will also likely be tied
to generosity for better or worse. For example, conflict in Yemen
has created a crisis in which more than half the population lives

in poverty and is food insecure. Yemenis are suffering from malnutrition.[106] Rather than accepting the humanitarian crisis as inevitable and insurmountable, the United Arab Emirates pledged $1.2 billion dollars to help support education and health care and to help develop Yemen's infrastructure. To call to mind the old proverb, rather than just giving Yemen a fish, the UAE is investing in helping Yemen learn to fish. As education, basic health, and infrastructure improves, Yemen is likely to finds its way out of conflict and to continue to develop.

On the less positive side, parts of the Middle East have been portrayed as hotbeds of barbaric religious fanatics who are corrupt and ungovernable. Those portrayals seem to be supported in the media by depictions of ISIS fighters as bloodthirsty and medieval, showing mass hangings and ISIS prisoners locked into cages. Certainly, ISIS fighters show no generosity to those the organization deems its enemies. However, those depictions do not capture the complexity of societies in which ISIS takes hold. For as many are as put off by ISIS's totalitarian style government and ruthlessness, others are won over by the organization's generosity. For example, *Time* magazine reported in 2016 that ISIS members donated $800 to pay for a man's wedding, gave free fuel to the man's brother, and paid for house repairs for a third person.[107] In helping residents with such basics, ISIS gains their respect and allegiance.

In a sacred world, generosity is a sacred act. In a mundane world, generosity can be mutually beneficial, and we ignore that at our peril. In looking at the Middle East, we can choose to see radical stereotypes. We can also choose to see the rise of Arab feminists working to improve opportunities for women, the interest of Arab youth in democracy, and the attraction of Western values for many of those who have been educated abroad and who have returned home to try to improve education, infrastructure, and economic possibilities.[108] In fact, the attraction of Western values is a large part of why so many Syrians fleeing the bloodshed in their country want to come to the West. To work together with such people to support them in achieving their goals takes generosity; it takes the acknowledgement that people's goals for themselves might not align with our own schemes to amass wealth or power. For some, wanting better education, the chance to drive, marriage, food security, and democratic government is enough. And in being generous through schooling, opportunities for resettling, contributing to infrastructure growth and so on, the West can gain long term allies, even though those allies will not fill our coffers or provide markets for our weapons.

True generosity takes compassion. It requires the heart, not just handouts. It's difficult to compel anyone to give from the heart, especially to give to someone who has terribly wronged that person. Being able to give in such circumstances combines the values of compassion, forgiveness, and generosity, and it takes effort. In fact, we could argue that true generosity *must* take effort: if I toss to you only what I don't need, that's not true generosity. That's just housecleaning. An example of a story that shows how compassion, generosity, forgiveness, and effort work together comes from Iran. In 2004, an Iranian woman, Ameneh Bahrami, lost her vision in an acid attack. Her attacker, Majid Mohavedi, threw the acid in her face, leaving her scarred as well as blinded, when she turned down his marriage proposal. Bahrami brought charges against Mohavedi, and he was imprisoned. Imprisonment would not be the sole punishment. Islamic law has a provision called *qesas*. *Qesas* is the equivalent of an "eye for an eye," and in this case, the provision was literal: the court decreed that Mohavedi should be blinded by acid, although in one eye only, in retribution for his vicious attack. It was to be carried out in 2011.

The sentence made Bahrami feel relieved. In 2011, Mohavedi was brought out as his victim witnessed, and those who were present described his fear and anguish. The doctor prepared to blind Mohavedi, but first turned to Bahrami to ask whether this was still what she wanted. Only one thing could save Mohavedi's sight, and that was Bahrami's ability to forgive and give clemency. Islamic law allows a victim to grant that mercy. Astoundingly, Bahrami gave it. Mohavedi was spared. Weeping in relief, he told Bahrami that she was "very generous." In our own culture, which often clamors for death and eye-for eye justice, Bahrami's example shows the power of generosity. She didn't forgive Mohavedi because she was squeamish. Instead, she explained, "I did it for my country, since all other countries were looking to see what we would do."[109] Bahrami's generosity thwarted a punishment that many in the world lambasted as cruel and unusual and took ammunition away from those who would have been happy to publish a story portraying Iran as backward and barbaric. By doing so, Bahrami demonstrated both compassion for another and her ability to overcome her own bitterness.

TZEDEKAH

Some two thousand years earlier than the birth of Muhammad, life was no less difficult in the lands of the Torah, the biblical Palestine. As in the Arabian peninsula, life in Palestine tended to be tribal in nature and varied in form from nomadic enclaves to settled towns. There were no social welfare systems, food banks, or soup kitchens. Orphans had few rights of inheritance; widows had none. The poor were at risk, not just in matters of justice but often for their own survival. The generosity and hospitality that one person showed to another could determine the life or death of the person who needed aid.

Generosity appears to be a trait that the God of the Torah
wanted the Hebrews to practice. In Deuteronomy, for instance,
God makes clear how those with means should treat those who are
poor, insisting that if a poor man gives his cloak to a rich man as
a pledge for a debt, the rich man must return it at sunset so that
the poor man can protect himself in it from the night's cold.[110]
Whether a stranger or fellow townsman, the poor person was not
to be defrauded; further, he was to be paid on the same day that he
worked because he needed the money for his sustenance.[111]
The gleanings of the field, the trees and the vines were to be left in
the fields and orchards and vineyards for those who needed them
for nourishment: the widows, orphans, and aliens.[112] Further, God
left no doubt in the minds of the Hebrews why He commanded
these acts of generosity: "Remember that you were once slaves in
Egypt. That is why I command you to observe this rule," He said.[113]
Just as God had led the Israelites out of their bondage in Egypt, He
expected his followers, those He had freed, to follow His example
and lead their fellow humans out of the bondage of poverty and
hardship through their generosity. Yet again, people were reminded
that they and those around them were no different at the core.

The God of the Torah led by example. Again and again,
after He had revealed Himself, humans infuriated Him. God's
destructive capabilities were clear—we read about flooding,
plagues, destruction, pillars of salt, and more in the text—but the
God of the Torah repeatedly showed generosity in allowing the
survival of humanity despite people's transgressions.

In the story of Cain and Abel, for example, people usually focus
on the first murder in the Bible. The story at first hardly seems
compassionate. Nor do we at first think about the role generosity
(or the lack of it) plays in the story. The stage was set for Abel's
killing when God liked Abel's offering to Him better than he liked

Cain's. The story tells us that Abel, the shepherd, gave to God "one of the best firstlings of his flock," while Cain, the farmer, gave "an offering from the fruit of the soil."[114] Why did God like Abel's offering better? Should we think that God had a special taste for lamb? The problem wasn't that God is a carnivore. Instead, the writer of the text suggests that Cain did not give the best offering that he could, but Abel *did* give the best that he could. "Best" was and is relative. When God later gave the law to Moses, He made it clear that he didn't expect His followers to beg or steal in order to give to Him. If a person had sheep, then he should give the best ram. If a person couldn't afford sheep but had birds, then she should sacrifice the best bird. If a person couldn't afford birds but had a bit of meal and oil, then the best that the person could give was a cake made of meal and oil, and to give that was good enough.[115]

The lesson here is that whatever Cain gave God that day, whether it was a rutabaga or an onion or a bit of wheat or whatever he gave, he could have given more and could have given better, but didn't. God knew he had been slighted. That's why he favored Abel's efforts. When Cain killed his God-favored brother, God was clearly not happy. He could have struck Cain dead, but that would have been a limited punishment. What would Cain have learned from that? What would *we* have learned from it? Instead, God went a step further. He took away Cain's livelihood. Nothing would grow in the soil ever again for Cain the farmer, and he was doomed to a nomadic existence of wandering the earth. Cain knew exactly what this meant. He had no protection. He was at the mercy of the merciless, and he told God, "My punishment is too great to bear" because he knew that anyone at any time could and would, sooner or later, kill him on sight.[116]

However, compassion and generosity saved Cain. God could have said, "So what?" Many would understand if He had, because many have no problem understanding the concept of vengeance. That is why people support the idea of capital punishment; vengeance seems reasonable to them when a transgression is serious. Less understandable in such circumstances is generosity, but that is exactly what God showed. God told Cain that he would not be killed, and He promised "If anyone kills Cain, Cain shall be avenged sevenfold,"[117] then put a mark on Cain so that no one would be tempted to kill him. Cain found a wife, established the nomadic peoples of what became the Holy Land, and his descendants went on to form settlements. God's generosity helped to give birth to the people who became the Israelites, the ones He later chose to receive His word.

Throughout the Hebrew Bible, God acts as a role model of generosity. Which of us would contemplate that God and think of Him as weak? The thought is ludicrous, so we can see in God's model that generosity is a strength, not a weakness. It is an attribute, not a flaw. Throughout the Torah, God makes clear that he wants humankind to follow His model. For example, He specifies a Jubilee every fifty years in which people are freed from servitude and their debts are annulled. Families return to properties that they may have lost. God decrees that people should be generous even to the land in that year, not sowing or reaping or picking the grapes, just as He decrees that they should do every seventh year to allow the ground to regenerate after its generosity to those who cultivate it.[118] Throughout the text, generosity is presented as a virtue.

Millennia later in the 1100s, Moshe ben Maimon, more famously known as Maimonides and sometimes as Rambam, wrote in the Mishneh Torah about the levels of tzedekah, or charitable giving, one of the cornerstones of Judaism. The most important level, Maimonides said, was to help a person become self-sufficient. After that come two levels of anonymous donation. In the more important of the two, neither the giver nor the receiver knows each other. In the lesser, the receiver does not know the giver. The least important level is that which is given grudgingly or meanly after someone requests it.[119] In other words, Maimonides suggests, the greatest good is to give from the heart because it is the right thing to do with the intent of helping others realize their potential. The model for this good is God, who again and again in the Hebrew Bible attempted to help people realize their potential, even though humanity again and again forgot about Him and His laws.

In today's world, many in developed countries have access to resources that our ancestors never could have dreamed of, yet generosity of spirit, of will, or intention still means the difference between life and death. The story of Leiby Kletzky is a sobering and terrible example. On his first day of walking home from school by himself in Borough Park in Brooklyn, with his parents just a few short blocks away, nine-year-old Leiby got confused and asked a man for directions. It was such a simple request, so easily granted, if only the spirit of generosity had been in the man that he asked. Instead, the man brought Leiby to his house and then killed him when he realized that the boy's disappearance had spurred a massive search. We hear these stories so often that we become numb to them. Consider, though, that after doing the unthinkable, the killer could not even leave the child's body intact for his family to view and find solace and closure. What a stark contrast that person is with Leiby's father. Stunned with grief over the loss of his little boy, Leiby's father proclaimed, "God gives and God takes. Thank You God, for giving [Leiby] to us for nine years. We have to thank You for what You gave us."[120] In Nachman Kletzky's greatest of losses, he still was able to praise generosity, something from which the murderer had long since turned away.

SACRIFICE

In the story of Christianity, God Himself is the One to lose His only child to murder by the Romans. However, Jesus' death does not come as a shock. Almost unthinkably, it is a script that is pre-written. Christians see the crucifixion as the ultimate act of generosity of God the Father, who sends His son to die to redeem sinners, and of God the Son, Jesus the Christ, who willingly goes through with the plan rather than turning away from the agonies that he knew faced him. For the Romans, crucifixion was common, so much so that at various times citizens could view so many bodies hung on crosses outside the city that the hillsides were barren of the trees used to make them.

Jesus of the Gospels idealizes generosity because he sees clearly that people are trapped by wealth and material possessions. The way to God, Jesus insists, is not through amassing wealth. It's quite the opposite. Jesus exhorts his followers to give up not five percent of what they have, not ten percent, but all of it.[121] Only by breaking the shackles of the material world can we properly focus on the world of the spirit, Jesus seems to suggest. To Jesus the only world that mattered was the world of his Father's kingdom. Seeing the sectarian fighting and social problems around him enabled him to see that attempted revolt was inevitable and would result in the Roman destruction of Jerusalem.

In a way, it seems as if Jesus turned the laws of God upside down. God gave laws to Moses about inheritance, for example, but when a man came to Jesus and demanded that Jesus tell the man's brother to share their inheritance, Jesus shrugged him off, telling the man that he was not a judge. Instead, He told the man a parable

about an individual who had a great harvest of grain, but no place
to store it. To that individual, the answer to the dilemma was
simple. He would tear down his barns and build bigger ones. Then
he'd have nothing to worry about. All would be good. But did God
agree? No. According to Jesus, God called this man a fool because
the man was storing up the grain for himself rather than giving
away what he could. Walking in avarice meant that the man was
not walking with God.[122]

As importantly, Jesus understood the relationship between the
giver and what was given, as he demonstrated when he went to
the home of a righteous Pharisee to share a meal. The Pharisees
observed table fellowship rules, meaning that sinners were shunned.
Just as Amish or Mormons or Orthodox today may shun a person
who does not follow the religion's rules, the Pharisees did likewise.
Into the house, though, came a woman who was being shunned for
her sins. She brought ointment with her, and she knelt and wept at
the feet of Jesus. Her tears washed his feet, which she then anointed
with the sweet-smelling ointment.

Truly, the Pharisee must have been horrified by this display.
What was a sinful woman doing in his house? Why was she
touching a man who was not kin to her? Jesus could not have
helped but see the Pharisee's discomfort. As a response he turned to
Simon, who accompanied him, and He asked Simon who would be
more grateful: a person whose debt of fifty days' labor was forgiven
or a person whose debt of five hundred days' labor was forgiven.
Simon rightly acknowledged that the one who owed the bigger debt
would be more grateful. Jesus' point was twofold. By her caring
for Jesus despite being an outcast, the woman had shown more
generosity than Jesus' wealthier and presumably more "moral" host
had shown.[123] In return, God's generosity in forgiving the woman's
sins was far greater than any that He might extend toward the

Pharisee, who was so careful to live an upright life. Jesus wasn't suggesting that everyone should go live a life of sin so that God could show how magnanimous He is. Rather, Jesus was showing that if God's heart is big enough to forgive the greatest debts, who are we to do otherwise? That is our model: to do the most that we can do, not the least, because doing for others lessens our attachment to ourselves.

DANA

In the Karnataka state in India, the Drepung Loseling Monastery in exile keeps alive Tibetan Buddhist teaching and traditions. It is home to almost 300 student monks who come from Bhutan, Tibet, and the Himalayan regions of India. One of those monks, Rinchen Dorjee, is dear to me. He is about forty years old now, and I think of him often. Each month, I look at a photo of him with shaven head, kindly face, broad smile, and maroon robes, and I hope that he is succeeding at his studies. I imagine him one day bringing the Dharma to others. I wonder if he will ever come to the West. I ask myself why I never write to him, but I know the answer: I think that maybe he does not read English, and I do not write in Tibetan or Sanskrit, and so communication seems awkward to me. I write out a check, as I have done every month for years, ever since Rinchen Dorjee was in his mid-20s, and I send it off to the monastery's education fund in Atlanta, Georgia. Then I go on with my life for another month.

I am not related to Rinchen Dorjee. In fact, I have never met him. All I know of him is that smiling photo. Surely, he knows nothing of me. The check I send does not go into a special account for him; I know that much. It goes to help all the monks. He is just my poster monk. I picked him out of a table full of photos of Drepung's monks to support. I like to think that my choosing him was some kind of karma. The monks pray for the donors at year end, and I like that idea, although I am not sure their praying has any personal benefit for me, especially if they don't know that I exist. Sometimes I fantasize about saving money to go to India. I imagine going to the monastery, knocking on the door, showing someone the picture and through gestures indicating that I would like to meet Rinchen Dorjee. I imagine bringing him socks and other small gifts from America. I imagine that he would be friendly but confused, wondering who this American woman is and why she is bringing him socks.

Why do I send a check every month for someone I have never met and will probably never meet? I can give you absolutely no logical answer. I can tell you that it doesn't make me feel proud of myself. I don't have any idea that I am somehow personally responsible for the continuation of Buddhist teachings or anything of the sort. I don't brag about the donations. To be honest, I just like the idea that this friendly-looking monk might get a little more food each day, like an egg, if I send some money each month. An egg seems like a basic food to me. So out comes my checkbook, and, hopefully, in goes the egg to Rinchen Dorjee.

Generosity, or *dana*, is a central value of Buddhism. In Buddhist thinking, what I extend is not the most important form of generosity. It is the generosity of material goods, and material goods aren't the primary focus of Buddhists, although I remain convinced that obtaining an egg or some heat is a perfectly reasonable material concern. Instead, the highest form of generosity is expressed in how we feel toward others and the way in which we treat others. As in Judaism, Buddhism has levels of giving, the least of which is the stingy kind of giving at the bottom of Maimonides' ladder. The person who gives in this way doesn't do so from a good heart. Instead, the compulsion might be annoyance, impatience, or even wanting to look good in front of others.

Barbara Lazear Ascher writes about this kind of compulsion in her essay, "On Compassion," which links empathy to generosity.[124] In her essay, Ascher paints a typical New York City scenario. A crazy-looking homeless man is fixated on a baby in a stroller; an old, reeking man frequents a bake shop. The mother of the baby gives the homeless man a dollar, and the owner of the bake shop gives the old man a cup of hot coffee and some bread. Why? Ascher questions whether fear, annoyance, or true compassion motivates the mother and the shop owner. She makes the point that real generosity is not born out of fear. What we give out of fear or out of annoyance is a transaction; it is a buyoff, our security, our comfort, our continued fantasy for whatever the currency may be. As Ascher writes, "We do not wish to be reminded of the tentative state of our own well-being and sanity," but that's exactly the benefit of generosity. It allows us to acknowledge our limits and to give to others out of that acknowledgement of shared fragility. Compassion isn't an innate trait, Ascher argues. It must be learned, and one way to learn it is through giving born of pure kindness.

The next kind of Buddhist giving is related to the Golden Rule. This generosity offers to others what we would like to be offered. That may sound selfish, but it's selfish only if we are hoping someone will do likewise for us, so we have to be willing to look into our hearts to see what the real motivation is for the giving. Finally, there is the highest form: the generosity that has absolutely no self-interest. In fact, it might even hurt us. Generosity at its highest level becomes one of the Buddhist perfections, *dana-paramita*, or the perfection of giving, in which one's intentions in giving are selfless.

Another past life story of the Buddha shows *dana-paramita* in action. In this Jataka story, the Buddha before he was the Buddha was a silvery elephant. One day he met a terrified man in the forest.

When the man realized that the elephant was not going to hurt him, the elephant approached the man and had him climb up. The elephant fed the man and took him to the outskirts of the city, where he left him kindly on the road.

Once the man reached the city, he saw elephant tusks for sale and learned that the most expensive ivory was cut from living elephants. The greedy man thought of the elephant's kindness only so far as it could benefit him. He went back to the forest and pled his case, explaining to the elephant bodhisattva that he was very poor and could be relieved of his poverty if the elephant would give him the ivory from his tusks. The elephant agreed and let the man saw off the length of his tusks. The man took them off and cleared his debts, but that was not enough for him. Soon he returned and begged the elephant to let him have the rest of the stump, and again the elephant agreed. Already the elephant had shown more generosity than most of us could imagine; in fact he had turned my former boyfriend's joke upside down, in essence showing the man, "What's yours is yours, and what is mine is yours, too."

Unfortunately, the man wanted all that the elephant had to give. He came back a third time and begged to be able to cut out the root of the tusks. Many have seen the photos of how poachers mutilate elephants to get every last ounce of ivory from their skulls. Their great trunks are hacked away, and their faces are slashed open. That is what the elephant bodhisattva let the man do to him, and in agony, just as elephants still experience today from that cruel trade, the bodhisattva slumped over and died.[125]

The elephant could not have been more generous in wanting to relieve the hardship of another living being, just as the man could not have been more selfish. The story, however, has a satisfying ending. Selfishness does not pay. As the man leaves the forest with the bloody roots of the tusks, the earth opens up in anger at what it has witnessed, and the man is swallowed into the fiery depths of hell.

"To be generous in giving and righteous in conduct" is one of the thirty-eight blessings of the Maha-Mangala Sutra, the Buddhist scripture that is a Discourse on Blessings. A Chinese sutra, the Filial Piety Sutra, encourages us to contemplate generosity in giving from a source so common, so right in front of us, that we might overlook that source: our own parents. Marrying Confucian ideas of the importance of respect for elders with Buddhist ideals of generosity, the Filial Piety Sutra shows us how difficult it is to match the generosity of our mother and why we are obligated to do our best to attempt to match it. "There are ten types of kindnesses bestowed by the mother on the child," says the Buddha in the sutra:

> The first is the kindness of providing protection and care while the child is in the womb. The second is the kindness of bearing suffering during the birth.
> The third is the kindness of forgetting all the pain once the child has been born. The fourth is the kindness of eating the bitter herself and saving the sweet for the child. The fifth is the kindness of moving the child to a dry place and lying in the wet herself. The sixth is the kindness of suckling the child at her breast, nourishing and bringing up the child. The seventh is the kindness of washing away the unclean. The eighth is the kindness of always thinking of the child when it has traveled far. The ninth is the kindness of deep care and devotion. The tenth is the kindness of ultimate pity and sympathy.

After listing these acts of generosity for his disciples, the Buddha goes on through the sutra to describe each in detail, explaining the pain that the mother feels in birth, the toll that pregnancy and birth takes on her body, and the burden of love that the mother feels for the child. When he finished, according to the sutra, his disciples were in tears.

In *The Dhammapada,* greed is a bond, and generosity is not seen as beneficial if it is just an empty action. Generosity means seeing the value in others, especially the perfected ones we are exhorted to emulate. "Whatever gifts and oblations one seeing merit might offer in this world for a whole year, all that is not worth one fourth of the merit gained by revering the Upright Ones," the text tells us.[126] To see the worth in others and to put others above ourselves is a form of generosity.

In the end, generosity is about community. Hinduism, too, reflects on this. In his book *The Call of the Upanishads,* the late Indian philosopher Rohit Mehta writes, "Social obligations demand that a person must know how to receive from the community—but he should also know how to give to the society to which he belongs. He who receives but does not give has not known his relationship to society.... The teacher tells the student, "Give always with faith – do not give if you do not have faith. Give generously—but let your generosity be tempered with modesty. Give with sympathy, but also give with propriety."[127] For Mehta, the *Upanishads* show how our generosity keeps our society functioning with health. There is a fine line between feeling grateful for the generosity of another and feeling beholden to another. While feelings of gratefulness often spur the receiver to do his or her own acts of generosity, to feel beholden can be a force of destructiveness, creating feelings of resentment and anger. To put it another way, there are times I may need charity, but I don't want to feel like anyone's charity case.

THE BENEFITS OF GENEROSITY

One immediately recognizable model of generosity is Oprah Winfrey. Yes, Oprah gave away cars and coats to viewers like a fairy godmother, but she has also given millions to establish a leadership academy for girls in South Africa, to help rebuild the Gulf Coast in the aftermath of Hurricane Katrina, to help organizations that take in abandoned babies and provide education for children in developing countries, and more. Giving is Oprah's brand and her trademark; she understands that "money is one of the things that truly unites us,"[128] just as generous actions and thoughts are also a form of universal currency.

We might wonder, "Why bother? Why not let others struggle?" We might be tempted to look back at the early Israelites and their struggle to survive against the Babylonians, the Assyrians, the Persians, the Seleucids and more and think, "Right. The lesson from the story is to take care of what's yours, and whack anyone you don't know. Better safe than sorry. If you have more than someone else, then you must have worked harder than they did, so you deserve it." The more callous amongst us might think that is the way of the world, and that the struggle for survival results in the survival of the fittest. That kind of idea led to the mistaken idea of Social Darwinism in the late 1800s, a misguided theory that some in society were fitter to survive than others so that those less "fit"— people in poverty, for example—should not be helped so that they could naturally just die out.

That's not Darwin's concept, though. Darwin theorized that those best able to successfully adapt are most likely to reproduce. If we take Darwin's theory at face value, we should think that the most selfish animals are the most likely to reproduce. However, when we consider the world of animals, we find that individuals in all kinds of species cooperate in a variety of different ways. In certain species of monkeys, for example, a member of the group will vocalize to alert other monkeys if a predator enters the scene, even though the predator can then more easily attack the calling monkey. This phenomenon, which humans share, is called altruism, and the core of altruism is generosity, because altruistic behavior benefits the recipient, not the giver.

In fact, sometimes altruistic behavior is given at the *expense* of the giver. Consider the earlier stories of people who donated organs. Not only is living organ donation compassionate—a donor is able to mentally and emotionally put herself into the situation of the other—it is altruistic because giving away an organ gives the donor no physical benefit, causes the donor physical pain, and could potentially cause the donor grave danger. Now, consider that science has discovered that evolution tends to favor altruists.[129] In other words, generosity—altruism—is a trait that nature values and wants to reproduce. As an example, think for a second about ants, who keep their queen alive at their own expense, the result being the continuation of the colony.

Here's an unremarkable story having nothing to do with religion, with missions, or with feeling a religious need to do the right thing. In the summer of 2011, it was not a matter of whether Yankees shortstop Derek Jeter would get his 3,000th hit. It was a matter of when. On July 9th, the magical hit happened, making Jeter only the 28th player in American baseball history to achieve that benchmark. Up popped the ball, a home run...and out reached 23-year-old Christian Lopez, who caught it from the stands. Imagine for a moment being massively in debt, winning $100,000 on a spur of the moment lottery ticket that you purchased, and then handing the ticket away as a gift to a successful business person. Could you do it? Lopez did the equivalent. Although he had student loan debt of over $100,000, and although he could have sold that historic ball for at least that amount, he simply gave it to Jeter, a highly paid professional ball player. Why? Because he believed that it was the right thing to do.

Lopez' act of generosity brought him reciprocal generosity that shocked him: two sporting goods executives pledged him $50,000. Additionally, one of the two pledged an additional percentage of Yankees merchandise sold at his shop over a week's period. Shoppers could contribute through their purchases to Mr. Lopez' unexpected good fortune.[130] If the shoppers were aware that choosing to shop during the week would benefit Mr. Lopez, and if they did not know Mr. Lopez and Mr. Lopez did not know them, then the shoppers' decision to shop would be high on Maimonides' ladder of worthiness of generosity to others. In that case, both the shoppers and Mr. Lopez (and the store owner, thanks to the publicity and whatever tax write-off he might earn) benefit. Other times it might be harder to see the advantage to ourselves from being generous. Perhaps we cannot imagine the myriad ways in which it may reward us.

The story of Linda Mussman and Claudia Bruce shows us one possible way. When Linda needed to move her theater in New York, a friend suggested that she call Claudia, who had a van. Linda's response was "This is New York. Generosity is not so simple."[131] For Claudia, who no doubt had a busy schedule and many of her own obligations with which to contend, lending the van and helping with the move would be a hassle, and Linda recognized it. The act didn't need to be as dramatic as giving away a baseball or a million dollars or a dream vacation. Claudia offered the van and her help, and her generosity opened the door to love between the two, who later married.

I remember going to a farm stand years ago with my daughter and a friend who has no children. My friend bought some fruit;

I bought some little items for my daughter. For myself, I bought just a tiny thing, a honey stick, as money was very tight in those days. I remember that I felt delighted at the thought of sucking the sweet honey from the stick, but my daughter, who was ten at the time, saw it and asked for it. Without a thought, I gave it to her. I remember the look of surprise on my friend's face. Some might read this story and automatically think that I spoil my daughter, but I don't. In fact, she would be the first to tell you how "mean" I am to her because I generally don't indulge her in what she wants. In Buddhist thought, though, to be a parent means that your heart should not be entirely your own. As I think back on it, giving away that honey stick was an act of nothing more than love. Real love, I think, needs to be fed by generosity. I don't mean the kind of generosity that a gold digger or a user hopes for. I mean the generosity of spirit, the kind that a loving parent extends to a child on so many different levels: generosity of time, of discipline, of nurturing.

That brings us, yet again, back to nature. Where would any species be if parents did not show generosity to their offspring? How can society function if we are not willing to give to people and organizations who need what we have to offer: meals, heat, services, expertise, time, goods? Generosity is so very important as a value in the wisdom texts of the world because in generosity there is no mine and there is no yours. In the world of the Infinite, there is just reciprocity, and it makes the universe go around and around.

Order

In the summer of 1998, Beijing was stifling hot. I tromped
into Tiananmen Square along with eight compatriots, our
tai chi instructor, and our local Beijing guide. Red flags with
yellow stars flapped around the perimeter, and an enormous
portrait of Chairman Mao gazed down on Chinese citizens and
foreign tourists alike who were gathered below his immortally
painted likeness. At what seemed like random intervals, armed
police in their green uniforms stared humorlessly across the
concrete expanse.

Our guide had plans for us in some building or another, but
I had other ideas. I had been captivated by my glimpse of Mao's
refrigerated tomb, which elevated itself periodically so that the
snaking line of gawkers could file by and pay respects. I had to see
his corpse, I decided. For much of my life, I've been a solo traveler,
so I thought nothing of slipping away from my little group and into
the line, which seemed to only inch along.

After about fifteen minutes, our guide magically appeared next
to me. "Come with me, please," she directed. Her tone made it
clear that this was an order, not a request. In case I had any doubts,
she immediately followed the statement with, "We are not waiting
in the line. That is not on our schedule for today." Reluctantly and
feeling somewhat annoyed, I gave up my place in line and followed
her inside a building, where she asked me to sit.

"When you go off on your own like that, you make it
impossible for me to do my job," she told me in a pleasant but very
matter-of-fact tone. "You are guests of China, and I am paid to
make certain that you all have a good time. When we must stop
what we are doing for fifteen minutes so that I can find you, your
fellow guests are not having a good time, and I am failing at my

job. That is why it is important for you to follow directions and stay with our group."

As an adult, I don't think I've ever felt quite so ashamed of myself. I tend to be stubbornly independent, and I come from a culture that prizes independence. This was the first time that I truly comprehended that focusing solely on what I wanted to do could have an adverse effect on people around me. In short, I was out of order. I was flouting Chinese ideas of order and was inconveniencing my fellow travelers, who had paid just as much as I had for a trip that we all had scrimped for. Unlike me, they were following the rules.

Rules are often easy to hate. History has shown us that rules will be changed over time. They are dynamic, not static, because that is the nature of this world, this universe, and this existence. However, rules keep order. Order is how we function. It's how we organize ourselves. Order isn't meant to be mindless and robotic, and it isn't etched in stone; that's called totalitarianism. Real order is meant to free our focus, curtail our fears, and afford us liberation from the mundane so that we can focus on the Infinite: God, enlightenment, the Dao, or whatever one wants to call It.

BEFORE THE TEXTS

Think for a moment about what life would be like if gravity "went out" for brief periods at random intervals or if at odd times Earth flung itself out of orbit and exchanged places with Mercury for a short while and then Jupiter the next time around. Imagine if you went out to your garden to pick your tomatoes, which normally just fall into your hand, but as you grabbed one, it bit you hard. We trust that such things could not happen because we trust in an orderly universe.

In reality, scientists believe that the universe operates from chaos. In a scientific worldview, "chaos" means that very small actions have big and not necessarily linear results. For example, a commonly used example is that a butterfly beating its wings in one place can cause, through a series of causes and effects, a tremendous storm somewhere else. In other words, even chaos isn't haphazard.

The story doesn't stop there. I really like how astronomer and physicist Adam Frank explains the next step: "Even the effort of your cells doing their moment-to-moment work, purging their innards of poisons, allows life to create astonishing islands of order. Each of our bodies, each of our lives, represents a triumph. Life *is* order and structure hammered out, for just a time, to give the blind universe its sight."[132] Humans have a place in the universe and can survive on Earth because the natural laws that currently govern our planet and solar system, such as the Universal Law of Gravitation and the laws of thermodynamics, allow us to survive. Orderliness surrounds us in laws of mechanics, motion, energy, mathematics, relativity, chemistry, and more. Without them, life as we know it would be threatened.

The same is true in the relatively small sphere of humanity. The human body, for instance, behaves according to rules. Without food, the body will die. Without water, the body will die even faster. Normally, the organs of the body interact in orderly ways and cells divide in orderly ways. Disease stems from disorder. For example, when cells run amok, disorders such as cancer and polycystic kidney disease occur and threaten the survival of the body. When cell division is orderly, health prevails.

Rules help people socially as well as physically. What we know about humans from the archeological and anthropological record is that to survive, humans must group together. Grouping together, though, can be as dangerous as it is beneficial. Individuals often have competing interests. What benefits one may not be what's good for the group. One person's self-interest may suggest another's demise. For humans to survive together there must be some kind of order.

The idea of order is older than the ideas of a supreme God, enlightenment, or the Dao. In early human societies, order helped people to flourish. One of the earliest examples of the role of order in bolstering human populations can be found in an Israeli cave dating from the Lower to the Upper Paleolithic periods. University of Arizona anthropology professor Mary Stiner discovered through her analysis of cut marks on bones that the Lower (earlier) Paleolithic hunters were neither specialized nor efficient in carving meat. Ritual was absent; people cut off what they could and grabbed whatever they could grab. In contrast, the bones from the Middle (later) Paleolithic showed evidence of ritual carving. Meat was cut and distributed by skilled butchers, and their individuality can be recognized by the pattern of cuts on the bones just as stone cutters can recognize who shaped a stone by that cutter's "handprint" of cut marks.[133] Meat is important. For early human societies, it was a crucial source of proteins and fats, both of which sustained strength and provided energy. It was also a difficult resource to obtain. Paleolithic hunters had to chase down the animal on foot, kill it with a stone spear or drive it over a cliff, and then butcher it with knapped stone hand tools. Greater efficiency and greater order in the processing and distribution of meat could very likely have meant greater survival and reproduction rates for those Middle Paleolithic bands of humans.

As humanity grew, travelled, and began to settle in permanent settlements, order was expressed in at least three main ways. One was the order of design. Where people lived was often determined by and reflected power relationships. A ruler might live in the equivalent of a palace in the center of a city while the common people might live on the outskirts of the settlement. We still see this sense of design order around ourselves today. Physical infrastructures such as streets and roads connect people within areas and connect areas. The more developed a place is, the more developed its infrastructure is in a circular relationship that both reflects and enables economic expansion and power.

A second type of order that accompanied the development and expansion of human society was the order of ritual. Rites were developed for specific purposes meant to benefit the group performing them. Evidence of ritual has been found all over the world. Ritual appears to be associated regularly with development of settled human culture and early religious thinking, especially in Iron Age cultures, and one piece of evidence for ritual is often the evidence of sacrifice, including human sacrifice. The Shang Dynasty of China, for example, was a warring culture, and the Shangs' war-making, prisoner-taking, and enslavement helped to ensure that they would have an ample supply of sacrificial victims. Sacrifice of humans was important to help placate the gods and the spirits because the gods and spirits were the beings who helped to ensure the success of the rulers. A settlement was as successful as its rulers in cultures where warfare was common.

We also have evidence of bog bodies from Iron Age Europe, and although some of those remains may have been the result of murder, others clearly appear to be a result of sacrifice. As in China, the sacrifices were meant to appease the gods and spirits who inhabited the bog lands. The bogs were a source of both fuel and metal for the inhabitants of the time, as well as a portal to the realm of gods and spirits. The bogs are where Grauballe Man met his end, his throat slit from ear to ear as he was offered

as a sacrifice, probably to appease the goddess of fertility. His
sacrifice might have taken place after a bad harvest. In an article
in *National Geographic* magazine a decade ago, Eamonn Kelly of
the National Museum of Ireland pointed out the close relationship
between people and the gods in Iron Age Ireland. Irish kings
"married" the fertility goddess, Kelly said, and when things went
awry, human sacrifice was the cost to put them right again. Kelly
points to mutilations, stomach contents and the like as symbols
of the ritual sacrifice, arguing that each facet "honored a different
aspect of the goddess—fertility, sovereignty, and war. It's controlled
violence," Kelly explained. "They are giving the goddess her
due."[134] Early cultures believed they owed such debts to beings
more powerful than themselves who would benefit them in return.

In the old pre-God order of ritual, humans were the currency
that could keep the many specialized gods and spirits appeased. In
a limited way, sacrifice still occurs today. In India, those looking
for riches and other benefits in the world may (rarely) sacrifice a
child to Kali, the most fearsome of the Hindu deities, even though
human sacrifice is not a practice sanctioned by Hindu scriptures
or mainstream Hindu priests. It is hard to sustain any kind of
harmony, though, when a key facet of the society is regular ritual
slaughter of citizens. Without harmony, growth is difficult. Two
crucial differences can be found between such sacrifices today
and Iron Age sacrifices. First, the modern sacrifices are motivated
by personal greed,[135] not for the purpose of benefitting an entire
human settlement that may be suffering from famine, drought, or
prolonged warfare that may be interpreted as anger of the gods.
Second, the practice of sacrificing humans to the gods has been
supplanted by the third part of order: law.

Law is ancient, predating belief in God. However, modern
law in many cultures is intimately connected to God. As human

society moved away from belief in many erratic and often amoral gods, and as human society grew to be more complex, views of the Infinite changed. Judaism and then Christianity and Islam saw God in part as lawgiver. In Eastern religions, while the focus was slightly different, a sense of the Divine was also associated with "laws." In all the so-called modern religions of the world, order is a crucial component. The universe may thrive in incessant chaos, but humans do not. If we cannot control ourselves and cannot live in healthy social relations, we are stuck on the bottom of Maslow's pyramid, fighting for survival rather than at the top, striving to appreciate the Infinite.

LAW

One of the earliest sets of laws in human history is the Code of Hammurabi, which dates to 1780 BCE. The Code specified rules to which citizens were held accountable and formalized contracts. The wording of those contracts influenced the writers of the Torah, who wrote down the contracts between humans and God—such as the covenants God made with Noah, Abraham, and Moses—and the recitation of laws.

The transition from a focus on many gods and spirits to belief in one God brought with it a new kind of order, one that focused on serving God as the highest authority. We see this first in the covenant with Noah. The Noah story in the Hebrew Bible is important because it is a kind of bridge. It references earlier Mesopotamian flood stories as it introduces a new kind of God that is both personal and contractual. This God does not operate purely by whim. In the story, God has the power to completely obliterate humankind and regrets creating humans because He sees that people are wicked. Instead, God uses an earthly method: a contract, the first in the Hebrew Bible. First, God assures Noah that in return for building the ark, gathering the creatures and their food, and trusting in God, He will save Noah and his family from the flood that would obliterate the rest of humankind. After the flood waters subside and after Noah releases the animals and his family upon the dry earth, God clarifies the pact: "See, now I am establishing my covenant with you and your descendants after you and with every living thing that was with you...that never again shall all bodily creatures be destroyed by the waters of a flood; there shall not be another flood to devastate the earth."[136] The rainbow, a sign of the agreement, was the equivalent of a contractual seal.

God's next covenant was established with Abraham. God told Abraham, "Between you and me I will establish my covenant, and I will multiply you exceedingly...My covenant with you is this: you are to become father to a host of nations."[137] God told Abraham that He would make him fertile in his old age and that he would be the forefather of kings. God would be the God of all of Abraham's descendants. God promised to adhere to this contract, but Abraham and all the generations after him were expected to also keep it. In addition to the honor that Abraham's descendants needed to show God, each male also became a party to the contract through circumcision. The forfeit of the piece of flesh and the pain accompanying the circumcision paid the contract's consideration.[138]

God as described by Judaism and its holy books shows humanity the importance of order through God's own actions as well as through handing down law for people to follow and administer. In Torah, what God does and does not do often depends on how humans act in the contractual relationship. Order keeps equilibrium. In the musical *Fiddler on the Roof*, the protagonist Tevye points this out. "Because of our traditions, we've kept our balance for many, many years," Tevye says. "Every one of us knows who he is and what God expects him to do."

For the Hebrews, who would become the Jewish people, order and tradition was established through Mosaic rules, specifically the 613 mitzvot in the Torah. Rules gave the Jewish people identity. Rules reflected the concerns of the culture at the time and tried to establish an identity of order and purity that the Hebrews believed would be pleasing to God. Some of those rules are practical ones, such as isolating oneself if one shows signs of leprous or other contagious skin diseases.[139] Quarantine laws persist today, and challenges to those laws in the United States by invoking the Fourteenth Amendment have not survived because of the importance of those laws to preserving social health and order. Some of the Mosaic rules are meant to specify marriage and family relationships, which could otherwise be fraught with tensions and potential violence. For example, Deuteronomy provides a means for divorce, which must be undertaken formally and in writing,[140] and Leviticus prohibits incest.[141] Both Leviticus and Deuteronomy prescribe civil laws governing property rights and business practices and lay out criminal laws governing courts, damages, and punishments.

As we read through the list of rules in those books, we can easily see that many are meant for people to live peaceably together in close quarters with a growing population and an influx of immigrants. Those rules fit that society at that time, more than one thousand years before the birth of Jesus (13th-14th century BCE). Clearly, not all of the Mosaic social rules fit modern society. It's unlikely that a reasonable and compassionate person would argue today, for example, that criminals should be burned to death or that we should keep slaves.[142] Even Tevye experienced change. The irony of the musical (and Sholom Aleichem's stories that were the basis for it) is that blind tradition will not save Tevye and his family. What enables the family's survival is Tevye's eventual ability to understand that times change, that people must change with the times, and that certain laws and traditions can be let go without damaging the relationship between humans and God. In fact, being able to discern the difference can even deepen the relationship. Such an idea has helped to influence Reform and Reconstructionist Judaism in our own time.

Other rules transcend time and change, and those are the mitzvot that focus on God and people's dealings with God, including through how they treat each other. Therefore, Judaism commands that people acknowledge that God exists and that there is no God but God.[143] People are commanded to love God and to fear God; people are expected to acknowledge that God is far mightier than humankind.[144] People are to pray to God and to imitate the goodness of God.[145] The way that we are to imitate the goodness of God is by what we carry in our hearts: not to stand by when another life is being threatened, not to hurt others through our speech, not to harbor hatred, and not to seek revenge.[146] In a full circle, such laws also help to maintain the social order. Vengeance begets vengeance; hatred begets hatred; a cavalier attitude toward life allows devastation. The two world wars of the twentieth century show the truth of these assumptions.

By the time of Jesus not all Jews practiced all the Mosaic rules. Society had changed. However, the idea of order in Jewish life was still very important. The Dead Sea scrolls pertaining to the Qumran sect of Essene Jews provide evidence of how important their idea of order was. The Qumran sect lived at a time when many Jewish people believed that the end times were imminent. Jesus himself seemed to believe this, which could explain His focus on becoming ready for the kingdom of God. It would seem as if there could be no better time for complete and utter anarchy and lawlessness, no

more opportune time for *dis*order, than the impending end of the
world. What incentive is there to hold back?

Instead, the community at Qumran focused on God and
established and maintained order. The sect was a small Jewish
group living together in an intentional community that was
isolated from the rest of society. The community was led by a
single male leader who helped to control the membership through
the establishment of laws. Laws existed against sex, guffawing,
and assisting those who were expelled from the community.
The Community Rules established precise statutes governing
community life, and they included systematized punishment for
transgressing the law, because the law promoted harmony. Without
harmony, there could be no purity. At least one scholar has argued
that impurity was the "Phantom Menace" of Qumran because
impurity jeopardized holiness, and holiness was what the Qumran
inhabitants believed would lead them to victory over the sons
of Darkness.[147]

In Judaism, then, God's laws provided a new order for a new
people. Law did away with the practice of human sacrifice: by
the angel's stopping Abraham, the practice of human sacrifice
was shown to be unnecessary and began to end, and by the time
of Moses, a law was enacted that an innocent person may not be
killed.[148] Order was how Judaism was kept intact even through the
destruction of the Second Temple, the Jewish Diaspora, and the rise
of rabbinic Judaism. In part because of the biblical insistence on
order, this relatively small religion is alive today.

Law – a sense of order – is how a group turns itself into a
people. When the American colonies became independent from
Great Britain, their first act was to establish basic rules, the Articles
of Confederation. Soon enough the weaknesses of the Articles
were discovered. The Constitution that replaced them, which has

remained the supreme organizing and governing body of law in the United States for over 200 years now through its ability to be amended and interpreted, provides the order that allows for a national identity as Americans.

Similarly, around the world, wherever people form themselves into groups, order provides identity and the ability to live together. Even though indigenous peoples and societies in North America have very different worldviews and spiritual views than non-indigenous people, for example, they create order through laws that stem from traditions and they create systems of governance. Those systems may not conform to the systems used by the dominant culture, but that's irrelevant. They provide structure that fits the culture. No culture, no society, can exist in a total absence of structure, ideas of right and wrong, and a means of enforcing what is acceptable and what is not.

CANONICAL HOURS

At Mount Melleray Abbey, nestled into the Knockmealdown Mountains outside Cappoquin in Ireland, day begins in the dark at 4:00 a.m. with Vigils. It ends at 8:00 p.m. with Compline. At Mount Melleray, it's not unusual to follow up Compline with a biscuit and a cup of tea and a brief chat before retiring to bed. In other monasteries, Compline starts the Great Silence that will not break until Vigils arrives eight hours later.

Between Vigils and Compline are the other Divine Offices. On a weekday, Lauds takes place at 7:15 a.m., which was when I started my day, followed by community Mass at 7:45. Terce, an office of psalms, comes at 9:30. Sext, rich in symbolism of being the time of the day most favorable to the prayers of humans ascending to God, comes in midday at 12:15, after which lunch awaits. None, the ninth hour, arrives at 2:15, followed after supper by Vespers at

5:45 p.m. Vespers is the most solemn of the daily offices and ends
with the Magnificat, the hymn of praise to the Blessed Virgin Mary.
It is little wonder that communities of monks, such as Cistercians,
are called "orders."

In the green farmlands of Mount Melleray, the Cistercian
monks keep a small herd of cattle for dairying. Gardens dug into
rich loam provide vegetables. Between offices, different monks have
their different jobs to do. I could almost always find Brother Peter
in the kitchen telling stories and jokes. He used to help take care of
the cattle, but by the time I stayed at Mount Melleray, he was too
old for that. On a rotating basis, one monk is the Guestmaster who
assists the laypeople coming for retreats. The regimen of most of
the monks is to avoid the guests to focus on prayer and the order
of the monastic life. Seamlessly the monks move back and forth
between fields, kitchen, guesthouse, and Divine Offices. The offices
are the skeleton that supports the flesh of each day.

In addition to the structure of the seven daily offices plus the
community Mass, each monk each day engages in *lectio divina*.
Lectio divina is meditative scripture reading, but it is not just the
passive act of sitting with book in hand and thinking about what
the words mean. Rather, it is "an encounter with God. In it the
monk centers his whole attention on seeking God. He listens to His
voice, and he lets his mind and heart be formed by God's creative
Word. By tasting His Word, the monk comes to know God in a
personal experience of His love."[149] This kind of meditative focus
takes more than effort. It takes a sense of orderliness. Order is
what enables communal monastic life to be successful. Order is
what opens the space within and around the monk to be able to
meet God and to commune with the Infinite because, thanks to the
offices, the monk is never far from God. To survive in the mundane
world, people all must acknowledge it, work with it and in it, and

eke their existence from it. However, as anyone who has worked himself or herself to death, divorce, or distraction knows, it is easy to be caught up in the whirlpool of distractions of the mundane world. A life lived amongst the Divine Offices and *lectio divina* keeps the mundane world in perspective and God at the forefront of the seeker's heart and mind.

This kind of focus is freeing. Far from entrapping us, such structure can provide us with a form that supports us. I'll be honest: I went to Melleray to run away from life for a short while. When I walked through the doors of the guesthouse, I was a psychological mess. I felt numb. I felt as if I had forgotten how to talk to others. As I told Guestmaster Father Kevin Fogarty later, I felt as if my soul had been taken away. My soul felt gone. I knew why I felt as I did. The sequence of bad personal decisions I had made was bitterly apparent to me as well as to my friends. It was on the advice of one of them that I had made the call to Father Kevin, piled into my little red Ford Fiesta, and wound my way from County Clare through the startling purple heather and rhododendrons of the mountains between Cork and Waterford down to Cappoquin.

I discovered that the Cistercian sense of structure directed all of our lives and afforded some of us the space to heal. I did not know at the time that Mount Melleray is known for helping people to recover from alcoholism. I met one of the people the Abbey had helped while I was there. He told me the story of finding himself at the side of the road one bitterly cold New Year's Eve and realizing that he was going to die. Filthy and disheveled, he scrounged a ride to the Abbey, and there with the support of the monks and the regularity of the offices he began to rebuild a life without alcohol.

I learned the power of order one morning at Terce. I had attended both Lauds and Mass, and I sat in the pew like a zombie through both. I watched and listened, but I felt nothing. I was as detached as if I were an alien sent to the Abbey to report back to my superiors as objectively as possible. At 9:30, I made my way back into the chapel and sat at the end of an oaken pew. In front of me was a beautiful stained glass window flanked by painted figures on the walls. Wooden arches clasped together at the peak of the ceiling and sprang out of the white walls like aged brown arms. Arched windows lining both side walls swept light into the chapel as the monks filed in. A monk announced that the psalm would be 102, and I opened my prayer book.

"Lord, hear my prayer, let my cry come to you," the monks began to sing. Their voices swelled and cascaded, filling the space. "Do not hide your face from me now that I am distressed. Turn your ear to me; when I call, answer me quickly." Without willing it and powerless to stop it, I could feel the cemented pain inside myself start to splinter and crack. "For my days vanish like smoke; my bones burn away as in a furnace. I am withered, dried up like grass, too wasted to eat my food. From my loud groaning I become just skin and bones. I am like a desert owl, like an owl among the ruins. I lie awake and moan like a lone sparrow on the roof."[150] Unbidden, unwanted, and utterly needed, the tears poured down my face. As the monks finished singing the psalm and filed out, I sat for a moment, no longer feeling alone and no longer utterly broken. I sat as if in the arm and the breath and the breadth of God, who had heard my despair through the song of the monks, and in that long, quiet, fraught moment, I began to heal.

Order brought me that healing, but order is not a panacea. Problems don't magically disappear just because there is order. Monasteries are not full of robots who mindlessly march from office to office the way that the Calvin's robotic duplicate marched from class to class to home in the comic strip "Calvin and Hobbes."

Monasteries are full of people with very different backgrounds, ideas, beliefs, temperaments, and energy levels. Order doesn't erase all the problems from daily life. Order simply provides a predictable stopping place where, at a particular time, a particular sequence of events will happen in a prescribed way.

In that moment there is single-minded focus on a common task. As Kathleen Norris wrote in her book about Benedictine life, *The Cloister Walk*, the orderliness of monasticism is not a way to fulfill each person's needs, just as the structure of marriage is not going to be a way, most often, to fulfill all of the needs that both people of the couple bring to the marriage. Rather, as a monk said to Norris, "What we have to struggle for...is a shared vision of the why...It's a common meaning, reinforced in the Scriptures, a shared vision of the coming reign of God."[151] Even if one doesn't believe in God, the attempt to share vision benefits relationships of all sorts.

That humankind should focus on the coming kingdom of God was the central message of Jesus and the vision he wanted to share. To gain the kingdom of God, Jesus suggested, individuals needed a new kind of order. In the society of the time, wealth and its achievement were paramount. Wealth brought power. Much of today's society is focused on the same idea.

For Jesus, though, wealth was a hindrance. Focusing on earthly concerns could only separate people from the kingdom of God, not fold them into it. To Jesus, order needed to be established by community and be focused on God. Anything that got in the way of focus on God was a distraction to be eliminated. He proves that in both Matthew and Luke when He is tempted by Satan during his forty days and nights of fasting in the desert. In both stories, Satan takes Jesus to a high place and shows Him all the kingdoms of the world in their entire splendor. Satan is willing to give it all to Jesus, if Jesus will just worship him instead of God.[152]

In today's reality TV shows in which people backstab, eat insects, and publicly humiliate themselves for a chance at a million dollars, who would turn down Satan's deal? Unlike them, Jesus did. He did not turn away from the central commandment to worship God and serve God alone. Serving and worshipping God was the order that cemented Jesus' world. It was his reason for living and preaching. As a result, He was able to see more than what was. He could focus on what would come.

Law was important to Jesus. That idea is obvious in the Sermon on the Mount. "Do not think that I have come to abolish the Law or the Prophets," Jesus told the masses. "I have not come to abolish them but to fulfill them."[153] For example, the purity laws in Leviticus 14 dictated sacrifices to be made after a person healed from leprosy and other skin diseases. Such purity laws were a vehicle for a person both to give thanks for healing and to be reestablished in the community. In the Gospel of Mark, when Jesus heals a leper, he instructs the healed man to be quiet about the healing and to offer the Levitical sacrifices.[154] That instruction shows his respect for the law.

Jesus also insisted on some flexibility of law to changing circumstances. Even the earliest of the Gospels provide stories that not all of God's laws are permanently fixed. Mark, for instance, recounts the story of Jesus and his disciples walking through a field of grain on the Sabbath. As they did, the disciples picked grain to clear a path. I've walked through corn mazes with my daughter, and we've lost each other on purpose in the tall walls of grain, but at least we had paths already cut for us to wind our way through. How impossible it would have been for us to get through the field of corn without a path having been cleared, just as it would have been impossible for Jesus and His disciples to do so. However, picking the grain constituted work, and work on the Sabbath was forbidden by the law handed to Moses. When the Pharisees confronted Jesus about this, He told them, "The Sabbath was made for man, not man for the Sabbath." To Jesus, a new "law" was needed to keep the focus of humankind where he believed it needed to be: on being able to enter the kingdom of God through Jesus's ministry. Whether or not it was permissible to pick the grain so that the minister could walk through the field was just a distraction.

Order is relative. If we look at the times in which Jesus lived and preached, we see an enormous transition occurring on several levels. On one level there was an upending of the old pre-God social order of the Romans. For the Romans, human death by various forms of execution was not terribly different from the concept of human sacrifice. Deaths appeased both the voracious state and the masses. From a Roman perspective, Jesus himself was just one more human sacrifice to keep the state and social machinery running smoothly.

The sacrifice of Jesus is also a demonstration of order. It's the outcome of a hierarchical relationship in which Jesus the human being acknowledged the authority and supremacy of God by being willing to fulfill his destiny. As a human, Jesus had a choice. He chose to keep order in every important way: by imploring the Jewish people not to revolt but to submit to the state; by adhering to what He saw as the inviolable laws of God while rejecting laws and traditions that He believed kept people from God; by voluntarily offering Himself up to torture and death as He believed God had commanded Him to do. Through seeing out the role that he had been assigned, Jesus would bring a new order, one that would be flexible and encompassing enough to spread over the entire globe, giving approximately two billion people today an avenue by which to try to know the Infinite.

SYSTEMS OF SUFISM

One by one, the Mevlevi Sufi dervishes drop their black cloaks, symbols of their earthly tombs. Beneath the cloak each wears a white short coat over a voluminous white skirt, under which are white trousers. The white garb symbolizes burial garments, in which they are about to "die" to mundane existence to achieve union with God. Their tall hats represent their tombstones. Apart from their master the sheikh, all are dressed alike. They are equal. Each in turns bows to the sheikh. Then each one steps precisely into the music. Their arms are at first crossed over the chest, as if the men are dead; then their arms open out in prescribed movement as each dervish begins to turn. The feet of each are placed just so as the dervish whirls faster around an internal still point, a point of emptiness. For those moments, the world spins out of existence. There is nothing but the dervish and the Infinite, ecstatically one.

Islam is as legalistic as Judaism, and Sufism is an expression of Islam. However, Sufism's focus is mysticism and the direct personal experience of God. At first glance, mysticism's focus on the self might seem incompatible with order, which focuses on cohesion within a group. However, mysticism in many different spiritual paths stresses the master-student relationship. There is a common realization and warning that the mind is a trickster, completely capable of deluding practitioners and leading them down paths further and further from a true experience of the Divine. Such paths can even be dangerous to the practitioner's mental health. Therefore, these spiritual paths stress the need to rely on the wisdom and experience of a master who has traveled the path under the tutelage of a previous master, and so on back through time in a lineage. Over time, Sufism developed into various schools or orders. Those orders form a kind of "institutionalization" of learning, rather like spiritual universities. J. Spencer Trimingham's book

The Sufi Orders in Islam goes into detail about the fundamental organizational aspects of Sufism, which has spread across the world. There is a North American branch (Sufi Order International, also known as SOI) founded by Hazrat Inayat Khan in the early 1900s that is not even necessarily dependent on Muslim identity.

With the sometimes exception of SOI, Sufism accepts the Qur'an, but it is ordered by guided experiences. To be a Sufi is about more than just spinning. In fact, the turning is just a small part of Sufism, and turning is about not losing balance. Keeping one's balance when the world is spinning around the axis of the self takes a well-ordered mind. To achieve that sense of order, abiding by the counsel of the sheikh is the first important task within Sufism.

As a poet and music enthusiast, I believe in the rules that govern both poetry and music, and it's through both poetry and music that I have developed my appreciation of Sufism. That appreciation has helped me to understand that the ecstatic in Sufism is not found through abandon. It is found through method and through relationship. The famous Sufi poet Jelaluddin Rumi alludes to this in one of his poems:

> Longing is the core of mystery.
> Longing itself brings the cure.
> The only rule is, Suffer the pain.
>
> Your desire must be disciplined,
> and what you want to happen
> in time, sacrificed.[155]

The great Persian lyric poet Hafiz suggested that we are kept from union with the Infinite by all of our distractions and the clamor of disorder that we let invade our daily lives:

...If you had the courage and
Could give the Beloved his choice, some nights,
He would just drag you around the room
By your hair,
Ripping from your grip all those toys in the world
That bring you no joy...[156]

he insisted in one of his poems. To Hafiz, as to Rumi, experience
of the Infinite and union with the Divine takes more than the
effort that it demands. It also needs the constraints of order, which
paradoxically will allow the Sufi to be utterly intoxicated on
achieving union with the Beloved.

Similarly, Sufi qawwali singing allows the ability, through
percussive, vocal, and musical structure, to create a trance-like
state. Songs performed by a group of musicians called a qawwali
party follow a predictable arrangement in which the side singers
will repeat verses and refrains that the lead singer presents. The
qawwali is accompanied by handclapping from the chorus and
percussion by a tabla player. Often, at least one musician will
provide a drone from a harmonium. Just as the dervish trains
under a master, so too does the head of the qawwali party. For
example, the great qawwali singer Nusrat Fateh Ali Khan who
died in 1997 was leader of the Ali Khan party and belonged to a
family that has sung qawwali for over 600 years. Nusrat identified
his nephew, Rahat, as his successor when Rahat was just a young
boy, and he trained him in the art of qawwali for the next two
decades. Upon Nusrat's death, Rahat became the party leader,
the person responsible for helping to lead both the party members
and the audience to an ecstatic state through his ability to follow
ancient patterns and vocalize to a meditative space where humans
and the Infinite can meet. Sadly, qawwali has become an art form
under pressure. The Ali Khan party essentially disintegrated with

Nusrat's death because Rahat was seen as still unprepared, and fundamentalists have targeted qawwali, killing Amjad Sabri of the Sabri Brothers party in 2016. A decline of qawwali would be the decline of centuries of musical and devotional structure.

The poems and the songs of Sufism are not spiritual texts. The texts of Sufism are the Qur'an and the hadiths, or sayings of the Prophet. "O you who have believed, remember Allah with much remembrance and exalt Him morning and afternoon," the Qur'an directs,[157] and it also places God intimately close to humans, asserting "...We have already created man and know what his soul whispers to him, and We are closer to him than [his] jugular vein."[158] Sufism yearns to experience that intimacy through the remembrance and exaltation that the Qur'an directs.

Not surprisingly, many in mainstream Islam see Sufism as heresy, because mainstream Islam focuses on a different kind of order, an external order as opposed to an internal order. This external order is known as the Five Pillars of Islam. First is the articles of faith, which is the recitation of the creed: there is no God but God, and Muhammad is His messenger. Order is further established through the five daily periods of worship, or *salat*. The remaining three pillars are the directive that those who can must fast during the lunar month of Ramadan; *zakat*, obligatory alms-giving; and pilgrimage at least once in a lifetime to Mecca by those who are healthy enough to make the trip and who can afford to do so. All five of the Pillars encourage a Muslim to be continually mindful of God and God's compassion.

In the Qur'an, order is both unity and salvation. "...Hold firmly to the rope of Allah all together and do not become divided. And remember the favor of Allah upon you—when you were enemies and He brought your hearts together and you became, by His favor, brothers,"[159] Allah tells Muslims. What to do and why to do it are spelled out for believers: "...fear the Fire, which has been prepared for the disbelievers. And obey Allah and the Messenger that you may obtain mercy."[160] For the devout Muslim, submission to God's will is the very cornerstone of the faith; the word "Islam" itself means submission. The difference between the mainstream Muslim and the Sufi is the expression of submission. For the mainstream Muslim, submission is order in following the law of the Qur'an and the hadiths in their specific details. For the Sufi, submission is conquering the ego. Order is the awareness and the true bliss of the self once reunited with God. It is an experience of that wholeness in which the sense of self as a separate entity is transcended.

STRUCTURE IN THE EAST

In India, the Vedas gave way to the Upanishads in part because of the pressures of a growingly complex Hindu society. Vedic ideas had led to stratification and compartmentalization of social classes resulting in what we now call castes. The development of Jainism and Buddhism both put pressure on the ideas that gave rise to castes—both of those religious systems reject the notion of caste—and because of that pressure came the transition in Hinduism from belief in many gods and goddesses, some fearsome and demanding human sacrifice, to belief in one Supreme God, Brahman. Neither Jainism nor Buddhism focus on the idea of a creator God, but both as well as Hinduism focus on the importance of order. In the thinking of these religions, humans are part of an ordered universe and must rely on order to achieve enlightenment, the dispelling of all illusion. The method is meditative equipoise.

In the Upanishads, the old order of Vedic rituals including human sacrifice is overturned, just as the Torah overturned old ideas and supplanted them with law. Rather than social law, though, the new order in the Upanishads is constructed of paths to God, and those paths are all achieved through the cultivation of the self. The paths are the four yogas. These are not the hatha yogas that Western practitioners are most familiar with, the series of physical exertions such as Bikram yoga that are meant to help strengthen and preserve the body so that the practitioner might have more time in the earthly body to work toward liberation. Rather, these are devotional yogas or practices.

One of the devotional yogas is jnana yoga, the path of learning and knowledge. In this path, the yogi learns through studying scriptures with a teacher then discovers how to identify with God rather than with earthly existence. Another path is bhakti yoga, in which the person focuses pure love on an aspect of God that he or she can relate to. For a Hindu, that might be Ganesha; for a Christian, that might be Jesus. A person might show devotion by reciting prayers or chanting God's name, such as Sikhs or Hare Krishnas might do. My Catholic grandmother showed it by reciting the rosary. Third is the path of karma yoga, or the yoga of work. This doesn't mean work like going to the office; rather, it is the tremendous effort of working to live without generating karma so that the practitioner can be liberated from rebirth and find unification with God. The final form of yoga is raja yoga, a deeply meditative and psychological form of yoga that uses some of the postures of hatha yoga to develop utter concentration and meditative ability so that the practitioner can dissolve all the mental barriers between God and self.

Hinduism is a pragmatic religion, and the devotional yoga that a Hindu practices isn't dictated. Rather, the practitioner chooses the path that best fits her or his personality. India's largest export, Buddhism, also emphasizes the idea of a path. This path has the same stepping stones for all Buddhists; however, they are not "laws." Rather, they are guideposts that prompt the Buddhist to reflect deeply in order to speak and act beneficially.

In Buddhism, the Eightfold Path provides the sense of order.
The Four Noble Truths assure the Buddhist that suffering can
be eliminated through enlightenment, and the Eightfold Path is
part of the way a Buddhist can reach enlightenment. To adhere
to the path requires the Buddhist practitioner to use right speech,
do right work, and perform right actions. She must use accurate
recollection and right concentration, and exert right effort. He must
have right views and right understanding. At those times when
I resisted the temptation to shout at our dog for barking, I was
using right intention to develop my compassion. When I don't lie to
telemarketers or wallow in the latest juicy gossip, I am choosing to
use right speech. When I ignore a married person's pass or hand the
extra $20 bill back to the clerk who gave it to me by mistake, I am
using right action.

Buddhism teaches that these steps on the path all accumulate
merit in future lifetimes to help me reach enlightenment. In the here
and now, I am more likely to practice kindness to others and to
act ethically. As a Hindu, similarly, I might use karma yoga to act
ethically. Acting ethically has social benefits; ethical interactions
lessen our perceived need to defend ourselves and our sense of
mistrust and suspicion.

China absolutely recognized that action and inaction have
social consequences, although China's traditional sense of order
reflected China's differences from India's culture. Confucian
thought emphasized order in China. Confucius acknowledged the
existence of a Supreme Being, and this Supreme Being prized order,
which was based on the duties inherent in human relationships. For
Confucius, the highest possible good was social order because the
best possible social order would reflect divine harmony. In other
words, in Hinduism harmony with God was the focus and could
have benefits on Earth. In Confucian thinking, harmony in earthly

society was the focus, and Heaven was its own kind of separate society. Confucius believed that moral force must combine with harmony on all levels of living. This is done through hierarchical relationships. In Confucian thinking, a ruler owes certain duties to subjects; subjects owe different duties and allegiances to the ruler. The same is true of relationships between spouses, parents and children, siblings, and friends. To know one's place in any relationship, in Confucian thinking, is to know the correctness that must govern the relationship, and acting with correctness is in harmony with cosmic order in which, for example, the sun warms the planets in our solar system according to the planet's distance from the sun, and the planet maintains its regular orbit.

In the *Analects*, Confucius repeatedly stresses the rules. "Respectfulness, without the rules of propriety, becomes laborious bustle; carefulness, without the rules of propriety, becomes timidity; boldness, without the rules of propriety, becomes insubordination; straightforwardness, without the rules of propriety, becomes rudeness," he tells his disciples.[161] The "rules of propriety" are essential to Confucius. By them, one's "character is established." Order establishes cause and effect to create the outcome one wants; lack of order leads to unwanted effects. For example, when he was asked what the first step was to fixing government, he replied that correcting names of things would be the first step. His reply was met with incredulity, and he explained,

> If language be not in accordance with the truth of things, affairs cannot be carried on to success. When affairs cannot be carried on to success, proprieties and music do not flourish. When proprieties and music do not flourish, punishments will not be properly awarded. When punishments are not properly awarded, the people do not know how to move hand or foot. Therefore...what

the superior man requires is just that in his words there may be nothing incorrect.[162]

Repeatedly throughout the *Analects* Confucius stresses the difference between the right way of doing things and the wrong way. Both have consequences, but the preferred consequences come from discerning action that conforms to divine order. Although humans were not trying to merge with the Divine, they needed to imagine it to live in a similarly perfected way.

Chinese Daoism's sense of order was more nebulous than Confucianism's. In Daoism, everything is ordered by the Dao, which is constantly in motion. Circumstances change because the Dao is ever changing. To quote the Borg from *Star Trek*, "Resistance is futile," or at least ill-conceived, because the Dao is going to do what it does. To Daoism, our hope for healthy life and society is to understand the order of things and the role that we play in that order.

Inherent in Daoism are the ideas of yin and yang. Often, these are simplified in Western thinking as opposite forces. It is more accurate to think of yin and yang as forces that are simultaneously complementary and in tension. The forces both wax and wane to their most extreme in both directions, after which they shift direction. As the *Dao De Jing* explains,

> Being and non-being create each other.
> Difficult and easy support each other.
> Long and short define each other.
> High and low depend on each other.
> Before and after follow each other.[163]

The text offers the Daoist a method to live by the Dao that at first sounds like the complete antithesis of order: non-being and not-doing, or *wu wei*. To put it simply, if the Dao is the Way, then a way is order, not anarchy, and we find practical wisdom in the text for how to live a harmonious life:

> In dwelling, live close to the ground.
> In thinking, keep to the simple.
> In conflict, be fair and generous.
> In governing, don't try to control.
> In work, do what you enjoy.
> In family life, be completely present. [164]

Other methods that the Dao champions may seem at first to be more esoteric, such as:

> Express yourself completely,
> then keep quiet.
> Be like the forces of nature:
> when it blows, there is only wind;
> when it rains, there is only rain;
> when the clouds pass, the sun shines through.[165]

If such methods are harder to understand, though, perhaps that is because Daoism suggests that enlightenment is in the here and now. Realizing our place in the Dao and living in harmony with the Dao is true enlightenment. In that sense, it has natural connections with Buddhist ideas. Likewise, a Hindu ascetic would recognize the wisdom in that passage and its suggestion that self-control and careful observation help a person to connect the sacred and the mundane. As Lao Zi writes,

> Each separate being in the universe
> returns to the common source.
> Returning to the source is serenity.[166]

In other words, order is not just the way to the Infinite. Order is the Infinite itself. Whether a Hindu practices one of the four yogas, a Buddhist practices the Eightfold Path, a Confucian follows the relationships spelled out in *The Analects,* or a Daoist tries to live in harmony with the Dao, the common goal is to transcend earthly squabbles, jealousies, competitions, hatreds, and ignorance to perfect both oneself and the world.

BENEFITS OF ORDER

Order means more than just the local police department handing out traffic tickets or speed zones on roads. Importantly, it doesn't mean the emphasis on "law and order" currently being espoused in the United States, a concept more rooted in punitive measures than in creating true social safety. It's more than zero tolerance policies in schools. In fact, it's true that a shadowy aspect exists to order, a dark side that a protestor can point to and say, "Look at the terrible consequences of order, especially the order of law." For instance, we can and must condemn the orderly execution of millions of Jewish people along with Roma people, Jehovah's Witnesses, homosexuals, Soviet prisoners of war, and political dissenters in Nazi Germany. We can and should decry the Stalinist purges. We can and ought to criticize Mao Zedong's insistence on his disastrous agricultural policies that left millions of Chinese people dead from famine. We can and need to disparage any expression of shariah law that encourages men to bury a woman in a pit, leaving her head exposed so that they can cast rocks at it until she is dead, or to mutilate people as punishment for petty crimes. Americans can easily find examples of excess carried out in the name of order: police brutality and killings across the nation and torture at Guantanamo Bay are just two examples prominent in the news.

Excesses aside, though, order is what lets us live and function together. We may not even think about the many small ways in which order benefits us and our societies. Order lets us find books and articles in libraries. It prompts us to construct classifications such as species, genus, and family to better understand the natural world in which we live. Being messy has certain advantages, researcher Kathleen Vohs and other researchers found, but order in the form of neatness correlates to generosity and aversion to crime.[167]

Order also allows us to communicate. Anyone who has tried to have a conversation with others who continually interrupt knows how frustrating that can be. When listening doesn't occur, true communication is difficult. Researchers have studied how effective communication takes place, and one key facet is a sense of order through taking turns to speak and listen. That includes pausing.[168] On a larger perspective, order allows towns and cities to be built and grow. A sense of order allows us to pay bills, meet deadlines, create schedules, and organize our daily tasks. Further, even though chaos may be the nature of the universe, much of life on Earth is demonstrated by a sense of order. For example, even twenty years ago when the science of the brain was not as advanced as it is now, scientists discovered that the brain cells responsible for processing visual images arrange themselves in geometric mosaics. Dr. Mark Huebener of the Max Planck Institute wrote in response to the imaging of the cells that "Our maps of the working brain are so orderly they resemble the street map of Manhattan."[169] Order itself allows us the experience of being human.

Despite the benefits of order, humans often tend to disorder. It can be seen in crime statistics, violence, hoarding, and other irregular behaviors. The reasons vary. For example, people who hoard may do so because they are feeling an unusual attachment to the objects or animals that they hoard. The objects or animals may make them feel safe, loved, or in control. Even though their hoarding may spiral out of control, they may be trying to create a sense of safety and order for themselves. The root causes of violence are many, including genetic causes, but environmental risk factors include a combination of poverty, lack of education, and unstable family life. Without the sense of order that comes from basic needs being met and feeling loved, people may become susceptible to violence; the lack of order becomes expressed in a different (or even similar, for those in violent families) disorder.

If we are unwilling to admit that rules and order are beneficial to ourselves in relation to others, it might seem tempting to flout the rules. When we realize that rules can serve a purpose, we can see how to create constructive ones that can benefit our families and relationships. I was reminded of that a few years ago when I was chatting with my friend Cristina. She told me that she and her husband didn't sleep in on weekends. Their rule was to get up at the same time on the weekends as they did during the work week. They did that because her husband hates alarm clocks. Cristina used to get up early to make the drive to a demanding job. To benefit their relationship, she was willing to forego the alarm clock, but the rule needed to be established that they got up at the same time every day so that she wouldn't run the risk of oversleeping during the week. Such a small compromise and sense of order benefitted their marriage. From Alcoholics Anonymous' Twelve Steps to anti-clutter professionals to how-to books that lay out the process for self-improvement, evidence surrounds us that order is an asset to our lives, as the world's spiritual texts indicate.

Do we want to live in suspicion that others will rip us off, or do we want to create a society in which people are highly unlikely to rip each other off? Do we want to live in anxiety because we live in chaos, or do we want to set up regular times to have dinner with our families, to talk to each other, to establish boundaries to keep various parts of our lives separate? Look at the popularity of media that encourages us to de-clutter rather than to hoard. At heart, we like order. In a perfect world, order helps keep our children and ourselves safe from predators. It helps us walk the streets without fear, as I can easily do in Southern China. In America, we think we need guns to keep order, yet we see every day that guns contribute to the chaos. Instead, we need the will and commitment to design rules that keep us safe and healthy and to live by them.

Acknowledgement

"Now I lay me down to sleep," I used to pray as a child in my bed. "I pray the Lord my soul to keep. If I should die before I wake, I pray the Lord my soul to take." It's a ritual that is still played out nightly in families who practice some form of Christianity, just as common as saying grace at meals in thanks for the food on the table. Now that I think back on it, I realize it's no wonder that I sometimes am anxious. It seems odd in our child-protective world for small children to be praying not to die in their sleep and to go to heaven in case they do. In another way, though, the idea is utterly functional. From a very young age, the idea was instilled in me that there was more to life than just me and that life itself was a precarious thing, a gift that could be lost in an act as simple as tucking myself into my bed below the portrait of the thorn-encrusted, bleeding Sacred Heart of Jesus.

My prayer was an act of acknowledgement. In the spiritual texts of the world, we can find other forms of acknowledgement. "Put no other gods before me," God told the Hebrews, and the rule became a core belief of Judaism and then Christianity. He told the Hebrews to keep holy the Sabbath, too. Why? Did He just want people to take a rest every seven days, as He had done when he created the universe? No. He didn't want people just to take a day off. He directed people to literally keep the day *holy*. For the Hebrews then and modern observant Jews today, the Sabbath was and is a day for remembering God. An Orthodox person will do no work on the Sabbath because to do so profanes its sacredness; to work takes time away from remembering God. To keep the day holy in remembrance of God acknowledges the existence of God.

I learned about acknowledgement in my travels. In Tunisia, as I walked the glistening white sands that slid gracefully up to the densely blue Mediterranean and wound my way through the marketplace in Tunis or the side streets of Kairouan, five times a day I would hear a male voice call out over a loudspeaker: *Allahu akbar. Ash hadu, an la ilaha illallah. Ash hadu anna Muhammad ar rasullullah. Hayya alas salah, hayya allal falah, Allahu akbar, la illaha, illallah.* The piercing song from the muezzins is the Muslim call to prayer, the *adhan.* It's not a call that says, "Time to come pray, get a move on." Rather, it means, "Allah is greatest. I bear witness that none is worthy of being worshipped except Allah. I bear witness that Muhammad is Allah's messenger. Come to prayer; come to success. Allah is most great; none is worthy of being worshipped except Allah." I acknowledge You, the prayer says. I know You are, and I know that You are greater than I am.

In the courtyard of the Six Banyan Buddhist temple in Guangzhou, the enormous port city located on the Pearl River in southern mainland China, people light incense and deposit it in a large burner. The faithful perform prostrations, kneeling down and touching their foreheads to the ground, hands clasped, in front of the gilded statues of the Buddha. In 2004, as I did again when I returned in 2017, I did likewise, although my brand-new daughter laughed at me, a Caucasian woman paying homage in front of the serene Chinese faces that loomed above me. I was there with other adoptive families to be blessed by the monks. All of us were new families. Most were beaming married couples with their new babies in their arms. Amongst us on that trip, I was the sole single mother and the sole adoptive parent of an older child. While I absolutely wanted the monks' blessing, I also wanted to pay homage. I was not "worshipping the Buddha." I was giving thanks for connecting the red thread that had brought my daughter and me together across a vast ocean, different languages, and nine years of her life.

A scientist would call the match between my daughter and me simple chance. A non-believing bureaucrat would call it bureaucracy at its most effective. For me, acknowledging that maybe the Infinite played a role in our match takes nothing away from our adoption agency, the Chinese Center for Children's Welfare and Adoption, the American Embassy, our indefatigable social worker, our Guangzhou guide, and the many others from the local police department to the FBI to the Department of Homeland Security who played their seemingly random roles. I appreciate their work and their decisions, but I choose to also appreciate the Infinite's role. A Vietnamese student once said in our class, "I may be a Buddhist, but I'm a God-fearing man," and I'm right there with him. My view is that there's no harm done by my thanking something that might not be real. On the other hand, if I don't give thanks, and that Other *is* real, then I have been both egotistical and ungrateful.

For me, as for so many others in the world, to believe in the world of the sacred is to acknowledge it. All the spiritual texts of the world make the need for acknowledgement clear. For a Jewish person, a Muslim, a Christian, a Sikh, or a Hindu, the Other is God. For a Jain, the Infinite is karma. For a Buddhist, the Other includes the possibility of enlightenment and the existence of the buddhas in celestial realms. For the Daoist, it is the Dao. For a Confucian, it is a celestial sense of harmony. For a scientist, maybe it is a Grand Unified Theory. The Infinite is bigger than and beyond us. If we cannot or will not acknowledge the world of the Infinite, then it is tempting to see ourselves as the most important facet in our universe.

We may think of ourselves as invincible and infallible, but we are not. The danger of not acknowledging the Infinite is that we can become narcissistic, enamored with our own human image, and convinced by our own self-interest and ideas of self-importance. We may never think about the larger order of things. We may not stop to contemplate whether our actions reflect a sacred path because we may not stop to consider that the world of Infinite even *is*.

We live in a time when we are forced to question our old paradigms. For instance, do humans truly have dominion over all other creatures? Is exploiting other creatures/beings for our own profits unethical? Are we creating environmental catastrophe in our hunger for profits and convenience? What are the consequences of the slaughter of other humans in wars and genocides? What are the ethical implications of our new genetic and pharmacological technologies? As we consider the answers to these questions, to think that the highest call to which we answer is our own self-interest is foolhardy.

Acknowledgement connects to the other virtues. Effort pushes us out of our comfort zone. Compassion demands that we feel what other beings feel. Generosity asks us to give, even if the giving is painful. Order enables us to constrain ourselves. Like all of them, acknowledgment of the Infinite, however we conceptualize it, recognizes that something more important than our self-interest exists and should compel us.

Acknowledgement isn't meant to be grudging or reluctant. Acknowledgement of the Infinite is the axe with which we can crack and destroy our own ego-grasping. It dares us to discover what is truly moral rather than whether we can establish a consensus that we think the act or stance is okay. To acknowledge the Infinite means to ask and listen for the answer: What does God want? What would Jesus do? What karma will X accumulate for us: beneficial or harmful? What is most harmonious with the Dao? What is *truly* right and good?

RECITATION

Guru Nanak Dev was the first of the Sikh gurus and the founder of Sikhism, one of the five most populous religions of the world. His words open the *Adi Granth*, also known as the *Sri Guru Granth Sahib*. "People beg and pray, "Give to us, give to us", and the Great Giver gives His Gifts. So what offering can we place before Him...What words can we speak to evoke His Love? ...[C]hant the True Name, and contemplate His Glorious Greatness,"[170] the text tells the Sikh faithful. For a Sikh, acknowledging God means having a relationship with God.

Sikhism rejects everything that it sees as blind rituals. The way to God, for a Sikh, isn't found through fasting, through asceticism, through idolatry, or through superstition. To a Sikh, the Muslim practice of fasting during Ramadan is blind ritual because Sikhs don't believe that spirituality is developed through the amount of food that one does or doesn't eat. Sikhs reject the idea that fasting can bring one closer to God. Similarly, Sikhs see the Catholic practice of making the sign of the cross on oneself as another blind ritual. So is the Jewish practice of male circumcision. For Sikhs, the whole objective of life is to lose one's separateness and to be reunited with the one God, and the only way to do that is through the constant acknowledgement of God.

Simran is the Sikh term for the constant meditation on the Divine Name. One way this constant meditation is achieved is through repetition, which is called *japana* or *jaap*. Sikh Guru Ram Das wrote, "He who calls himself a Sikh...should meditate on the divine name after rising and bathing and should recite *Jaap* from memory, thus driving away all evil deeds and vices... He who recites the divine name with every breath and bite is indeed a true Sikh...."[171] The recitation of the name and the continuous meditation on God has two functions. One is to keep the idea of

God close to the practitioner in every waking minute. The other is to consider what that closeness means. By keeping the idea of God close at hand every moment, we must reflect carefully on what we choose to do and not to do. From this perspective, God is not a distant eye whose very act of watching influences us, as in Michel Foucault's panopticon. Rather, God is as close as our breath, an intimate presence that acts as a steadying influence to keep us on the "right path," whatever that may be.

Reciting rosaries has a similar purpose. I remember reciting the rosary as a child and thinking that the time the recitation took was interminable. Compared to *jaap*, though, the time spent in that rosary recitation seems like the blink of an eye. Referring to God, Guru Nanak Dev wrote, "I bow to Him, I humbly bow...If I had 100,000 tongues, and these were then multiplied twenty times more, with each tongue, I would repeat, hundreds of thousands of times, the Name of the One, the Lord of the Universe."[172] The recitation means to help the Sikh practitioner live according to Sikh principles, which include helping those in need and working actively to be useful in the community while striving to live a life of truth, benevolence, and cleanness of mind and body.

The *Adi Granth* explains various reasons why the faithful should continually remember and acknowledge God: "Remembering God, the pain of death is dispelled. Remembering God, death is eliminated. Remembering God, one's enemies are repelled. Remembering God, no obstacles are met. Remembering God, one remains awake and aware, night and day. Remembering God, one is not touched by fear. Remembering God, one does not suffer sorrow.... In the remembrance of God are knowledge, meditation and the essence of wisdom.... In the remembrance of God, duality is removed.... In the remembrance of God, one attains honor in the Court of the Lord. In the remembrance of God, one becomes good. In the remembrance of God, one flowers in fruition."[173] In the Sikh view, acknowledgement benefits both this life and whatever afterlife awaits us.

For a Sikh, to acknowledge God and to keep the idea of God close in mind at all times means to also keep the idea of God close at hand at all times. One of the five articles of faith worn by Sikhs is the *kirpan*, or small ceremonial dagger. The *kirpan* is the symbol of willingness to defend the helpless members of the community against tyranny and injustice and to cut though the shroud of deception to free the truth. The other four articles are uncut hair covered by a turban to remind the Sikh to live according to the will of God, a ceremonial comb to keep the hair groomed, a metal bracelet worn on the right wrist as a visible reminder to do only what is right with one's hands, and drawstring underwear that serves to dissuade the Sikh from acting hastily out of lust in addition to protecting his or her modesty and allowing for freedom of movement during combat situations. The Sikh *khalsa*, or membership, is committed to doing the right thing, not just thinking about the right thing to do.

In the larger world outside the Sikh *gurdwara* or worship hall, wearing the five articles of faith and staying focused on the existence and nearness of God sustains Sikhs in their identity as "warrior saints." The story of Dr. Tejdeep Singh Rattan, a captain in the United States Army, is one example. Captain Rattan was one of two Sikh soldiers who, in 2010, were allowed to retain their articles of faith while on active duty. The right to wear the articles had been rescinded by the military in 1984. Captain Rattan, who was born in India's Punjab, said, "History portrays Sikhs as warrior-saints and I believe that is what Sikhs are. That's what our life is all about...There is a line in the Sri Guru Granth Sahib that translates to 'Good for all,' which means that all men are my brothers. If something happens to them, I must go and

protect them."[174] In an article on the Army website, Rattan went on
to state,

> "This is actually very important for the Sikh community.
> The reason I am here is to serve, as well as educate. When
> my little kids grow up, if they want to serve in the Army,
> they can and they will have the safety to serve. Maybe my
> elders won't be assaulted when they walk down the street.
> I was not born in the United States, but it is my home
> and I am an American...Our country was built by people
> like me, from different parts of the world, from different
> races and religions. I hope my desire to serve in the United
> States Army shows my commitment to my country. I am
> willing to lay down my life for America. I ask only that my
> country respect my faith, an integral part of who I am."[175]

For Rattan, acknowledgement of God means acknowledgement
of the need to defend his adopted country, just as so many Sikhs
volunteered at Ground Zero in Manhattan in the wake of the 9/11
attacks. Ironically, since those acts of terrorism, hate crimes against
Sikhs have risen across the United States. Those hate crimes are
motivated in part by one of the Sikh articles of faith, the wearing
of the turban. Because they have been stereotyped by people who
believe that only Muslims wear turbans, Sikhs have been bullied,
beaten, shot, and even murdered. Such attacks stem from deep
prejudices rather than from any attempt by the perpetrators to
do "right." Such attacks are justified by no religion. Even the
authoritarian God described in The Baylor Religion Studies, the one
who is imagined to be incessantly displeased with humans, doesn't
tell humankind to hurt others based on the clothes they wear. Still,
despite the targets that the turbans sometimes create, devout Sikhs
continue to wear them in the belief that acknowledgement of a

higher power and their relationship to that power is as important as life and security itself.

ACCEPTANCE AND ACTION

The God of the Torah makes the expectation of acknowledgement very clear, including in the stone tablets that he gives to Moses. In those tablets, God promises love to those who love Him and follow His laws.[176] To me, though, there is no clearer and no more touching story about acknowledging God than the story of Job. As readers, it is easy to get so caught up in the story that we forget that the unknown writer of the book, a human lost to us through the passage of thousands of years, created the dramatic poem to explore profound philosophical questions, including what is good and what is evil?

In the prologue, Satan offers God a challenge. God has blessed Job, Satan tells God, so it is no wonder that Job praises God. Satan's proposition is that Job praises God only because he has been blessed. In a kind of cosmic poker game, God takes up Satan's wager. So the trials of Job begin. Job first loses all his livestock and all of his children to various calamities. When he does, he is as distraught as any person would be, throwing himself to the ground in dismay. However, he neither writes off nor forgets God. Instead, he says, "The Lord gave, and the Lord hath taken away. Blessed be the name of the Lord."[177] Not satisfied, Satan presses his cause further, and the result is that Job is smitten with boils from head to foot. When Job's wife encourages him to curse God, Job cannot acknowledge God through a curse or an expression of anger at God. Instead, he admonishes his wife and asserts, "We accept good things from God; and should we not accept evil?"[178] Job's comment is complex; he is acknowledging that his suffering is caused directly by God, yet he simultaneously accepts God's handiwork.

Three of Job's friends, Eliphaz, Bildad, and Zophar, visit Job after hearing about his misfortunes, and they talk at length with him, trying to reason through his problems. Eliphaz tells Job, "In your place, I would appeal to God, and to God I would state my plea."[179] Bildad reinforces Eliphaz's suggestion, arguing with Job that if he pleads to God for mercy, God will restore all that he has taken from Job, if Job is truly blameless. Their advice has a bit of "blame the victim" built in. Their responses suggest that maybe Job has done something to deserve punishment, even if he is unaware of it. Their advice also seems to underestimate God. It's as if they think that God might have made a mistake and not realized it but will own up to it and fix it if Job just points it out to Him.

Job, however, isn't having it. His response is to acknowledge the complexity of God. He sees clearly that God is not a being who simply hands out goodies, like an ice cream truck driver, nor is He capricious and amoral like the Greek gods whose motivations so often tended to be self-interested. "God is wise in heart and mighty in strength; who has withstood him and remained unscathed?" he asks.[180] He lists out the wide array of God's attributes and actions, and he concludes that God destroys both the innocent and the wicked.

A reader could almost be forgiven for thinking that Job is a simpleton and a fool for maintaining such allegiance to a God that seems arbitrary. Job is no fool, though. Job has vision that pierces the blindness of so much of humanity and expresses that vision by admitting that while he thinks he is blameless, he cannot possibly *know* if he is truly innocent. He can fool himself, he points out. In this admission, Job recognizes that there is a higher order, a higher knowledge, and a larger scheme of things than that able to be perceived by humans. Job is conceding that God is greater than humankind.

Job is also aggrieved. He argues with his friends, and his arguments again and again lay out the differences between humans and God. In one of the most poignant passages, he asserts that if he could, he would stand before God and present his case and argue his worthiness in the hopes that God would heed him. However, that is not going to happen, Job concludes, because he cannot find God. God is not in a place and is not able to be perceived. Neither is God intelligible. To even be able to converse with God, Job would have to "learn the words with which he would answer, and understand what he would reply to me,"[181] and Job's comment is an admission that to understand God is impossible. We can recognize that which we cannot truly understand, though, and that recognition carries with it its own benefits, as Job explains when he tells his friends that to man, God said, "Behold, the fear of the Lord is wisdom; and avoiding evil is understanding."[182] The two go hand in hand. By being cognizant of God (or whatever higher power we choose), we are encouraged to exercise our free will for good rather than for evil, not because we imagine a carrot (Heaven, blessings, enlightenment) or stick (punishment, hell), but because we are moral beings.

Most importantly, through his long and self-righteous speeches Job is not just talking about God. Job is talking *to* God, and he begs for direct answers, just as any of us who have ever begged, "Why me, God?" To Job, God is not some abstract concept. God lives, and Job knows it, and Job believes that the chasm between himself and God, between human and the Infinite, can be bridged.

As it turns out, he is both right and wrong about that. God is fed up with listening to Job when He finally answers, and his answer is the world's first *Jeopardy* moment: all the answers he gives Job are in the form of questions. "Have you an arm like that of God, or can you thunder with a voice like his?" God demands to know.[183] Obviously, Job can do nothing and know nothing and be nothing like God can, and he knows it. When God has finished pelting Job with questions, Job simply agrees: "I know that you can do all things, and that no purpose of yours can be hindered."[184] Perhaps even more importantly, he tells God, "I have dealt with great things that I do not understand; things too wonderful for me, which I cannot know. I have heard of You by word of mouth, but now my eye has seen You."[185] Job doesn't mean this literally. He and God are not sitting across a hassock from each other in a tent drinking coffee. Job is saying here that prior to this he thought he knew about God. He knew what he had learned from others. Now it is personal. Now he can bear witness. Now the encounter and the knowledge is authentic. He owns this experience, and his knowledge of God, is now intimate.

God next rebukes the friends of Job, whose comments to Job show only what they *think* they know. Job acknowledges what none of us want to acknowledge: that we cannot know everything about the realm of the sacred Infinite, and we certainly cannot know it intellectually as an abstract concept. The heart of faith is accepting that we are limited and that there is a point at which our senses and our reason only get in the way. What is bigger than us and beyond our physical senses and sense of reason is the Infinite? For Job, this Infinite is God.

It's precisely because the Infinite is beyond our physical senses and reason that we must acknowledge its existence. What we can see, touch and feel is part of the mundane world. We can slot it all neatly into the box that we have created for it. The box for "tree," for example, tells us quickly that the tree is unlikely to harm us, that it acts to help clear the air, and that, depending on the species (yet another box) it might be used to build boats, houses, furniture, or other goods. The box for "shark" tells us to be extremely cautious since "shark" is filed under fast-moving predator with rows of sharp teeth. What is in each of our boxes is usually predictable and acts just like the labels tell us it should. In contrast, the story of Job tells us that the Infinite cannot be put so easily into one of our boxes. It is different from the rest of our schema. To acknowledge the Infinite means to engage with a world with few if any signposts.

PROPHECY

The story of Job is not the only story of the acknowledgment of God in the Hebrew Bible. Nevi'im, the books of the prophets, is the second major section of the Bible after the Torah. Perhaps because it is said today in Judaism that the time of the prophets is over, it is worth thinking about those ancient men who received messages from God.

I sometimes wonder would it would be like to be God's mouthpiece on Earth. I think that it must be terrifying, especially depending on what message God might be delivering at any given time. To acknowledge God means more than just saying, "Yeah, I believe in God. Can I have dessert now?" For the prophets, acknowledging God meant first hearing God, then really listening to God, and then relaying the message of God, and it had to have taken tremendous courage because then, as now, God is not a static smiley face. Those same four general images of God that people have today, the authoritarian God, the benevolent God, the distant God, and the critical God described in the Baylor study, are the same images that the prophets had. As circumstances changed, the God that they acknowledged changed too, in all His complexity. The biblical prophets were not carrying today's "God loves you, don't worry" kinds of messages and could not have been terribly popular.

The Minor Prophets provide an example of how the view of God began to change as events unfolded leading to the Assyrian conquest of Israel in 722 BCE, which led to the Jewish Diaspora and hundreds of years of foreign domination of the Jewish people. Hosea heard God tell him, "I will not be your [Israel's] God."[186] Instead, the warrior God who had made appearances in the past and championed Israel gave way to an image of God as lover: "I will also banish bow, sword and war from the land," said God to Hosea, "And I will espouse you forever; I will espouse you with righteousness and justice."[187] Hosea's view is loving and hopeful.

That's not at all the same God that Amos acknowledged as the Assyrians destroyed cities and settlements and deported inhabitants. The God that Amos acknowledged is frightening in His omnipotence and terribleness, a wrathful God who will judge Israel. This God told the kingdom, "I will call you to account for all your iniquities."[188] The God who spoke through Amos could not be appeased by blood, nor was this God a consolation or helpmate; "I loathe, I spurn your festivals," He told Israel. "I am not appeased by your solemn assemblies. If you offer me burnt offerings...I will not accept them...Spare me the sound of your hymns...But let justice well up like water, righteousness like an unfailing stream."[189] By acknowledging these aspects of God and His dissatisfaction, Amos reflected on the fears of his place and time as well as the realization that the people could have done better. If God wants effort, Amos seems to tell us, then perhaps people had made the wrong kinds of effort. If God wants order, it is for justice rather than injustice.

Amos seems to speak out of a sense of uncertainty, guilt and a new understanding that came from hearing God. Micah, who prophesized "Someday they [the chiefs of the House of Israel] shall cry out to the Lord, but he will not answer them; at that time he will hide his face from them in accordance with the wrongs they have done,"[190]echoed Amos' sentiments, but by listening carefully Micah also was given knowledge of the remnant that will be protected "from Assyria, should it invade our land, and should it trample our country."[191]

For the prophets of the Hebrew Bible, acknowledging God meant first and foremost that they saw God as an active agent in the world. For them, God was not the distant clockmaker who put the universe into action and then stood back and let it take its course. Rather, the prophets believed that God wanted something from people.

To be clear, "prophecy" doesn't just mean telling the future. To truly know the future takes omniscience. Rather, prophecy reveals God's intent. To reveal God's intent, the prophet must know God's intent. To know God's intent, the prophet must acknowledge God and try to understand the desires and purposes of God. The Hebrew prophets looked at their world, and they listened to the voice of God in their heads. They tried to grasp what God wanted and planned, and they spoke what the outcome would be if people continued on their present course. They tried to identify what was wrong with the present course not from their own perspective, but from God's.

Also, by acknowledging God, they could share the knowledge of God that they were granted, as if over centuries they were building an enormous metaphysical jigsaw puzzle portrait of the Divine. By 520 BCE, for example, Zechariah saw a far different image of God than Amos had. Zechariah described this God as having softness in His heart for His people: "They shall be my people," God says, "and I will be their God – in truth and sincerity."[192] The God who spoke to Zechariah wasn't a pushover, though. He was still a warrior who sounded the ram's horn and manifested himself with arrows and sling stones.[193]

There is another layer to the prophets, however. They show us that what we experience is much greater than just ourselves; we are not the only cause of our fates. Other influences that we may not even imagine also come to bear. Malachi, for example, suggests a sense of cosmic conflict when he prophesizes that all "shall come to see the difference between the righteous and the wicked, between him who has served the Lord and him who has not served Him. For lo! That day is at hand, burning like an oven. All the arrogant and all the doers of evil shall be straw, and the day that is coming... shall burn them to ashes."[194]By the time of Malachi, the Jewish people were looking forward to a messiah, a priest and warrior-king duo who would liberate them and deliver them from their conquerors, but the Dead Sea Scrolls suggest that the messianic idea was also connected to the idea of a cosmic battle in which righteousness would overcome evil.

If we cannot or will not acknowledge a moral power that is deeper and more universal than our own desires, then we are left with the problem of sorting out the difference between what is righteous and what is evil. If we acknowledge only the primacy of the human mind and human will, then it is easy to fool ourselves into believing that whatever we do is righteous because we say it is. What any of us wants is determined by our cultural upbringing, our experience, our histories. What we want is produced by the mundane world. What the mundane world produces is not necessarily righteous; it is generally born of self-interest. For example, Nazi Germany acknowledged the might and power of the German people, the so-called Aryan race, and argued the righteousness of eradicating the disabled, the aged, the Roma, and the Jews from German society. It convinced itself of the righteousness of *lebensraum* as it annexed states and killed millions in the process. ISIS is focusing on what it sees as its righteous goals right now in the Middle East in its quest to create a "pure" Islamic state. Its righteousness is marred by violence, rape, and mayhem. Many could reasonably argue that the United States' use of torture in its "war against terrorism" is an example of mistaking evil for righteousness. Without much difficulty, most of us can think of other examples of terrible acts that have been undertaken with the assurance that they were somehow noble.

For the prophets, acknowledging God meant seeing ourselves as having power but also being part of a larger scheme, one in which we would ultimately be accountable and in which our actions would set off reactions that we could not control and that could have terrible consequences. Acknowledgment meant accepting that values of right and wrong had to be assigned to behaviors. The prophets believed that people should consider their actions and they believed that what happened on this earth was connected to actions that people decided to undertake. Lack of seeing a bigger picture than one's own wants and needs meant that people could act in ways that might not be beneficial to anyone in the long run.

A simple and common model gives us an example of how such behaviors work: ants. In an interview on National Public Radio's *Fresh Air* program, Mark Moffett, author of *Adventures Among Ants*, described some of the behavioral similarities between the insects and humans. Ants, for example, have a strong sense of order, and their need for infrastructure depends on the size of their colony. Like humans, ants developed agriculture (and Moffett pointed out in the interview that ant agriculture has many of the same problems besetting modern human agriculture, such as depleting of resources and the dangers that accompany monoculture). Most importantly, most species of ants have a powerful sense of what we would call, in human terms, tribalism. Ants have very small brains and appear to have very little brainpower. In a sense, ants are programmed by eons of evolution to do what they do, and what they do very well is to defend by attacking whatever they perceive as an "outsider." Ants war and kill, and they do so easily. Ants are not ethicists. Ants do not have morals. Ants are not philosophers. Ethics and philosophy are human talents. Therefore, ants stage all-out war in which the smallest and weakest often are made the first casualties and in which territory is conquered to gain its resources, resulting in massive death, and then discarded once the resources are consumed.

Without being willing to see a larger scheme of things, the fallback position of humans is to act like ants. We attack perceived enemies wantonly. We erode our resources. We do rather than truly think. The prophets, beset by attackers, understood more than 2,500 years ago that acknowledging the Infinite allows us to be "bigger" than our insect brethren in more than just size. Acknowledging the Infinite allows us to imagine our potential rather than relying on our present capabilities. Rather than doing what we do simply because we can do it, acknowledgement of the Infinite prompts us to look beyond ourselves and question what we should do, and to what end, and whether it is, in the simplest terms, good.

LOOKING FOR HARMONY

Along the Li River in China's Guangxi Autonomous Region, the Karst Mountains of Guilin rise out of the mist in fanciful shapes and beckon to human imagination. Here is an apple; there is an elephant, all fashioned out of Devonian limestone dating back approximately 350 million years. Time, water, and geological process have sculpted the shapes. Rainwater has chiseled away at the stone that was thrust up out of the earth when

India and China's plates rammed together to create the soaring Himalayan range.

An art buff who takes the guided cruise down the Li River to the town of Yangshuo might experience the sensation that he or she is part of a Daoist painting come to life. I have exactly such a watercolor painting in my living room, a memento of a trip to the region that I took in 1994. Rounded mountains tower in the background, solid and hard in the bluish grayness, although their edges are softened, especially as they meet the water at their base. Between them birds dart, and on the edge of the river a tiny farmer tends a water buffalo bigger than himself. The buffalo is just a spot of black amongst the cool colors. The painting is realistic—maybe I should say "naturalistic"—but it's more than just a pretty, everyday scene. Such landscapes acknowledge the Dao and acknowledge the place of humans in the grand scale of nature.

In a true classical Daoist painting, most of which are centuries old, the mountains are yang, a strong, masculine energy. They dominate the painting with their aura of stability and solidness. They are balanced, though, by two types of yin: air and water. In modern times, people worry about painting their rooms the right color and where to hang mirrors, concerned about a New Age consumerist interpretation of *feng shui* that might help or hurt their luck, their finances, and their love and family prospects. The Daoist paintings, however, are representations of classical feng shui belief: *feng* is wind and *shui* is water, and to the ancient Daoists, wind, water, and mountain all had specific subtle energies that intersected with varying results depending on their balance. While the stone mountain is stable, changing only minutely over lengthy periods of time, water is continually dynamic, constantly moving and travelling. In comparison to the mountain, it is "soft," yielding, yet it is also profoundly powerful, as anyone ever caught in a strong current or bowled over by a wave will attest. Air is subtler still. We cannot see it or touch it, yet it provides tremendous resistance, as cyclists and pilots know, and it possesses energy mighty enough to provide electricity or to flatten homes and toss cars as easily as if they were Matchbox toys.

In this balance of the Daoist painting, there is life. Trees sprout out of the mountain in a variety of branched angles, their contorted shapes showing that they are not just matter but manifestations of energy as well. The pines signify the ability to endure throughout a long life of competing pressures, to eke survival not out of deep, rich loam but out of hardscrabble and precarious locations. Always, too, are the signs of humans: a fisherman on the water, a small pagoda in the distance. We are of this world, the painting says. We cannot be absent from it. If we were absent, no painter would exist to paint this scene. However, the painting is the inverse of the ones we draw with bright crayons as children, the ones in which we and our parents and our pets dwarf the lollypop trees and stick flowers that crouch beneath the boxy house. In the Daoist painting, the painter acknowledges that humans are but a very small part of a much larger balance. We are one force, but by no means the most powerful force. As Lao Zi writes in the *Dao De Jing*,

> The Dao is great.
> The universe is great.
> Earth is great.
> Man is great.
> These are the four great powers.
>
> Man follows the earth.
> Earth follows the universe.
> The universe follows the Dao.
> The Dao follows only itself.[195]

If people walk into the Asian art section of any metropolitan museum and view the painting as just a pretty picture, then move quickly on to the next, the message of the painting can be easily lost. The painting is not just an imaginative ideal; it is instructional. The message is consistent amongst Daoist painters, and the message is that we achieve harmony by understanding our place in the order of things and not fighting it. We are not everything, the Daoist painters say. The Dao is. We are an important but ultimately very small part, and when we forget that and don't acknowledge the Dao, then we create disharmony. We set into action a chain of causes and effects that may well backfire. As explained in the *Dao De Jing*,

> When man interferes with the Dao,
> the sky becomes filthy,
> the earth becomes depleted,
> the equilibrium crumbles,
> creatures become extinct.
>
> The Master views the parts with compassion,
> because he understands the whole.
> His constant practice is humility.
> He doesn't glitter like a jewel
> but lets himself be shaped by the Dao,
> as rugged and common as stone, [196]

which is a message not terribly dissimilar to the ones that the Jewish prophets tried to give people in their own time.

To the Daoist, acknowledging the Dao is not an empty exercise. Rather, doing so allows the Daoist to live an authentic life and a well-balanced one. In the *Dao De Jing*, Lao Zi writes,

The Master keeps her mind
always at one with the Dao;
that is what gives her her radiance.

The Dao is ungraspable.
How can her mind be at one with it?
Because she doesn't cling to ideas.

The Dao is dark and unfathomable.
How can it make her radiant?
Because she lets it.

Since before time and space were,
the Dao is.
It is beyond *is* and *is not*.
How do I know this is true?
I look inside myself and see. [197]

There is no separation between us and the Dao, the passage
tells us, except for the false separation that we create when we
forget that we are part of something larger and believe that we are
all there is and that we are the ultimate power. The Daoist also
remembers that death awaits him or her as it awaits everything.
Trying to escape death is useless, so what matters is how we live.
As the *Dao De Jing* tells us,

Each separate being in the universe
returns to the common source.
Returning to the source is serenity.

If you don't realize the source,
you stumble in confusion and sorrow.
When you realize where you come from,
you naturally become tolerant,

> disinterested, amused,
> kindhearted as a grandmother,
> dignified as a king.
> Immersed in the wonder of the Dao,
> you can deal with whatever life brings you,
> and when death comes, you are ready.[198]

What immortality there may be is not found in plastic surgery procedures or being frozen and shot into space or in expensive naturalistic embalming that over time will disintegrate into nothing but skeleton, because the forces of the Dao are greater than the forces of our hands. Acknowledging our relative smallness allows us to see our respective place in the cosmos. Immortality can be found only by returning to the true source, by becoming one with the Dao, just as the Sufis slowly twirl their way to become one with God. Such immortality is impossible when we look for it within our own technologies in the form of a pill or elixir or new life-prolonging machine. We must acknowledge the Infinite, even if we don't understand it, in order to understand the possibilities that lie both outside ourselves and deep within ourselves since we are never separate from the Dao.

Acknowledging the Dao is not nature worship or anything remotely like it. Nor should it be simplified, as it so often is, into a pop phrase such as "Go with the flow." We need discernment; if "the flow" is taking a machete to our friends and neighbors, as happened in Rwanda in 1994, or stampeding at a soccer match, as happened in the 1989 Hillsborough disaster in England, killing more than 90 people, the last thing we should do is "go with the flow." Rather, acknowledging the Dao means actively seeking out the spark of the Infinite in everything, the "shouldness" rather than the "isness," and discerning that harmony. It's both a realization and a recognition.

This is a concept that cuts across religions. In her *Revelations of Divine Love*, 14th century mystic Julian of Norwich wrote of God putting a little thing as small as a hazelnut into the palm of her hand. When she wondered what it was that God was showing her, God answered "It is all that is made."[199] The smallness of everything that is made astounded Julian, and then he showed her the truth: that "this is the cause why we be not all in ease of heart and soul: that we seek here rest in those things that are so little, wherein is no rest, and know not our God that is All-mighty, All-wise, All-good."[200] Julian's revelation shows us that what we think is so enormous, so overwhelming, so noteworthy, such an accomplishment, is miniscule compared to the sense of satisfaction that we can potentially find in knowledge of the Infinite of everything past, present, and future.

Later in the same text, Julian makes an even clearer explanation about the need for acknowledgement. She tells of a vision of the sea-ground, filled with hills and dales that were covered with seaweed and gravel. "Then I understood thus," she writes: "that if a man or woman were under the broad water, if he might have sight of God so as God is with a man continually, he should be safe in body and soul, and take no harm."[201] Her vision is reminiscent of an underwater Daoist painting. In everything, in all of us, there is a sense of something much more complex than what appears on the surface. Think of that in very practical terms. Each of us appears to be "just us." However, within the "just us" is a DNA sequence that connects us to ancient ancestors. It connects us to people not born yet. It may affect our physical and mental health in ways that we have not yet experienced. We are not "just us." To see the bigger picture, all we have to do is be willing to look deeply and trust that we will discover more than we might at first think because, in Julian's words, "God willeth to be seen and to be sought: to be abided and to be trusted." [202] The *Dao De Jing* echoes Julian, telling readers, "My teachings are older than the world. How can you grasp their meaning? If you want to know me, look inside your heart."[203] Acknowledgement prompts us to look.

MEETING THE DIVINE WITHIN

I've known Westerners interested in Eastern religions who, whenever meeting someone new, clasp their hands together in a prayerful pose and say "Namaste." In fact, my son's cross-country team practices yoga, and he comes home making "namaste" jokes every so often. Sometimes I get the impression that people think "Namaste" is an exotic equivalent of "Hi. Glad to meet you." To a certain extent, it is, but "Namaste" means more than that. A rough translation of the word is "I bow to the Divine within you." In other words, when I see you, I see something and someone holy, and if I see something and someone holy when I see you, then I am less likely to see you as an enemy. If I see holiness when I see you, and if I see holiness throughout life, then I see that you and I are connected. I see that we both have a Divine spark. If we are the same, and if I cherish myself, then I must cherish you, too. Acknowledgement allows for compassion. Compassion stems from acknowledgement and prompts us to recognize the worth of others.

Like the person who says "Namaste" with full awareness of what she is saying, Arjuna bowed to Krishna. He saw the Infinite. When Arjuna of the Pandavas and his cousin Duryodhana of the Kauravas went to Krishna to ask for his assistance in their battle, Krishna was sleeping. He awoke with Duryodhana at his head and Arjuna at his feet. As Krishna opened his eyes, he beheld Arjuna before he noticed Duryodhana. However, Duryodhana insisted on being allowed to make the choice between Krishna and his army before Arjuna could. A person might suppose that Arjuna just took the leftovers in the choice. Krishna himself asks Arjuna, "For what reason is it that you have selected me who will not fight at all?" However, Krishna is exactly what Arjuna wanted. "It hath been always my desire to have you for driving my car. I, therefore, ask you to fulfil my desire cherished for a long time,' Arjuna tells Krishna.[204]

Arjuna knows that he is able to go into this battle; he has been trained to fight. He also knows that the battle is about more than the clash of forces, which is a concept that has completely escaped Duryodhana. For Duryodhana, might is the only answer. Lots of countries today believe the same thing. The biggest and most powerful army is believed to get the best results. That's just what the Soviets thought when they invaded Afghanistan in 1979, except that they eventually lost their battle, just as America eventually gave up its battle in Vietnam. At present, the world is watching a war of words between America and North Korea, except that this time nuclear weapons are in the mix with the potential to create global catastrophe. What Arjuna saw in that fateful moment was that the army was a limited agent of power. Only the Infinite is limitless. With Krishna as a manifestation of the Infinite on his side, Arjuna knew he would win.

Winning wasn't the whole point. After all, as we've already seen, Arjuna didn't really want to fight, although he did his duty. Really, the point of this part of the epic is that Arjuna saw something more important than the all-important family tribe, more important than the continuation of the Pandava name, more important than earthly power, and more important than winning. What's more important is understanding that things are the way they are. We have roles to fulfill, and the social order depends upon us fulfilling our roles. Arjuna understood that what happened on that battlefield was going to affect generations. His

choice of Krishna as his champion is an admission that his ability
to correctly see the long-range causes and effects is limited. As
logical as humans may be or think they are, they cannot imagine all
possibilities. Krishna represents omniscience, which we would love
to have, but don't have.

Fortunately for Arjuna, Krishna spells out the benefits of
focusing on Him at the end of the *Bhagavad Gita*. Krishna
tells Arjuna,

> By devotion one truly understands what and who I am in
> essence. Having known Me in essence, one immediately
> merges into Me. One attains the eternal imperishable
> abode by My grace, even while doing all duties, just by
> taking refuge in Me. The Lord abides in the heart of all
> beings, O Arjuna...Seek refuge in Him alone with all your
> heart, O Arjuna. By His grace you shall attain supreme
> peace and the eternal abode. Fix your mind on Me, be
> devoted to Me, offer service to Me, bow down to Me, and
> you shall certainly reach Me.[205]

This is where a skeptic might throw up her hands in
exasperation. "It's not possible to reach God," one might say,
"because there is no God." Different language can ease that
frustration: focus on enlightenment, and you will reach it. Focus
on perfection, and you can find it. Focus on infinity, and you will
overcome your limits. Focus on something bigger than yourself,
because you are not the whole shebang.

Several centuries later and almost 3,000 miles away, the writer
of the Psalms of the Hebrew Bible would echo the words of Krishna
and the motivation of Arjuna. Similar to Arjuna wanting Krishna
as his charioteer, the psalmist wants God and writes, "I will say
of the Lord, he is my refuge and my fortress, my God, in whom I

trust."[206] As if second guessing Duryodhana, the psalmist writes, "It is better to take refuge in the Lord than to trust in man."[207] In an echo of Krishna's own sentiments, we read in Psalm 16:

> "Keep me safe, my God, for in You I take refuge:
>
> I say to the Lord, "You are my Lord;
> apart from you I have no good thing."
> I say of the holy people who are in the land,
> "They are the noble ones in whom is all my delight."
> Those who run after other gods will suffer more and more.
> I will not pour out libations of blood to such gods
> or take up their names on my lips.
>
> Lord, you alone are my portion and my cup;
> you make my lot secure.
> The boundary lines have fallen for me in pleasant places;
> surely I have a delightful inheritance.
> I will praise the Lord, who counsels me;
> even at night my heart instructs me.
> I keep my eyes always on the Lord.
> With him at my right hand, I will not be shaken."

The God of Psalm 16 does not want acknowledgement to make people feel small and unimportant. The God of this psalm is not a contemporary slave master who expects people to bow and scrape before Him simply because he is powerful. Rather, the psalm shows us that focusing solely on our earthly existence will not make us happy. "Little gods" aren't going to help us because they are fallible, and they die off. Where are the ancient Greek and Roman gods today? We've discarded them, and even the ancient learned Greeks came to see their gods as limited and all too much like humans. Instead, Krishna and the psalmist tell us that we need wisdom much bigger than what we can imagine. The first step to that wisdom is acknowledging that it exists and that we lack it. We aren't gods, no matter how much we might feel like one at times.

THE BENEFITS OF ACKNOWLEDGEMENT

Today we have different little gods, such as fame, wealth, and political power. We often hardly notice that they are as fleeting as the old gods. Many will want to resist the idea that focusing solely on our day-to-day existence can't bring us true happiness. For example, someone might think, "Well, if I were to win the lottery I would certainly be happy." We might be, but plenty of stories exist of people who won millions only to end up worse than where they began. Pentecostal minister Billie Bob Harrell, for instance, won $31 million in 1997. Within two years, he killed himself.[208] We might think that power would be a lovely thing to have, except that it's just as fleeting. For example, the government of Yemen is in transition, and who will ultimately end up with power in Yemen is anyone's guess at this moment. For years, liberals gained power in the United States, but as the result of the 2016 presidential election, their gains are being deconstructed. Power can be a trickster. Sheldon Silver, the longtime and very powerful Speaker of the New York State Assembly was imprisoned for twelve years in 2016 for corruption by misusing his position to amass millions. His considerable wealth and power diminished with his sentencing. Such stories are shockingly common. Power dissipates all too easily.

If happiness doesn't come from power and money, where might we "get" happiness? One message imparted by the spiritual texts is that happiness is not tangible. It is not fifteen minutes of fame on a talent or reality show. The earth should come with a warning sticker attached to it, spiritual stories seem to suggest. We can look at the stories of stupendous talents who crashed and burned—Jimi

Hendrix, Kurt Cobain, Amy Winehouse, Judy Garland, Philip
Seymour Hoffman, Malcolm Lowry, even the Singing Nun, Jeanine
Deckers—and realize that they are simply the public faces of the
many people who seek happiness and success in this world only
to succumb to misery. Nor do we need to seek happiness through
fame to become devastated. Many search for the happiness of just
getting by, having enough to live on and support their families.
Many fail at that, such as the thousands of farmers in India who
have committed suicide over the last decade over their economic
plight. Some commit suicide because the government will pay
compensation to their families, thereby securing their families what
they couldn't achieve: enough to live on, at least for a while.

   If earthly life is at best fleeting and at worst a misery, then what
hope do we have? The major religions of the world have similar
answers to the question. Krishna tells us that in God we will find
peace and happiness. The Buddha tells us that in enlightenment,
oneness with the Divine, is peace and happiness. The Buddha's
fourth Noble Truth is the way to end suffering. In his letter to the
Philippians, Paul tells us that the peace of God "transcends all
understanding."[209] Allah tells His faithful through his prophet,
Muhammad, that the Holy Qur'an "guides those who pursue
His pleasure to the ways of peace, and brings them out from the
darkness into the light."[210] The Nicene Creed asserts that believers
"believe in one God, the Father, the Almighty, creator of heaven
and earth, of all things seen and unseen." When I prostrate myself,
laying myself flat out on the floor, I chant "*Om namo Manjushriye,
namo sushriye, namo uttama shriye soha*": To Manjushri (Buddha
of wisdom) I prostrate, to incomparable glory I prostrate, I
prostrate with my body, speech and mind." The words are meant
to bring me peace. My only surety is in something other than
myself. The message is consistent throughout the world's scriptures:

acknowledge what is greater than oneself, trust in it, and find tranquility and true happiness.

One doesn't need to trust in God specifically. Some invoke and acknowledge a Muse. Even those people who just offer good thoughts to others are acknowledging something larger than themselves.

Prayer for the well-being of others is one example. Prayer has been noted to work for people even when they don't know they are being prayed for. Nurse Martha Loeffert notes that when prayers are offered for people, "a feeling of love, compassion, empathy, and deep caring is conveyed to them. Although atheists may not believe in prayer, they recognize these emotions and are gratified by knowing that they...are loved and deeply cared for."[211] I was impressed by the power of prayer in late 2014 when Zen Master Thây, Thich Nhat Hanh experienced a devastating brain hemorrhage. He was 88 years old, and his prognosis was not good. People all over the world sent the monk thoughts and prayers for healing. His disciples spent time at the hospital with him and visualized his healthy cells as healing bodhisattvas to repair the damage to his brain. Certainly, he had excellent neurologists and neurosurgeons and Western medical care, but at the end of 2014 one of those doctors asserted that they were "witnessing a miracle" as Thây recovered.[212] Medicine worked, but all who were involved believed that prayer did, too.

Acknowledgement is important in other areas, too, such as addiction recovery programs. Methods such as Alcoholics Anonymous, Narcotics Anonymous, Gamblers Anonymous, and Debtors Anonymous all utilize the idea of acknowledgement to help people overcome addictions and self-destructive behaviors. The first three steps of AA are "1. We admitted we were powerless over alcohol and that our lives had become unmanageable; 2. Came to believe that a Power greater than ourselves could restore us to sanity; 3. Made a decision to turn our will and our lives over to the care of God *as we understood Him.*"[213] The goal of the twelve steps is to take account of oneself, to reach out to others, including those the addict has hurt, and to have a spiritual awakening as the result of careful and honest self-examination that will encourage one toward healthier behaviors. Addicts learn that they don't need to solve everything by themselves. Instead, they learn that they don't have to be perfect.[214] Research seems to indicate that frequent participation in twelve-step programs produces results, even though people may have false starts and even though no program is 100% successful.[215]

Nor does a person need an addiction problem to benefit from the idea of acknowledgement. It helps our relationships at home and work. Acknowledgement of others comes from seeing and hearing the value that others have to offer. It's hard for people to live together harmoniously in society when some feel as if they don't have value because others will not listen to them or see them as equals. Without an understanding that our own frame of reference, our own desires, and our own vision is not all that matters, it's hard to imagine how civil rights, including women's rights and LGBTQ rights would have been achieved. Some may argue that those rights should not have been achieved, but future generations may wonder why certain rights took so long. At one point in time, for example, slavery was controversial to the point that it led to a war that almost tore the country apart, but today most Americans do not believe that any ethnic group should be enslaved. Few would argue today that women should not vote. When members of societies, families and workplaces are systematically denied rights and their value is systematically overlooked, harmony cannot follow.

Collaboration is another powerful outcome of acknowledgement. In our imaginations the solitary genius or self-as-God image is a powerful icon, but the reality is that advances in the hard and social sciences, mathematics and even arts are more and more often made by groups of people working collaboratively.[216] For example, I may have written this book, but right up front is a page of acknowledgements that gives credit to the many people who contributed to it in various ways and made it possible. Acknowledgement works two ways, both in admitting the limitations of the individual and in crediting the efforts and contributions of teammates. Collaboration depends in part on some expectation of acknowledgement.

Finally, it's worth considering the heart itself, since the spiritual texts refer so often to striving for the Infinite with our hearts. Many people think that yearning after something with our hearts or reaching out in a heartfelt way is a metaphor, just a manner of speaking. However, at least one researcher has looked at scientific evidence in connection with Qur'anic verses. One verse in particular stands out: "And their hearts are sealed, so that they apprehend not (9:87)." Both the Qur'an and cardiac researchers have noted a link between the mind and the heart in which the heart influences the brain, and that the heart can "learn, remember, feel and sense" as well as provide substantive input to our lives by affecting both our thinking and our feeling.[217] Acknowledgement teaches us that we have limits, and in our hearts we may well know what they are, even as our hearts hunger to transcend them.

Truth

For any writer, at one point in time no more powerful sales engine existed than Oprah Winfrey. When Oprah picked a book for her book club, sales were practically guaranteed to go stratospheric. Her club helped introduce even established authors such as Elie Wiesel, Cormac McCarthy, and William Faulkner to a general audience, generating enviable sales. One author who benefitted from Oprah's star power was James Frey. In a now famous debacle, however, the author of *A Million Little Pieces* went from darling to demonized in 2005 after the public learned that he had made up important parts of the narrative that he had passed off as non-fiction. Oprah's support had catapulted Frey's supposed memoir into a bestseller, and when she found out that much of the drama of the book was invented and untrue, she brought him back to the show for an interview and a public dressing-down. "I feel that you betrayed millions of readers," she told Frey on the air. Although he tried to justify his actions, he had to concede the wrongness of what he had done.

When reading fiction, the reader knows not to mistake the story for truth or fact. Frey's dishonesty in calling his book non-fiction made dupes of the people who read him, profited him through buying the book, sympathized with him, and cheered him on for triumphing in a way that he hadn't. He was like a modern-day Walter Mitty, James Thurber's famous character who escaped into his fantasy worlds, but Frey took his fantasy out of his head and lived it as if it was real.

Ten years before the Frey fiasco, the groundwork was being laid for a different lie that would galvanize and astound the United States. In November 1995, then-president Bill Clinton began his now infamous relationship with intern Monica Lewinsky. When the story came to light, many Americans thought the entire investigation of the alleged affair was a farce and a conspiracy by Republicans to bring down a popular Democratic president. Regardless of the politics, one inescapable fact became clear over time: the president had lied under oath. His initial and feeble defense was that he had not lied—he simply defined sex as vaginal intercourse. Since he had not had vaginal intercourse with Lewinsky, he therefore felt justified in maintaining that he had not engaged in sex with her. He had been directed, however, to tell the truth, the *whole* truth, and his equivocation failed that test. Through ongoing investigation and pressure, the truth finally came out when Clinton offered, "I know that my public comments and my silence about this matter gave a false impression. I misled people, including even my wife." Because of his falsehoods under oath, Clinton became the third president in American history to face impeachment. The charge brought against him was "willful, premeditated, deliberate corruption of the nation's system of justice." Clinton kept his job, but the message was clear: the truth matters.

Yet truth is currently under siege. As the 2016 American presidential election made clear, social media is bombarded with false information, lies peddled as truth. Even academic articles might be fakes. At least two studies have turned up peer reviewed journals that accepted obviously hoax articles (and then blamed the hoaxers when their choice to publish the articles was exposed). It's become harder and harder for people to discern what is real from what isn't. Politicians tell blatant falsehoods and call the falsehoods truth. People high up in the American government claim that true information published in reputable news outlets is really lies. People who may not read critically or carefully get caught up in and pass along one deception after another. Citizens excuse much of it as a form of entertainment, adding to the problem: many people either do not know what to believe any more, or passionately insight that wrong information is right.

One of my own favorite stories about truth is a less obvious one, having nothing to do with politicians or mass media. When my daughter was young, I used to read her one chapter a night from the Monkey King stories. *Monkey*, by Wu Cheng En, dates back to the 1500s and is the basis for the popular Chinese *Journey to the West* stories and programs. My daughter was always anxious for me to read more because each chapter about the antics of the Monkey King, Sun Wu Kong, would end by telling us that only in the next chapter would we learn the answers we were awaiting.

The Monkey King was incorrigible. He created havoc. He was utterly in love with himself and his magical powers, just like we all are. *Monkey* was more than just a little bit of allegory. Sun Wu Kong's undoing wasn't that he was an out and out liar. He wasn't, not really. He just had no good relationship with the truth. He thought so highly of himself that he thought he was going to take over heaven, and he started to call himself the "Great Sage Equal to Heaven." Worse, he believed it. In his deluded and consistently drunken mind, the title was true.

Finally, the Buddha created the Monkey King's downfall. The Jade Emperor had sent his executioners to kill Sun Wu Kong and cut him to small pieces after he had tried to seize the Jade Emperor's throne, but the executioners failed. Sun Wu Kong's magical powers prevailed. Worse, since he had escaped death through his magic, he convinced himself that he was invincible. Therefore, when the Buddha made a bet with the Monkey King, his taking the bet seemed to be a no-brainer. "If you are really so clever, jump off the palm of my right hand," the Buddha told Sun Wu Kong. "If you succeed, I'll tell the Jade Emperor to come and live with me in the Western Paradise, and you shall have his throne without more ado."[218] Failure would mean many eons of penance on Earth, but failure wasn't in The Monkey King's vocabulary.

Monkey thought he had it made. The Buddha was a fool, Sun Wu Kong believed. Hadn't he, the Monkey King, just escaped his death sentence? Couldn't he somersault into the sky for 108,000 leagues at one leap?[219] Sun Wu Kong jumped. He travelled to the end of the world and the five pillars that marked it. Then he changed one of his hairs into a writing brush with his magical powers. With his brush and ink he wrote, "The Great Sage Equal to Heaven reached this place" at the bottom of the middle pillar.[220] After he finished, he pissed at the base of the first pillar. How proud of himself the Monkey King was when he returned to the Buddha to claim his throne! How quickly, though, his pride turned to shock when the Buddha told him to look into the Buddha's hand. There at the base of the Buddha's middle finger were the words Sun Wu Kong had written with his brush, and coming from the base of the Buddha's index finger was the unmistakable stench of monkey piss.

Whoosh! The Monkey King thought he could jump and escape, but he didn't see the truth. He hadn't seen the truth the entire time. The Buddha changed his fingers into the five elements of metal, wood, fire, water, and earth, and together they formed the mountain Wu Hsing Shan (Five Element Mountain) around Sun Wu Kong like the bars of a prison. He became trapped for eons as much by his inability to perceive the truth as by the steadfastness of the mountain.[221]

James Frey, Bill Clinton, purveyors of false information, lying public figures, the Monkey King. What they all have in common is the belief in themselves, in what they saw (or didn't see) as truth. Monkey was so deluded that he couldn't even see reality, although it was right in front of him. Frey and Clinton both concocted a truth. Hubris overtook all three. Each appears to have convinced himself that his actions were defensible. Each put more faith in his own importance than reality. Each was and is wrong. We need to care about truth because the desire for truth is universal. Truth binds us together. Truth is our only way to communicate with the Infinite, which the texts tell us *is* truth.

PEARLS OF PERFECTION

The Upanishads are full of verses that laud truth. "By truth is laid out the path leading to the gods...Truth alone wins, not untruth" one asserts.[222] Another insists, "Speak the truth! Practice virtue...Let there be no neglect of truth" [223] Yet another declares, "Truthfulness is excellent. What is excellent is truthfulness only. By truthfulness those who have attained the state of bliss never fall from there."[224] Truth is both the means of liberation and liberation itself.

Without truth, belief is impossible. Belief is possible because truth does exist. Belief in the truth enables Arjuna to come to know God. In the tenth chapter of the *Bhagavad Gita*, he says, "O Krishna, I believe all that You have told Me to be true."[225] Krishna has told him a list of all the qualities that come from him, and amongst these is the quality of truthfulness.[226] Krishna goes on in that chapter to list all of his various attributes, and he ends by telling Arjuna, "Whatever is endowed with glory, brilliance, and power; know that to be a manifestation of a fraction of My splendor."[227] In other words, Krishna is saying that the truth is glorious, brilliant, and powerful, and that Infinite truth gleams far beyond what we are capable of imagining or even withstanding.

Consider for a moment the reluctant warrior, Arjuna. Each time he beseeches Krishna for answers, Krishna dependably provides them. What if Arjuna could not trust in those answers? What if

Arjuna were not assured that Krishna's answers would be the truth?
What would be the point of the conversation? The whole extended
dialogue, in which so much of Hindu philosophy is condensed, is
possible only because Arjuna can trust in and rely on the word of
Krishna. Krishna's word is real. That is the enormous difference
between truth and untruth: truth is solid and dependable. Untruth
is like quicksand, illusory and vacant. Though we may gobble it
ravenously, our hunger will never be satisfied by untruth.

In Hindu thought, truth is constant. Truth doesn't change
according to the color of the sky or the time of day. The Sanskrit
word for truth is *satya*, and the term implies something that is
free from any distortion. It's that clear, perfect truth to which
humans are encouraged to aspire, not just because that perfect
truth is a pretty gleaming jewel but because it is the standard for
how we should act and what we must do. The Yoga Sutras of
Patanjali Maharishi assert that "When there is firm grounding in
the perception of what is, or truth, it is seen that an action and
reaction, seed and its fruits, or cause and result are related to each
other; and the clear vision of intelligence becomes aware of this
relationship."[228] We are able to see the truth, and by seeing it we
are able to speak and act truthfully by understanding that truth
and untruth both have consequences. In fact, the Yoga Sutras
advise that the mental distress of humans is caused by "ignorance
of the truth" and our belief instead in our separate individuality
and grasping at the present physical life without understanding the
eternal nature of beings. We are distressed because we measure
time only by the span of our own lifetimes.[229]

How do we get past such ignorance? How can we perceive
truth? Ask mathematicians and they would point out that truth is
logical; logic provides the path. We can reason our way to truth.
The mathematician would be correct, but the Yoga Sutras tell
us that logic has its dangers: "In the case of the understanding

reached through logic or reasoning, there is confusion on account of the discrepancies that exist between the word...meaning... and imagination or assumption."[230] To get to real truth, we have to go beyond logic. It's only when we can clear our minds of our delusions about the self that "...the truth alone shines, without distortion, logic or reasoning."[231] This line of thought suggests that all the logical paths that are used to find the Infinite and infinite truth are doomed to failure, just as the logical arguments *against* the existence of God are untrue. In Hindu thought, the ultimate truth cannot be found by such methods any more than I can find a breathing, swimming fish by digging in the dirt of my vegetable garden. I will not find the fish there—I cannot find the fish there— but the absence of fish there cannot logically lead to a conclusion that fish do not exist.

At the very end of the *Bhagavad Gita*, Krishna asks Arjuna, "Has your delusion born of ignorance been destroyed?"[232] Krishna has shown himself to Arjuna in his entirety and has answered every question Arjuna has asked. Krishna's question isn't just polite. It carries great weight: only by perceiving truth can Arjuna act in clarity to truly fulfill his role through full knowledge. Without an understanding of truth, he is just a rock rolling through life, striking at random, resting where it will for no good reason, and causing unintentional consequences. Arjuna, in those last verses, has seen the truth. "By your grace my delusion is destroyed," he tells Krishna, "...and I shall obey your command."[233] In Hinduism, to perceive the truth is to act in harmony with God and thus achieve perfect enlightenment. First, however, we have to admit that we don't always want to see the truth and that we are blinded by our many ideas, beliefs, and perceptions that hang between us and the truth like so many layers of gauze curtains, letting in a certain amount of light but preventing us from seeing the vistas beyond them.

THE DIAMOND THAT CUTS THROUGH ILLUSION

Two of the steps of Buddhism's Eightfold Path are right speech and right perception. These can be translated as speaking the truth and seeing things as they are; in other words, seeing the truth. The act of becoming a Buddhist, taking refuge, means taking vows to speak the truth. In Buddhism, then, truth is both the means and the end. Enlightenment is truth, and truth is essential to reaching enlightenment.

The issue of truth is very complicated in Buddhism. The *Diamond Sutra*, also known as the *Vajra Prajna Paramita Sutra*, is one place where the problem is articulated. In the sutra, the Buddha and Subhuti are talking and the Buddha is explaining to Subhuti what ideas are mistaken and what ideas are not mistaken. Words are just figures of speech. Forms are illusions. Enlightenment and non-enlightenment are concepts, and as such they are not ultimate Truth. The essence of the sutra is that people must cut through all illusion. From a Buddhist perspective, not just the message, what is being observed or heard, is the problem. Buddhism is also concerned about the role of the observer. Objective knowledge in Buddhist thought isn't dependent on what observer is observing and who or what that observer might be. Objective reality is independent of whatever is observing it. Let's imagine an object, any object, and call it X. A bird, my cat, and I all line up and look at X. The three of us will see X differently, because our eyes do not work the same. I can see colors that the cat cannot see; the bird can see wavelengths that I cannot see; the cat can see in darkness and I cannot. The reality of X doesn't change depending on which of us is looking at it, just as the reality of the elephant earlier in the book doesn't change depending on which of the blind men is touching one part of it.

In Buddhism, the issue of objectivity gets trickier still. In Sanskrit, to exist means that something can be known and named. If I know X, and I name X, then there is a link between me and X. This link means that I can't be completely objective. In fact, Buddhism acknowledges that humans tend to distort everything all the time. We can't help it. What we perceive is just a product of our perceptions and their limitations. Naturally, that's useful. If we see something made of wood or metal that has legs and a horizontal surface at a certain height and a vertical surface that looks as if it could support our back, we call it a chair. If we stop and question our perceptions every time we see something that looks like a chair and ask ourselves whether the chair is really a chair or whether it has some other reality that we are ignoring because we are calling it a chair, we would never get anything done, and our legs would be very tired from standing up.

Given that chairs are just one item in a vast universe, one could easily think that the only "truth" in Buddhism is that everything is illusion and we are deceived all the time, especially because we depend on the senses. If that is the case, then how does a Buddhist take a vow to perceive things accurately and to speak the truth? The very heart of Buddhism is expressed as four truths. The first of the Four Noble Truths is that suffering exists. In Buddhism, that suffering is created by these distortions caused by our limited comprehension because our conventional views are incomplete. Truth, according to the great Buddhist philosopher, Nagarjuna, is that nothing— not you, not I, not the cat nor the bird nor the chair—is fixed in its identity. The Buddhist has a conundrum then. Humans experience the world through senses. Humans relate to the world through language. This is true of all humans in all cultures. However, both senses and language are incomplete ways of knowing anything.

Once we realize this, we realize that truth, at least from the
Buddhist perspective, is even more complicated than it is from the
Hindu perspective. Despite its complicated nature, the Buddha says
that disciples should strive for truth. "He who drinks in the Truth
will live happily with a peaceful mind," says the Buddha in the
Dhammapada; "a wise man always delights in the Truth taught
by the saints."[234] He assures us of the benefits of truth, stating
that "The wise find peace on hearing the truth, like a deep, clear,
undisturbed lake."[235] He closes his chapter on "The Wise Man"
with words that indicate that perceiving the truth utterly changes
us: "Few are those among men who have crossed over to the other
shore, while the rest of mankind runs along the bank. However,
those who follow the principles of the well-taught Truth will cross
over to the other shore, out of the dominion of Death, hard though
it is to escape....they are like shining lights, having reached final
liberation in the world," he promises.[236] Truth is not found; it is
not a place. It is a state of being, and achieving that state takes
extraordinary effort. Effort and truth go hand in hand.

To understand how hard it is, consider for a moment what kind
of creatures humans are. Like every other creature, we have a very
important drive: to survive. How we see and hear and smell and
taste and feel have all developed to help us survive. Therefore, what
we perceive through our senses seems real to us because that sense
of realness helps us to survive. Dr. John Dunne of Emory University
calls it the "Mesoscopic Perspective." Our perspectives are what
they are because our sensory capacities have emerged in a specific
environment in relation to a particular purpose. Our capacities are
not infinite. In fact, our capacities survey just a medium range for
our own ego-grasping purposes. Therefore, since our capacities are
limited, the truth we ordinarily perceive is likewise limited.

Here is an example. One day, years ago, I was living with my
married friends Dan and Ginny. The day was warm and summery,
and I had gone out through the kitchen into the back yard to enjoy
the sun. Dan was dozing in the family room. Suddenly, he was
awakened by my blood-curdling scream. He came dashing into
the kitchen, looking about wildly and shouting "What? What
happened?" Red with embarrassment, I pointed to the kitchen
counter. A thin black leather belt was dangling off the edge of
it. "I thought it was a snake," I admitted. I'm terrified of snakes.
My brain saw the image of something long, thin and supple and
immediately translated that image to "snake." The scream was an
instantaneous reaction as I froze in the doorway. My brain had
tricked me, quickly and decisively. Right there is the problem with
and the incentive for trying to search for truth from a Buddhist
perspective: my brain wants to convince me of things that aren't
real, and it's extremely hard to get past that gatekeeper.

A reader will think, "That is just an example of a mistake."
In Buddhist thought, mistaking conventional reality for ultimate
truth is the same kind of mistake. Take red. I see red because I
have the physical apparatus to see red. I call it "red" because that
is the name humans have collectively given the color. We would
not know "red" if no one ever showed it to us and said, "This is
red." I forget that red is a wavelength. I forget that other creatures
have absolutely no experience of red. I forget that in the dark, red
doesn't exist.

Despite the difficulty in Buddhism of achieving truth, it is
possible. After all, if truth wasn't real, then Buddhism couldn't
possibly have its Four Noble Truths. The fourth of those is that
there is a way to the truth and past the suffering. Truth does more
than tell us what is. Truth can also show us *how* to experience our
lives differently.

LIARS IN THE FAMILY

I remember the first time my daughter called me a "lousy liar." She had picked up the term at middle school, from her teacher no less, and she was laughing as she lobbed it at me across the dinner table for making up some ridiculous story or other as I do sometimes to make both kids laugh. I've always found that term really interesting because it has more than one meaning. Is a lousy liar someone who doesn't lie well, someone who is a louse because he is telling a lie, or both?

If ever there were some liars in the Hebrew Bible, it would have to be the family of Isaac, including Isaac himself. First, Isaac flees a famine by taking himself and his wife, Rebekah, to Abimelech's kingdom in Gerar, where God instructs him to stay. When the men of Gerar question Isaac about Rebekah, who is described as very beautiful, Isaac tells the men that Rebekah is his sister because he's afraid of being killed over her. It's miraculous really that no one molests her, and no one comes to Isaac to ask to marry her. The story seems surreal. It becomes even odder when Abimelech finally spies Isaac fondling his "sister." Rather than assuming incest, which certainly wouldn't have been unheard of, Abimelech confronts Isaac and says that it's clear that Rebekah must be Isaac's wife. Isaac doesn't deny it, and Abimelech is horrified. "How could you do this to us!" he shouts. It wouldn't have taken very much for any of the local men to have had sex with Rebekah, he exclaims, pointing out the obvious, and Isaac therefore "would have thus brought guilt upon us" for committing adultery. Not just the man who did the deed would have been guilty—Isaac was risking his wife's death too, as she would have been found equally guilty.[237]

In modern terms, the dysfunction of the family doesn't stop there. Isaac and Rebekah had twins, Jacob and Esau. Jacob was smooth, and Esau was red and hairy. Of the two, Esau was the first born. Isaac favored Esau, who as the first born had the right to inherit the family leadership on his father's death as well as a double share of any property that could be divided. He was also, as first born, entitled to a special blessing at his father's deathbed, one that would keep him close in relationship to God. However, Rebekah favored Jacob. When Isaac grew old and blind and lay near death, Rebekah heard her husband send Esau out to kill some game to bring back to eat. In return, Isaac was preparing to give Esau his blessing. As soon as Esau was gone, Rebekah sent Jacob out to get two kids from the flock, which she cooked up deliciously. With their furry skins, she made gloves, gauntlets and a neck covering for Jacob. She dressed her younger son in Esau's clothes, slipped the furry bits on his exposed skin—imagine how quickly she would have needed to do all this before Esau got home with his hares and ducks—gave Jacob the stew she had cooked up of the kids, and sent him to his father to pretend to be Esau to receive the blessing. Jacob could have said no. He had already bartered for Esau's birthright and obtained it, but he went right along with the ruse, lying to his father and pretending to be Esau. As a result, he got Isaac's blessing, and in that blessing, he received all his kinsmen as slaves and mastery over Esau.[238]

When Esau returned and learned what had happened, he was outraged. Who wouldn't be? Jacob and Rebekah's lie incited him to want to kill his brother. As a result, Rebekah sent Jacob away so that he could live. It's a wonder that Esau didn't want to kill his mother, too, because it must have been very clear to him that she had egged on Jacob. He must have watched her favoritism of his younger twin for his whole life. Maybe that favoritism was even deserved. Was Esau smart enough and stable enough to become the leader of a new nation? Still, Esau was duped by the dishonesty of his mother and brother. The story, though, has an interesting layer.

What Jacob did was dishonest. It was a lie. Innocent people were hurt by it. The writer of the story, through his characterization of all three family members, makes it clear that Esau, even though he is impetuous and dopey, is a sympathetic character. Jacob and his mother are clearly in the wrong. Yet the ultimate result was the fruition of what appears to be God's plan: Jacob goes on to become one of the Hebrew patriarchs.

If we are tempted to say in response, though, that God must not care about truth, we are wrong. One of the laws written in stone and handed to Moses by God is that people should not bear false witness. In other words, they should not lie. The psalmist consistently showcases how important truth is to God. In Psalm 15, for example, almost the whole poem is devoted to the idea of truth. When David asks God, "Lord, who may dwell in your sacred tent? Who may live on your holy mountain?" God answers,

> The one whose walk is blameless,
> who does what is righteous,
> who speaks the truth from their heart;
> whose tongue utters no slander,
> who does no wrong to a neighbor,
> and casts no slur on others;
> who despises a vile person
> but honors those who fear the LORD;
> who keeps an oath even when it hurts,
> and does not change their mind..."

Psalm 25 marries the idea of trust to truth. We can only trust that which is true. The psalmist asserts that God is Truth, stating "In you, Lord my God I put my trust; I trust in you.... Show me your ways, O Lord, teach me your paths. Guide me in your truth and teach me, for you are God my Savior, and my hope is in you all day long." Truth is a refuge, according to the psalmist.

The psalmist shows us as well the misery of deception. Psalm 52 lashes Doeg the Edomite, a herdsman and learned man who, in 1 Samuel, gives Saul only a partial story about the actions of David, who had gone to Abimelech pretending to be on a secret mission. Saul, who was jealous of David, called for Abimelech and all his company to be killed, and Doeg carried out the sentence. What is interesting about this psalm is that, to use the cliché, it is the pot calling the kettle black; David is as guilty of falsehood as Doeg. It's clear, though, whom the psalmist sees as having the larger guilt, as Doeg is addressed in disparaging words:

> Why do you boast of evil, you mighty hero?
> Why do you boast all day long,
> you who are a disgrace in the eyes of God?
> You who practice deceit,
> your tongue plots destruction;
> it is like a sharpened razor.
> You love evil rather than good,
> falsehood rather than speaking the truth.
> You love every harmful word,
> you deceitful tongue!

God will destroy Doeg in response, the psalmist insists. The world will laugh at him because he "trusted in his great wealth and grew strong by destroying others!"

The God of the Hebrew Bible is the model of truth. "The word of the Lord is right; and all His works are done in truth," the psalmist asserts.[239] To the Deuteronomist, that truth is clear and without distortion: "He is the Rock, his work is perfect; for all his ways are judgment: a God of truth and without iniquity, just and right is He."[240] The truth of God is a model for humans, one that transcends scripture. Mahatma Gandhi described truth similarly: "I used to say that though God may be love, God is Truth...But two years ago I went a step further and said that truth is God....It is the living embodiment of God, it is the only Life, and I identify truth with the fullest life, and that is how it becomes a concrete thing, for God is His whole creation, the whole Existence, and service of all that exists—Truth—is service of God."[241] Truth is a language, though, as well as a perception, and it's the language that the Infinite speaks.

TRUTH AND CONSEQUENCES

Humans may be blinded to the truth because of distortions caused by their senses. They may knowingly engage in untruth because it benefits them. There's another urge that pushes back against truth, though, and that's fear and discomfort. Sometimes we skirt the truth because we're afraid.

The knowledge of fear makes it easy for me to be sympathetic to Peter. In the Gospel of Matthew, Peter seems like a schmuck. Jesus, knowing that He is about to be crucified, goes to Gethsemane to pray. Matthew tells us how distressed Jesus was at that hour, and that Jesus tells Peter and the two sons of Zebedee, "My soul is sorrowful even unto death. Remain here and keep watch with me."[242] Like most of us at a moment of trial, Jesus wanted the comfort of companionship.

Almost everyone has a fear of dying alone. Why should Jesus have been exempt from that fear? Three times in my life I have sat with a dying person. One, mercifully, seemed to have little awareness. She'd had a massive stroke and was unconscious. She would die if her life support was turned off, the orderly told me, and the next day that is what happened, but that night I sat and held her hand and talked to her, hoping that whatever made her still alive, that mystery that separates being from not being in this lifetime, would hear me. I hoped to bring her some measure of comfort. None of us knows how we will exit this world, but often the exit will not be easy, at least not on a physical level. "Promise me," my mother begged me while she was still lucid, "that if I need you to, you'll give me an overdose of morphine." What daughter wants to promise such a thing? Despite my reluctance at doing so, I did promise (although she died naturally), because that is what keeping watch through my mother's decline from cancer meant, just as keeping watch for my friend Kim meant sitting with her days before she died, joking with her, and crying with her at what a fearsome and lonely thing death is.

Like my mother and friends, Jesus was fully human. Had He not been human, He could not have died a terrible, human death. Crucifixion was so common, as explained earlier, that Jesus would have had no question about what an excruciating ordeal He was about to experience. In that dark moment when, as a fully aware human, He wanted comfort, Peter failed Him. Peter fell asleep. Where was Peter's compassion? Where was his effort? Where was his generosity? On all accounts, Peter fell short for his friend, who loved him.

Peter's failures were not over. Matthew tells us that all of Jesus' disciples abandoned him when he was handed over to the crowd that led Him away to Caiaphas. Peter followed at a distance, though, and sat down inside the courtyard to watch and see what would become of Jesus. He watched the men inside pronounce a death sentence on Jesus and watched them slap him and spit in his face.[243]

What a shock this sight must have been to Peter. It's easy to imagine that he had not believed the truth that Jesus had told him:

that He would be betrayed, handed over, and killed. Why should
he believe such a thing? Traveling with Jesus must have seemed,
in many ways, like traveling with a modern celebrity. Where Jesus
appeared, crowds followed. In the Gospel stories, Jesus did the
impossible. Raise someone from the dead? Check. Feed a crowd
of thousands with a few fishes and a few loaves of bread? Check.
Turn water into wine? Check. There isn't a magician on television
today who could come close to what Jesus did, so His escaping
from a crowd and thwarting execution must have seemed like a no-
brainer to Peter. Maybe he just thought that Jesus was being overly
dramatic when Jesus foretold what would occur.

Now, though, Peter was confronted with the truth, and he must
have been terrified. This was ancient Rome, and his hero, the man
with whom he had been travelling, was being condemned. Guilt
by association would have been a real probability, and perhaps
for the first time Peter started to think, "If Jesus is really going
to be crucified, what are the Romans going to do to me? What
will happen to the rest of us disciples?" Peter's palms must have
grown clammy just at the thought of it when he went out to sit in
the courtyard. As the realization set in, along came a woman who
looked at Peter and said that she recognized him. His response was
swift: "I do not know what you are talking about!"[244] By now he
must have been spooked, and he headed for the gate, but his fears
were not over because another woman saw him and purposefully
pointed him out to others, saying, "This man was with Jesus the
Nazarene."[245] Her words presented a threat to Peter, and perhaps
his heart started to beat faster. For a second time, Peter swore that
he didn't know Jesus. The crowd wasn't buying it, though. People
began to gather around him, and this is the moment in which Peter
must have understood that his life was on the line. Surely Peter
was one of Jesus' disciples, the bystanders told him, pointing out,

"Even your speech gives you away." According to Matthew, "At that he began to swear and curse, 'I do not know the man.' And immediately a cock crowed."[246]

That sound, the sound of light, the sound of daybreak, is the sound that finally gets through to Peter. As he realizes that he is a liar, he starts to weep. He has not just lied to the crowd—he has lied to himself. Hadn't Jesus told him, after all, that he would deny Jesus three times before the cock crowed? Though Jesus had spoken the truth, Peter had been too blind to see it. Peter was caught in the delusion of his own hubris. When Jesus had told the disciples earlier that night at the Mount of Olives, "This night all of you will have your faith in Me shaken," Peter had bragged, "Mine will never be," insisting with the cockiness of someone who is sure he will never have to deliver, "Even though I should have to die with You, I will not deny You."[247] Peter could not see the truth of the situation: that miracles were not going to keep Jesus from a bloody end, that if Jesus was deemed guilty, then Peter and the other disciples would be guilty of aiding him, and that Peter was a human with human fears and failings, not a proto-Jesus. As light dawned, and with it the truth, Peter's ego was shattered. The destruction of the illusion of his sense of self reformed Peter. He saw the light, and his enlightenment shaped him into the rock upon which the church of Christ would be formed. In the Gospel of John, Jesus says, "God is spirit, and those who worship him must worship in Spirit and in truth."[248] Through his ego-death, Peter was filled with both.

All throughout the gospel of John, Jesus exhorts people to believe and reproaches them for not believing. "I am the bread of life," he tells the people. "Whoever comes to me will never hunger, and whoever believes in me will never thirst, but I have told you that although you have seen, you do not believe."[249] Jesus' point is that people are deceived. Jesus and the people observing him are like characters in two different stories, and people cannot see the truth of Jesus' story because they are caught up in their own literal language.

Jesus spoke in metaphors, but most of his listeners, even his disciples, were unable to understand his figurative language, much less understand that metaphors also speak truth. For example, when Jesus speaks of his body and blood as offering eternal life, his disciples recoil as if he is encouraging a cannibalistic feast. "This saying is hard," they protest. "Who can accept it?" Jesus, perceiving that they are shocked by his words explains to them, "It is the spirit that gives life, while the flesh is of no avail." It's not about our bodies, Jesus is saying, just as Krishna said, and just as the Buddha said. "The words I have spoken to you are spirit and life. But there are some of you who do not believe."[250] Their doubt was apparent, even if not to themselves.

They cannot believe because they are blind to the truth, and their blindness to the truth is a barrier that will keep them from God. It drives them from Jesus, who was their vehicle to God, and they fall away from him and return to their former lives. If the Indian philosophical scholar, Dharmakirti, were to evaluate them, he would point out that they suffer from conceptual illusion. The disciples and followers "see" and "hear" Jesus, but they cannot get past their preconceptions, which are the judgments and definitions that they bring to what they see and hear. Imagine seeing a mirage, and being convinced that it is water. For the disciples who cannot apprehend the Truth that is Jesus, the problem is just the opposite: they see the living Water, but they are convinced it is a mirage.[251]

John, the gospel writer who is referred to as the non-Synoptic writer because his views and story differs so dramatically from the dovetailed narratives of Matthew, Mark and Luke (they are called "Synoptic" because they all have "one vision"), tackles the topic of truth the most often of any of the gospel writers. He asserts that "the law was given through Moses, but grace and truth came to be through Jesus Christ."[252] He tells his readers that "he who does the truth comes to the light, that his works may be revealed, that they have been done in God."[253] In the gospel, Jesus famously tells his followers, "If you hold to my teaching...then you will know the truth, and the truth will set you free."[254] Ironically, his followers didn't understand his point, causing Jesus to admonish them, telling them, "because I tell the truth, you do not believe me!"[255] Later in John 14, he consoled his disciples, telling them that he would prepare a place for them, and that he could do so because he was "the way and the truth and the life."[256] Finally, when he is face to face with Pilate, he explains that he has come into the world to "testify to the truth." Jesus' truth was the imminence of the kingdom of God. Pilate's question in return is the question of the skeptic, of one who is limited, but it is also a very human question. "What is truth?" he asks.[257] Many of us still ask the same.

THE BENEFITS OF TRUTH

Of all the qualities explored so far in this book, truth is the most abstract. It's the hardest for many people to understand because it seems like mercury, quick and slippery, breaking apart and reforming. Philosophers including Aristotle, Aquinas, Kant, Kierkegaard, Nietzsche, and Foucault have all tried to define and understand truth, yet our truths often seem contradictory and difficult to ascertain, whether in our families, in courts of law, or in our own self-awareness.

"I'm not sure what is real," I've told my therapist, meaning that I'm not sure what is true and what isn't at times. That's one of the consequences of having grown up with an alcoholic parent. Maybe it's also a consequence of living in a society full of distortions.

Those kinds of distortions can alter our perceptions about very real people, stressing our society and relationships. For example, during a newscast in the summer of 2011, Chicago CBS television station WBBM reported on a shooting on Chicago's South Side. As part of the coverage, the reporter announced, "Kids as young as four were there to see it all unfold...and had disturbing reactions." A reporter asked the child, "When you get older, are you gonna stay away from all these guns?" The little boy, who was African American, crossed his arms and said, "Nooo." "What do you want to do when you get older?" the reporter, out of view of the camera, asked. "I'm going to have me a gun," the little boy announced, and that's what viewers saw and heard because that's what was shown to them. What they did not see or hear was the reporter following up the boy's response with "You are? Why you wanna do that?" to which the little boy responded, "I'm gonna be the police."

The station later apologized, but the damage was done. Stereotypes had been reinforced amongst viewers that young African American males are violent, even when they are little more than toddlers. What the station chose to show was *factual*, but it was not the truth. It was a distortion.[258] Had the station aired the whole truth, it could have made a small step to correct that stereotype and to decrease prejudice.

Truth also plays a role in our medical and psychological care. If we are unwilling to tell the truth to our doctors and therapists, the effectiveness of our care may be compromised. Sometimes the reverse problem occurs: our doctors and caregivers avoid telling us the truth. This can happen when unwelcome news such as a terminal or debilitating diagnosis must be delivered. The medical professionals might not be comfortable breaking the news, or they might have been asked by the family not to give the news. They might fear that the patient will lose hope. The result is that the patient loses autonomy and the chance to make important and informed decisions about care and living.[259] Truth gives patients the power of choice.

Related to this is the importance of true information. Advertising and pop culture are filled with claims that promise to improve our health, precisely because our health is such a source of anxiety for so many. However, staying well depends on a way to be able to discern truth from non-truth. A recent outbreak of measles from California's Disneyland traced to non-vaccinated people provides an example. Although vaccination is proven to work in the clear majority of cases, people are choosing not to vaccinate their children or to be vaccinated because of their beliefs. They insist that their beliefs are true. However, science disagrees with them. Science indicates that their beliefs are not true and that they are jeopardizing their children's health.

Nor do health benefits and drawbacks end there. Researchers Anita Kelly and Lijuan Wang of Notre Dame conducted a ten-week study that showed that people who lied less improved their physical and mental health. Many of us think that white lies are harmless to ourselves and others, but the study showed otherwise. Not surprisingly, the study also found that telling the truth improved the participants' various relationships, and that the smoother relationships were linked to health benefits.[260]

Truth affects almost every aspect of our lives. For example, our finances absolutely depend on truth. That's why so many laws exist that attempt to protect us, but it's still easy to be duped. In cultures in which brashness and swagger and ego can seem attractive, promising riches can be tempting for financial advisers. With truth, though, comes credibility. Clients and advisers can work more closely as a team and can avoid some of the pitfalls of emotional-based investing if advisers are up front about their failures as well as their successes.[261] Truth also enables our work relationships to be less fraught with drama, and it enables friends and family members to rely on each other. Truth may certainly be painful, but it is also the way for us to live in harmony with each other.

The problem is that we lie even when we don't need to. We exaggerate. We make stories more dramatic, or we fudge the truth a little, so people will be impressed by us or like us more. We lie to get what we want. We lie to control the actions of others. As a result, our relationships with family, loved ones, friends, coworkers, and bosses suffer. Neuroscientist Sam Harris explored this reality in his book *Lying* (2013). His conclusion: "By lying, we deny our friends access to reality—and their resulting ignorance often harms them in ways we did not anticipate."[262]

Here's a small example. A few years ago, I was taking a college class in Judaic studies and I connected with a woman in the class who I really liked. She seemed genuine, and I thought we could be friends. She assumed I was Jewish, though, and I didn't tell her the truth. I never out-and-out lied. I never said, "Yes, I'm Jewish." However, I also didn't tell the truth. I didn't say, "No I'm not Jewish." I wanted her to like me, and I didn't want to be perceived as an outsider. As the weeks of class and our conversations went on, I got dug in deeper and deeper. My new friend asked if my daughter had been bat mitzvahed and if she was planning to visit Israel through the Birthright program. I just stammered and evaded, trying to steer the conversation in a different direction. By this time, I was afraid to tell the truth. I knew that it would be clear that I had been misleading to begin with. The basis for friendship should be trust, and I was being untrustworthy. We communicated a bit after class, but I drifted away because I was embarrassed at my behavior. As a result, I lost out on what could have been a great friendship because I built myself a small prison of deception.

What happens, though, when the truth will hurt someone deeply? Often, our impulse for lying or omitting a truth is to protect others. We may see this as compassion. Is there benefit in telling a daughter that the man she thinks is her father is not, or just pain? Is there any gain from telling a neighbor that his wife is having an affair? These are questions with which ethicists grapple. The impetus for telling is important. So is the desired outcome. This is where the other virtues intersect. For example, perhaps it is generous to tell the truth. Perhaps it would be generous, depending on the circumstances, not to tell the truth and instead to encourage another person, one who is more vested in the situation, tell it. For example, is it my place to tell a neighbor that his wife is cheating, or is it his wife's place to do that?. Sometimes true compassion, the compassion that can see past the inevitable shock and tears is needed. As mentioned earlier, sometimes effort is the key.

My sister's story is one of thousands of how deceptions can cause pain. My sister grew up thinking she was half Ukrainian. She thought the Ukrainian side of her family was Eastern Orthodox. Recently, she has discovered documents that tell a very different story. Her father's family was Polish. They were probably Jewish. Why did her father lie about this? She'll never know – he is dead, and most of his family is dead – and she is angry. She doesn't even know who started the lie. As she puts it, she no longer is who she thought she was.

There are no easy answers here. I could say "Don't lie," even though that is precisely what my religion tells me. It may be what your religion tells you. Maybe you don't believe in religion, but you have a strong sense of honesty. Maybe, no matter your religious beliefs or lack of them, dishonesty is no big deal to you, not in this age of deceitful politicians and scripted for ratings "reality" TV and hoax videos. I can only say that all of the world's religious texts prize truth. It is a diamond in an expansive slurry pit of crap.

Mindfulness

The Guest House

This being human is a guest house.
Every morning a new arrival.

A joy, a depression, a meanness,
some momentary awareness comes
as an unexpected visitor.

Welcome and entertain them all!
Even if they are a crowd of sorrows,
who violently sweep your house
empty of its furniture,
still, treat each guest honorably.
He may be clearing you out
for some new delight.

The dark thought, the shame, the malice.
meet them at the door laughing and invite them in.

Be grateful for whatever comes.
because each has been sent

as a guide from beyond.

– Jelalludin Rumi[263]

Effort, compassion, generosity, order, acknowledgement, and truth: mindfulness is what makes them all happen. Awareness is in the name of our species: *homo sapiens sapiens*, the human who knows that he or she knows. We are supposedly aware. It's ironic, then, that one of our greatest human challenges is mindfulness.

Mindfulness is the practice of being fully aware and fully present in every moment. Without mindfulness, we are not awake. Without being awake, we are less likely to practice the actions that promote harmony. We are less likely to truly experience life. Those who believe in mindfulness believe that without it we will go through life as if we were sleepwalking. We will act in conditioned reflexes that are as predictable as the leg jerk that occurs every time the doctor or nurse hits one of us in the knee with a rubber mallet. We don't think about that leg jerk, and we don't control it. It just happens. We could easily say the same about so many daily experiences. Anger. Lying. Unkindness. Impatience. Judgment. Prejudice. Self-cherishing. Addictive and abusive behaviors. The list goes on. We're not guilty, we insist, because whatever "it" is, we didn't mean it. Alternatively, whatever "it" is, we may think we *do* mean it. We may be convinced we really do hate those people, whoever they are, or really do think that it's ok to exploit children or abuse others or hurt animals or do any of the things that other people watch us do and say, "What can that person possibly be thinking?" It's very possible that we have never deeply examined our beliefs or stood eye to eye with them.

All of the religions of the world prize mindfulness, although it is more obvious in some religions than in others. In Judaism, mindfulness might be practiced through reciting the Shema, entering the mikvah, or lighting a menorah. Mindfulness might be practiced at a Passover seder, when drops of wine are spilled so that Jewish people are reminded to take no pleasure at the suffering of the Egyptians and others. Hinduism may approach mindfulness through the daily puja or through the practice of yoga. For Christians, the doorway to mindfulness may be prayer or contrition. For Sikhs, wearing the *kara* and *kirpan* (the steel bangle and sword) are meant to evoke mindfulness of the infinity of God and the commitment to struggle and cut away one's own faults and weaknesses. Mindfulness is prized in the world's religions because it allows humans to be the ones who truly know that we know. It enables us to see the interdependence and interconnectedness of everything and to pierce the cottony haze in which our senses and emotions cocoon us. Although mindfulness takes great effort, it allows us to transcend all the distortions and achieve the depths of compassion, the golden light of truth, and our own freedom from bondage.

THE WISDOM OF VIGILANCE

Ecclesiastes in the Hebrew Bible is a wonderful study in mindfulness. It's easy to misread Ecclesiastes as a hedonistic and somewhat nihilistic "eat, drink, and be merry, for tomorrow we die" book. That would be a wrong understanding of it. The writer begins by telling us that "everything is meaningless." From the perspective of truth, it is exactly right; things have no inherent meaning. What things do have is their proper moment. The writer tells us,

> There is a time for everything,
> and a season for every activity under the heavens:
> a time to be born and a time to die,
> a time to plant and a time to uproot,
> a time to kill and a time to heal,
> a time to tear down and a time to build,
> a time to weep and a time to laugh,
> a time to mourn and a time to dance,
> a time to scatter stones and a time to gather them,
> a time to embrace and a time to refrain from embracing,
> a time to search and a time to give up,

a time to keep and a time to throw away,
a time to tear and a time to mend,
a time to be silent and a time to speak,
a time to love and a time to hate,
a time for war and a time for peace.[264]

What is important, the writer suggests, is for people to
understand these moments, pay full attention to them, and to enjoy
their work, "to be happy and to do good while they live."[265] The
times are important. If we are in a time of peace, our attention
shouldn't be on war. If we are in a moment that calls for the
discomfort and stillness of silence, we shouldn't break it with
nervous chatter. Step one is to pay attention to what is happening
around us. Attention comes from mindfulness.

Sometimes we pay attention to the wrong things and in
the wrong way, resulting in afflictive emotions, such as envy.
Ecclesiastes teaches us that neither happiness nor goodness can
be attained from envy. The constant striving associated with envy
distracts us and keeps us focused on the constant acquisition of
more, whatever it is that we want more of, such as goods, riches,
lovers, or children. The writer tells us bluntly, "The quiet words of
the wise are more to be heeded than the shouts of a ruler of fools.
Wisdom is better than weapons of war, but one sinner destroys
much good." [266] The more we compare ourselves to others, the
more we become fixated on whatever they have. Our actions
become like those of the windup drumming monkey I used to
have as a child: mechanical, frantic, and predictably set off by the
turning of the key. The lifeless monkey had no cognition, and when
we don't act from mindfulness, our own cognition is also limited
and conditioned.

Where do the wise of Ecclesiastes get their quiet words? They
get them from careful attention every moment. Proverbs tells

readers to "keep your heart with all vigilance, for from it flow the springs of life."[267] Vigilance is mindfulness. It is controlling the self, which doesn't like to be controlled. On a day-to-day basis the self is busy trying to please itself. It is too focused on promoting its physical comfort, trying to amass money, indulging in sensory pleasures, and trying to gain power to want to stop and be aware of what it is doing every waking moment.

In the Hebrew Bible, Solomon for many years was a model of mindfulness. In 1 Kings, God comes to Solomon one night as Solomon is dreaming and tells him he may ask for whatever he wants. If any of us had the chance to ask God for whatever we wanted, knowing it would be fulfilled, what would we ask for? The return of deceased loved ones? Wealth beyond measure? Fame? Vengeance? Would we ask for God to eradicate people we hate? How easily that list could escalate as we think of all the dissatisfactions in our lives and let our imaginations run free. The Benevolent God could become a kind of dark magician as our wishes multiplied as quickly and freely as the brooms carrying water in *The Sorcerer's Apprentice*.

Solomon, though, asked for nothing like that. Instead, he asked for "a discerning heart...to distinguish between right and wrong."[268] God left no question that Solomon wished for the right thing. Because he has wished to be wise, God gave him both wealth and honor in addition to wisdom.[269] Solomon went on to become renowned for his wisdom, until he reached old age, when his astuteness deserted him as it does to so many of us. Until that time, though, not only did he show mindfulness when confronted by God, he seemed to espouse it throughout almost his whole reign.

On the other hand, consequences follow lack of mindfulness in the Hebrew Bible. Perhaps the most poignant example is in Numbers, when Moses has his patience continually tried by the

Israelites. Moses was a reluctant leader to begin with. Leading the people out of slavery in Egypt was God's idea, not his, and he tried to talk God out of it. When Moses did submit to the will of God, the Israelites complained bitterly almost every step of the way. For years in the wilderness Moses put up with their grumbling and griping, and he tried to keep them turned to the way of God. At the same time, God gave Moses task after task after task. God presented Moses with dozens of laws governing what the people could and could not do. God had Moses perform a census of those who could go out into the army, a head count numbering hundreds of thousands. He had Moses number the Levites, more than 20,000 of them. Finally, after years of effort that would have exhausted a cadre of government bureaucrats, the Israelites arrived at the desert of Zin. They were tired and thirsty and no water could be found, so once again the Israelites kvetched and complained.

"Take the staff and assemble the congregation, you and your brother Aaron, and speak to the rock in their presence so that it will give forth its water," God told Moses. "You shall bring forth water for them from the rock and give the congregation and their livestock to drink."270 Moses picked up his staff and struck the rock, and water came forth, just as God promised. In his anger and his frustration, though, Moses forgot something key: he neglected to praise God for bringing forth the water. He was not mindful, even though he was otherwise obedient to the word of God. For this moment's entirely human lapse, he would never see the Promised Land, even after 40 years of leading the recalcitrant tribe. His punishment came because in that lapse, he forgot about the source of his power, God. Lack of mindfulness led to lack of acknowledgement.

As Moses learned to his lifelong regret, the kind of mindfulness that can ride the waves caused by other people and the ups and

downs of daily existence takes tremendous effort. The effort of
attention has a payoff, though, and it's our spiritual and even
psychological and physical health. It's possible that the three
cannot even be separated. In his bestselling book *Care of the Soul*,
Thomas Moore writes, "Spirituality doesn't arrive fully formed
without effort. Religions around the world demonstrate that
spiritual life requires *constant attention* (emphasis added) and a
subtle, often beautiful technology by which spiritual principles and
understandings are kept alive. For good reason, we go to church,
temple, or mosque regularly and at appointed times: it's easy for
consciousness to become lodged in the material world and to forget
the spiritual."[271] We have to accept our humanity, Moore argues,
and one way to come to terms with all the pain and beauty that our
humanity confers is through mindfulness.

In the Hebrew Bible, Isaiah warned the Israelites of the
consequences of focusing solely on the material word to the
neglect of the spiritual. God says through Isaiah, "the harp and
the psaltery, the tabret and the pipe, and wine, are in their feasts;
but they regard not the work of the LORD, neither have they
considered the operation of His hands. Therefore, My people are
gone into captivity for want of knowledge."[272] Isaiah's vision is
filled with anger, vengeance, and political awareness. He was a
prophet of the people in a sense, and that was precisely because
he was mindful. He saw what was happening around him, from
the machinations of rulers to the oppressions of the lowest classes
of commoners, the widows and orphans. He didn't indulge in
escapism. At the same time, he was acutely listening for God's voice
all the time.

Some might argue that prophecy is the antithesis of
mindfulness. It might seem like the prophet is focused on the
future and living in a world of fantasy. The prophet would see it

differently. Prophets didn't daydream. They were acutely aware of events and circumstances and interpreted what they meant from the perspective of God's will. Prophecy was a kind of limited omniscience. In contrast, many people do dwell mentally in the future, dreaming about what they will do when they get what they want and how their circumstances will change. Some are so caught up in their plans that they neglect the people around them each moment. They might even neglect to do what they need to do to fulfill those dreams. The future is never entirely predictable, and we are often blindsided by random events that may have been impossible to predict. Our dreams often do not come to fruition, or perhaps they do but at the great cost of friends and family or reputation. As the Hebrew Bible and other spiritual texts show us, neither living in the past nor living in the future is a wise path.

THE CLEARING OF BUDDHISM

In the early eighth-century text the *Bodhicaryavatara*, which is sometimes translated as the *Guide to the Bodhisattva Way of Life*, the great Indian Buddhist scholar-monk Shantideva writes, "Those who wish to protect their practice should zealously guard the mind...Untamed, mad elephants do not inflict as much harm in this world as does the unleashed elephant of the mind.... But if the elephant of the mind is completely restrained by the rope of mindfulness, then all perils vanish and complete well-being is attained."[273] Shantideva echoes the thoughts of the Buddha as expressed in the "Elephant" chapter of the *Dhammapada*. First the Buddha compares the mind to an elephant in a rut, and then he compares controlling the mind to a mahout guiding such an elephant. "Take pleasure in being careful," the Buddha said. "Guard your mind well. Extricate yourself from the mire, like a great tusker sunk in the mud."[274] To the Buddha, the elephant is both dangerous and in a forest. The only real clearing is mindfulness.

Perhaps the most famous visual image of mindfulness is the Buddha sitting under the bodhi tree, waiting for enlightenment. He wasn't just waiting, though. If he were just waiting, his mind would have gone off on all the mental adventures on which our minds take us whenever we are whiling away time. As I wait in line at the grocery store, for instance, I might be thinking about what chores I need to do when I get home or what time I need to meet a friend or whether I have enough ingredients in the fridge for supper. I might be recalling an incident from a day or week or month earlier that made me angry or happy or sad, or I might be thinking about some upcoming event with excitement or trepidation. One thing is certain: I am rarely completely in the moment or holding fast to any single mental construct as I wait in line at the store.

Unlike me and so many of us, the Buddha could keep up his concentration. His ability to sustain his focus, to follow his breath, and to restrain his mad elephant of a mind, keeping it focused laser-like on the "Now...now...now" is what enabled him to reach enlightenment. The cultivation of the ability took the passage of time and many wrong paths, including an attempt to reach enlightenment through extreme asceticism. His meditative mindfulness practice led to his discovery of the "middle way" between the extremes of asceticism and pleasure-seeking. His practice took enormous effort and generosity. It was generous because he focused himself for the eventual liberation of all sentient beings. The effort came because sitting and being mindful literally every second and every breath is so hard.

As I thought about this, I opened a meditation journal I wrote a few years ago during a Buddhist meditation class. It's full of notes about how easily I lost focus, how much pain I was in, how easily

I got distracted, and how much I fidgeted. I sounded like a first grader: "I was able to hold my attention pretty well for the first 20-25 minutes. Then I really lost it. I wondered if Rinpoche had fallen asleep. At one point, I looked to see if he was still breathing." For me at that point, 20 to 25 minutes was a real achievement. I can't imagine days and weeks and months in that single-focused state.

This mindfulness, though, is intimately related to truth. It is how truth is understood. In the *Mahasatipatthana Sutra*, the Buddha explains, "a bhikkhu, while going forward or while going back does so with clear understanding; while looking straight ahead or while looking elsewhere he does so with clear understanding; while bending or stretching his limbs he does so with clear understanding; while carrying the alms bowl and while wearing the robes he does so with clear understanding; while eating, drinking, chewing, and savouring he does so with clear understanding; while urinating or defecating he does so with clear understanding; while walking, standing, sitting, falling asleep, waking, speaking or when remaining silent, he does so with clear understanding."[275] In the same sutra, he explains that through the practice of mindfulness disciples learn to perceive "feelings as just feelings (not mine, not I, not self, but just as phenomena) in himself...he dwells perceiving again and again both the actual appearing and dissolution of feelings with their causes. To summarize, he is firmly mindful of the fact that only feelings exist (not a soul, a self or I). That mindfulness is just for gaining insight (vipassana) and mindfulness progressively. Being detached from craving and wrong views he dwells without clinging to anything in the world."[276] The Buddha's words can remind us that feelings are senses, just as much as the five senses that we commonly acknowledge.

It seems almost impossible to divorce mindfulness, in the Buddhist context, from meditation. All over the world on any

given day, millions of people are sitting erect, cross-legged in
meditation, as if they are living reflections of the Buddha. Certainly,
meditation is a vehicle for mindfulness, but it does not guarantee
success. Over the past decade, hundreds of my religion students
have attempted meditation in a group setting, just to get a sense of
what it is. Almost universally, they report two observations: that
the meditative experience is peaceful and calming and that they
found it impossible to still their minds for more than a second or
two. To successfully cultivate true mindfulness takes dedication.
It requires the willingness to hold fast to what is in our minds (the
idea of retention, *smrti*, literally means memory and refers to being
able to mentally hold fast to an object of attention without allowing
it to disappear), to act with awareness as we observe and clarify the
object of our attention without judging it and without emotionally
reacting to it.[277] It's a bit of a catch-22: we need consciousness to be
mindful, but without mindfulness, our consciousness is limited.

That's not to say that everything we gain from consciousness
and mindfulness is cheery and bright. One of Ursula Le Guin's very
famous short stories, "The Ones Who Walk Away from Omelas," is
like a study in what mindfulness can awaken within us. The story
shows us a utopia, Omelas, where life is absolutely, perfectly joyful
and everyone is happy. No citizen's life is miserable except for one
person's. A dirty, fearful, miserable, neglected child is caged in a
dark cell. The child is treated worse than we can legally treat any
beast. Not everyone comes to see the child, but all the citizens know
the child is there, and they all know that their happiness depends
on the squalor and misery of that small sore-infested scapegoat.
The existence of the child helps the citizens to have compassion
for each other and to appreciate the fineness of their lives, and that
truly is a kind of mindfulness.

Even more important, though, are the ones who view the child and walk away from utopia forever because the price of that child is too high a price for them to pay for their own perfect lives. The child is not a tourist experience for them; the child becomes an exercise and focal point in compassionate mindfulness. In our own world, where the gap between rich and poor continues to grow and where a person with a middle class Western lifestyle lives like an emperor compared to the poorest of the world's poor, such focus and attention can prompt us to question whether our own happiness is worth the misery of those who labor picking rags in dumps and handling the toxic wastes that we ship to them, all for a few meager coins that may not even be enough to fill the bellies of their hungry children.

When considering mindfulness, our lifestyles and happiness are crucial factors because in Buddhist thought, our cravings keep us from mindfulness. The Jataka tale of the tortoise helps to illustrate how this happens. Once, when the Buddha was born as a potter, he would dig the clay for his trade from the shore and the shallows of a lake near the mighty River Ganges. In a rainy year, the river and lake would unite as one, but in dry years they would separate, so the creatures that lived in the lake came to know which years would be dry and which years would be rainy by the patterns that they observed in the sky and the air and the quality of the water. When they perceived that the year would be dry, they would flee the lake and go to the river so that they could survive in the deep current fed by the massive Himalayan mountains. In the year of this story, however, even though the creatures perceived that there would be a drought, a tortoise refused to leave the lake because he was so attached to his home where he had been born. Soon the lake shrunk to nothing, and the tortoise had no water to cover him. All he could do was dig himself into the mud in the shallows where the potter came to dig. When the potter came, he plunged his spade into the

mud, knowing nothing of the tortoise, and split its shell. Then he
turned it out onto the ground thinking it was an enormous lump of
clay. Thus, the tortoise died, aware in his final suffering that he had
caused his own death by his attachment to his home, which had
caused him to abandon his true refuge, mindfulness.[278]

THE MINDFULNESS OF PRAYER

When I was a teenager, prayer was a race. I prayed on auto-
pilot, speeded up as if the prayer was a Chipmunks song. The
words hardly mattered. What mattered was getting the job done,
like cleaning my room by picking up my clothes, notebooks, art
supplies, and other odds and ends and throwing them all slapdash
into my closet, then closing the door. I knew the words to the
prayers, but they were mumbled off as though any extra second
spent on really listening to or feeling the weight of those words was
a second wasted. I could be out with friends, or tooling around
in my muscle car, or chatting on the phone, or doing anything
else once the chore of prayer was done. I suppose it didn't help
that in the Catholic Church, prayer was issued as a penance, so I
saw prayer as the price I had to pay to get right with God again,
which certainly didn't frame it as anything desirable. Penance is
considered a sacrament in Catholicism, so the Church didn't view
it as a punishment but as an avenue of reconciliation. However,
to a wayward and stubborn teen, there may as well have been no
difference between those two concepts.

That's a shame because prayer, no matter the religion, can
be a form of mindfulness, just as mindfulness can be a kind of
prayer. Imagine going outside and really seeing a leaf, a flower, or
an insect fully as it is. When we see a leaf, most often we flip right
into a conditioned state; we think "leaf," and that's usually that.
In a moment of true mindfulness, the word "leaf" becomes almost

irrelevant because we are not looking to sort this bit of chlorophyll-filled flesh into a mental box. Rather, we are seeing its many shades of green, perhaps some brown spotting, the intricate pattern of veins, the texture of the surface, the bas-relief of the underside, the serration of the edge, the fleshy prominence where it joins to the stem. As we fully immerse ourselves in seeing and experiencing, our sense of separateness from the leaf and the leaf's world slips away. As Ralph Waldo Emerson wrote in his essay "Nature," "Standing on the bare ground, my head bathed by the blithe air, and uplifted into infinite space, all mean egotism vanishes. I become a transparent eye-ball; I am nothing; I see all; the currents of the Universal Being circulate through me; I am part or particle of God."[279] If prayer is a way to bring us closer to the Infinite, this melting away of ego is a beautiful form of praying.

Emerson was one of the Transcendentalists who gathered and wrote in the first half of the 1800s in Massachusetts. These thinkers and writers were profoundly influenced by Eastern thought, including by the *Bhagavad Gita*. In many ways, it's easy to see Arjuna's conversation with Krishna in the *Bhagavad Gita* as a form of prayer. He is, after all, communicating with God, and prayer is the vehicle by which most people have that conversation, even if the conversation may often seem to be one-sided. In the *Bhagavad Gita*, however, the conversation isn't just one-sided; we have the benefit of God's answers to Arjuna. Krishna warns Arjuna that a mind that is captivated by the senses, roving carelessly from input to input, is like a boat on stormy waves, unable to reach "the spiritual shore." He goes on to tell Arjuna, "One attains peace in whose mind all desires enter without creating any disturbance, as river waters enter the full ocean without creating a disturbance. One who desires material objects is never peaceful. One who abandons...the feeling of 'I' and 'my' attains peace.... Gaining this state, even at the end of one's life, a person attains oneness with the Supreme."[280] It may, in fact, take us our whole lives to achieve this kind of concentration, as anyone who has worked to stay focused knows. That's because our minds are busy making movies every moment in which we star, sometimes as the victim, sometimes as the hero, but always in the leading role, and it takes diligent practice to realize that in larger reality we have only walk-on bit parts.

The concept of mindfulness is so important in Hinduism that the *Bhagavad Gita* devotes an entire chapter to it. The sixth chapter, the "Path of Meditation," is a how-to of cultivating mindfulness. Readers can even learn about proper meditative posture. It's not necessary to sit on a cushion to practice mindfulness, but a meditative practice that helps to limit some of the sensory input has benefits. For example, practicing inside with fewer distractions can eventually help one to stay more focused in the outside world, where we are bombarded by colors, shapes, desires, and emotions. Krishna reminds Arjuna (and us) of an important fact that is easy to overlook with all this talk of controlling and mastering: "The mind alone is one's friend as well as one's enemy," he points out. The mind is our friend because it allows us to experience the "…infinite bliss that is perceivable only through the intellect, and is beyond the reach of the senses. After realizing Brahman, one is never separated from absolute reality."[281] Reality is not the movie. Reality is only partially the world into which we walk when we leave the movie. Reality is the vastness of the Infinite, and our minds, if we harness them through prayer and other mindful practices, can ride us to that Infinity.

DEATH AND TRANSFORMATION

One frequent theme in spiritual texts that focus on mindfulness is the nearness of death and change. In the *Dao De Jing*, Lao Zi tells disciples to "Empty your mind of all thoughts." He advises, "Let your heart be at peace. Watch the turmoil of beings, but contemplate their return. Each separate being in the universe returns to the common source. Returning to the source is serenity."[282] There is more to the idea than "don't worry, be happy." To the Daoist, this serenity has real benefits: "Immersed in the wonder of the Dao, you can deal with whatever life brings you, and when death comes, you are ready."[283] That sounds as if it might be a recipe for a long and stress-free life at the end of which one simply lies down with a smile, looks back on many pleasant decades, and slips into oblivion, the afterlife, rebirth, or whatever one believes in. However, that's not the full meaning, and the full meaning is one from which many Westerners can benefit. We are utterly preoccupied with work, technology, family obligations, social callings and the like, and as a result, we are utterly heedless of death. Worse, we often feel as if we are immortal, that we can cheat death, and that we are fixable thanks to the many wonders of Western medicine. We are so busy racing through our random, chaotic, and ever-changing lives that we give no thought to that one inescapable, certain fact of our lives: that we will die, and we are unlikely to know when or how.

Some might ask why we should maintain our awareness of that fact, and the answer is that the reality of our deaths can influence how we live. "Can you coax your mind from its wandering and keep to the original oneness?" Lao Zi asks. "Can you step back from your own mind and thus understand all things?"[284] Through the entire text, the sage tells us to stop trying to shape the world and all in it to our own very limited views of what we want, especially because what we want changes from day to day, even moment to moment, as do we. If we can hardly decide in a restaurant whether we want the pasta or the fish, then it's pointless to try to bend the entire world to our whims. Such a desire can lead only to frustration and bitterness, a life lived in psychological and perhaps physical conflict, and when death comes we will have robbed ourselves of the life we could have had, a life filled with harmony and wonder.

The capacity to live that life is innate in us, Lao Zi reminds us: "Men are born soft and supple. Dead, they are stiff and hard.... Thus whoever is stiff and inflexible is a disciple of death. Whoever is soft and supple is a disciple of life.... The soft and supple will prevail."[285] The competing ideologies of the world and the drive to amass wealth encourage us to be hard and stiff, fixed in our views and our thinking to protect what we think we are gaining. In contrast, the way to softness and suppleness is mindfulness. "Close your mouth," the *Dao De Jing* tells us. "Block off your senses, blunt your sharpness, untie your knots, soften your glare, settle your dust...Be like the Dao."[286] Our task is to slip out of ourselves and into that leaf or image or moment and hold fast to it. From the perspective of Daoism we must become Emerson's "transparent eyeball," perceiving the Infinite and entering into it so that when death comes, we are as ready for it as we can be, having walked with it throughout our lives.

Death influences mindfulness in the Gospels, too. In the Gospel of John, Jesus gives his disciples the parable of the vine and the fruit. "Remain in me, as I also remain in you," he tells them. He describes himself as the vine and his disciples as the fruit of the vine, pointing out that "If you *remain* in me, and I in you, you will bear much fruit; apart from me you can do nothing." Jesus is not just exhorting his disciples to hold fast to his teachings. He is telling them to remain in Him, to be mindful each moment. He places a premium on mindfulness. This is their work, he suggests, and he echoes the writer of Ecclesiastes in telling them that to do this will bring them joy.

He is not asking them to be lemmings, to blindly follow their leader off a cliff. Rather, he knows that he is sending them off into the world with no earthly leader, for he is about to die. In their mindfulness is their ability to create change in the world through his teachings, which will bear fruit through them and their constant vigilance. That vigilance will not be supported through bickering or strife, because those are distractions. That is why, as Jesus approaches his death, the message he stresses is one of love and of compassion: "Love each other as I have loved you," he tells them.287 To do that in the face of their human emotions—their fears, their anger, their depression, and their struggles—would surely take their moment by moment mindfulness.

Although Jesus was aware of His own imminent physical death and subsequent transformation, the apostle Paul focused on a different kind of transformation in his own exhortations toward mindfulness. Paul explains very clearly in his epistle to the Romans what happens without mindfulness. "I do not do the good I want to do, but the evil I do not want to do—this I keep on doing," he writes. "So I find this law at work: Although I want to do good, evil is right there with me. For in my inner being I delight in God's law; but I see another law at work in me, waging war against the law of my mind and making me a prisoner of the law of sin at work within me."288 The law at work within us is our self-cherishing and our lack of attention. In the same epistle, Paul exhorts those who believe to "be transformed by the renewing of your mind." He tells the Romans, "Do not think of yourself more highly than you ought, but rather think of yourself with sober judgment," and reminds them to know themselves, to understand who they are and what they have to offer others, and to offer that willingly.289 Paul also reminds the faithful to live with humility and contentment, to be harmonious in their society, to live in peace with their enemies as well as with their friends.

Paul was referring to the literal belief that God's coming to Earth was imminent, but we would do well to take his advice in the metaphoric sense, understanding that mindfulness has the power to free us from entrapment: "Do this, understanding the present time: The hour has already come for you to wake up from your slumber, because our salvation is nearer now than when we first believed. The night is nearly over; the day is almost here. So let us put aside the deeds of darkness and put on the armor of light,"[290] he wrote, which means being fully cognizant, in every moment, of where we are, what is happening, what we are doing, and whether it is what we *should* be doing. Such harmony and contentment as Paul exhorted can't be achieved through knee-jerk reaction and the rule of emotion. It can only be accomplished through looking inward and governing the self.

THE INN OF THE MIND

The Rumi poem that opens this chapter seems counterintuitive. "Fish and guests stink after three days," a famous saying suggests. Most of us invite our guests with care. We welcome our friends and dread the arrival of those relatives we despise but are obligated to entertain for the sake of keeping peace in the family. Yet here comes Rumi, suggesting that we should run a guest house and welcome everyone.

The "guest house" to which Rumi refers is the mind. We might think, "Welcome everything in? Sadness, fear, frustration? Is he kidding?" Practically every psychological self-help book on the market advises against doing anything of the sort. There might not even be room here to list all the various pharmaceuticals such as Valium, Xanax, and Prozac, that have been developed with the aim of keeping those guests firmly *out*; the various so-called negative emotions are generally uninvited and unwanted. Rumi's idea of throwing open the doors sounds at first as if it might be a kind of madness.

If it is madness, though, then it is transformative madness. Mindfulness teaches us to examine these hurts, slights, fears, and miseries for what they are without judging them. When we can do so calmly and consistently, they no longer have any power over us. We see them for what they are, specters that we have created, so loose that the wind blows through them.

To believe that there is something more beneficial, a beautiful shore that we can reach, is our encouragement to mindfully welcome those guests, just as mindfulness is the way to reach the shore. As the great Sufi poet Hafiz wrote,

> "How
> Did the rose
> Ever open its heart
> And give this world
> All its
> Beauty?
> It felt the encouragement of light
> Against its
> Being
> Otherwise we all remain
> Too
> Frightened."[291]

In Islam, the concept of *taqwa* shows Allah as the light to which the faithful must open, and the path to that opening is keeping oneself from anything that will displease Allah. Mindfulness paves that path. In the Qur'an, Allah tells believers to "remain resolute, and be mindful of Allah, in order that you may succeed."[292] To submit and to avoid distraction, both of which are core values of Islam, we can welcome all the guests by seeing what they truly are. Invite them in, as Rumi says, because the mind is your house, and you are the master of it, not the other way around. These guests are clouds. We can blossom in the radiance that glistens beyond them.

Mindfulness brings us into that radiance. Mindfulness allows us to go beyond conventional reality to approach transcendent reality. For those who would scoff at such a notion, mindfulness can help us approach the nature of the world through a quantum physics perspective, which is no less than a focus on the Infinite through its attempts to create a unified theory of everything through focus on the most minute of particles and simultaneous dualities. Mindfulness is how we strip away our cruise control; it encourages us to seek the truth, to acknowledge that beyond ourselves, and to practice compassion and generosity. Mindfulness reminds us at the dinner table that many are hungry; it reminds us at the department store that many are poor; it reminds us at the fun party that many are suffering, and it encourages us to look within ourselves with honesty to assess what we can do and how we should act in response.

THE BENEFITS OF MINDFULNESS

To be mindful, we need to be fully aware of the moment that we are in, see it for what it is, be fully present in it, and accept it with equanimity. In the material world, lack of mindfulness at its worst can make us bad neighbors, problematic employees, poor parents, and unfaithful friends and spouses. For example, much of the world now has access to various kinds of personal technology, such as smartphones, and use of that technology has allowed people to connect with others in unprecedented ways. However, in many places it has also spawned an almost compulsive need for attention-seeking. One benefit has been a boon of creativity on many social media sites and through venues such as YouTube, but those same capabilities invite an almost breathtaking cruelty. Once my next-door neighbor told me about just such an example. Teresa had been walking home when she spotted a man on the ground outside the Dollar Store. He was jerking, twitching, and babbling. He may have been drunk or on drugs, or he may have been mentally ill. My neighbor is especially sensitive to that because her adult son struggled for years from mental illness because of his drug use. What incensed Teresa was that two female employees of the Dollar Store were standing outside with their phones capturing the man's struggles and laughing.

Teresa confronted the two young women and told them she thought that their actions were disgusting. She asked them why they weren't using their phones to call for help for the man. Immediately both young women became angry and defensive. "What are we supposed to do?" they demanded. "It's not our business." Their response even further shows their lack of mindfulness. They were clearly making the man's problems their business by filming the man and mocking him. When Teresa demanded to see the manager, the women ganged up on her and told her that she should mind her own business and that they weren't doing anything wrong. "I wanted to tell them that it could have been them or their relative or their friend on the sidewalk instead of him but for the grace of God," Teresa told me, "but I knew they would think I was some kind of Bible thumper." The point is that the grace of God doesn't even have to come into it; with a little bit of thought, most of us can understand that wanting to get attention for ourselves by making fun of and profiting from someone else's misfortune is wrong. That kind of self-absorption does nothing to make our society kinder or more compassionate. It is born of a complete lack of mindfulness, because from the perspective of social reality, Teresa is right: any one of us can be struck down by misfortune, and to forget that suffering can befall us is to forget an important part of our own humanity.

The idea of the slowing and introspection required by mindfulness can seem laughable. In this busy world, it can seem idealistic and impractical as well as pointless. However, it's hard to overstate the numerous benefits of this practice.

First, without even delving into the world of the soul or the spirit, mindfulness has benefits on the personal level. Mindfulness is not just seeing; it is monitoring. It is awareness of what one is thinking, feeling, and experiencing in every moment, and the awareness is clear and still rather than being drowned in the incessant background babble that our minds are so eager to provide. Psychological studies have shown that those who practice mindfulness are less likely than others to be neurotic and are more likely to be open-minded and conscientious.[293] Further, studies have shown that individuals with ADHD have less mindfulness than those without ADHD, but that many aspects of their ADHD, such as lack of organization and lack of inhibition, can be improved with mindfulness training and practice.[294] Training in mindfulness has been shown in studies to help people with depression and people with substance abuse disorders.[295] In short, these studies suggest that mindfulness is good for our mental health.

What's good for our mental health can also be good for our physical health. The Heidelberger Diabetes and Stress Study studied the effects of mindfulness-based stress reduction strategies on patients with diabetes, a disease that is becoming epidemic in the United States and that can compromise people's quality of life and shorten their lives. The mindfulness techniques resulted in "better health status and lower levels of depression."[296] Researchers also reported that the intervention improved patients' overall psychological health. It did not directly decrease the levels of proteins in patients' urine (kidney disease often accompanies diabetes), but patients' blood pressure improved. Researchers hypothesize that improved mental health may lead to further improved physical health for the patients and are continuing the study.

Another physical benefit for mindfulness comes in athletics training. Many good coaches train athletes in "process focus" rather than "outcome focus." The idea of "process focus" is basically mindfulness training: athletes learn to focus their attention on physical and physiological cues as they occur, with moment by moment awareness. The effect of such training is for the athlete to know what is happening in the now rather than dwelling on what she may have done wrong in the past or on the outcome that she wants to occur. In fact, coaches who use process focus believe that such techniques as visualizing winning are harmful because they can create mental stresses for athletes that can hinder their performance.[297]

The benefits of mindfulness include personal health and performance at work. Research indicates that mindfulness can benefit our organizations and societies. In fact, some organizations are investing in mindfulness training. The results include improved focus at work through decreased distractibility, and studies indicate that mindfulness is good for a company's bottom line, but they also underscore the improved health of the employees, particularly in decreased deaths from stress-related diseases.[298]

Further, studies support the idea that the benefits of mindfulness don't depend on where a person lives; the benefits are similar whether a person lives in the United States or in Europe or in the Middle East. Because this is true, researchers believe that mindfulness can play a key role in resolving domestic and inter-cultural conflicts.[299]

For a moment, let's imagine how mindfulness could work in the real world. If you're an American citizen, imagine Washington politics that are not mired in gridlock because politicians are reflectively and openly assessing the state of the economy and society without a view toward being reelected. Instead, they are working together to devise the best possible solutions to achieve the best good for the most people. They are not motivated by anger, by jealousy, or by fear, and since they are not operating from their own egos, they are able to find innovative solutions that make America a competitive marketplace, financially sound, and socially stable because people have access to means for advancement: they have education, they have jobs, they have basic health care, and they have pensions in old age.

The concerns of a European would be different but no less pressing than the concerns of Americans. One shocking scenario that perhaps could have been averted through practice of mindfulness occurred in the summer of 2011, when rioting broke out across London. Great Britain has a long history of community policing, and in the past the police were viewed benevolently by much of the law-abiding citizenry. At some point, that perception of the police started to change. What caused the change? What could have been done sooner to avert the hostile attitudes that people developed? When we're not aware, when we're not mindful, we don't even think to ask questions like that. Over the years, England had changed demographically, and its monocultural population had expanded to include many more people of color. The thinking of the police, however, seemed not to expand with the population. The police seemed to trust most white people, but their actions suggested that they distrusted people of color. For example, statistics from the Metropolitan Police in May 2011 showed that people of color were overwhelmingly disproportionally stopped and questioned, leading to a perception that the police were racist.[300]

As the rioting that August escalated, resulting in smashed shop windows, looting, and the arrests of over 1,000 citizens, Prime Minister David Cameron spoke of the country's need to fix the ills of its society, saying that the violence stemmed from "a complete lack of responsibility, a lack of proper parenting, a lack of proper upbringing, a lack of proper ethics, a lack of proper morals."[301] That may all be true of the rioters and the police alike, but the bottom line is that it was also caused by a lack of mindfulness. The moment we must ask the question "How did we get here?" or "How did this happen?" we must realize we haven't been paying attention along the way. We haven't been mindful, and our lack of mindfulness can affect our whole community. America has been seeing that in the various riots that have broken out for very similar reasons after men of color were killed by white police officers in circumstances that appeared not to require deadly force.

If nothing else, we can become happier in our daily lives through mindfulness practice. We can stop dwelling in our past feelings and experiences and see and feel and hear everything we have been missing, including the still point within ourselves.

Humility

Some years ago, I sat in a large, imposing office at my school being interviewed by the college's president and vice-president for a teaching position that I wanted very badly. I had applied for two openings. One was temporary, and one was permanent. Either would give me much needed benefits and stability for myself and my children, and I wasn't going to be choosy. I would happily take the temporary job. I had prepared for the interviews relentlessly. I had researched information about the school and its students even though I had taught there part time for years. I had a mentor look over my application and give me tips. I had practiced and timed my teaching presentation, and I had looked up the interests of the president and vice-president. My homework and readiness had paid off so far. This was my third and final interview. I offered confident answers until the vice president asked me, "You are being considered for the permanent position. Why should we choose you over another candidate?"

I stopped for a moment, then tears welled in my eyes. Both men looked away and were obviously uncomfortable. "I'm sorry," I said, grabbing a tissue and wiping my eyes and nose. "I didn't know I was being considered for the permanent job. I'm very grateful to my department for recommending me." I collected myself, thought a second, and said honestly, "I can't tell you that I'm any better than anyone else. I know others who have applied for this job, and they are very qualified. I work with them, and I respect them. All I can tell you is that I will work hard for you if you hire me."

I left the interview feeling discouraged. I thought I had blown it with my show of emotion after having come so far. At the same time, I decided that my tears had been honest, and if they had ruined the opportunity, then the job would not be a good fit for either me or the school. I went home and waited for the call that I expected, the one telling me "Thank you for applying, but we have selected someone with more control over her hormones, someone who doesn't cry in interviews." A few days later the phone rang, and I heard the Human Resources director's voice. "Just get it over with," I thought in distress. Then, to my shock, she offered me the job. I remember shouting with happiness. Months later, I was chatting with the vice-president, and he asked abruptly, "Do you know why we hired you?" I felt a bit taken aback, and shook my head.

"Because you are humble," he said. It turned out that my tears had actually *helped* me get the job.

Ego feels like our friend. Ego is the costume that we wear to show Western society that we have the qualities it expects: we are successful, independent, self-made, important, and proud. We are so used to wearing the costume that we believe it in, often utterly, and the thought of taking it off can seem unthinkable to us, as if we are nothing, invisible, without it.

From the vantage point and perceived safety of ego, we can be tempted to think that humility is for losers. It looks weak. We can see humble people as pushovers. That's how I felt about myself the day I burst into tears: I was a weak loser who must have blown the opportunity that could have been mine. Ego and humility had collided in that moment, because deep down inside I had known the truth when asked that question. Despite my favorable reviews, despite my hard work as an instructor and tutor, despite my committee work, and despite my many years of experience, I truly had nothing more to offer than anyone else had.

It can be hard to see the strength and power in humility. However, little is more powerful than taking off that ego costume and stepping into the world as we really are rather than as the construct that we have so carefully cultivated and the presentation in which we have invested so much effort. Little is stronger than admitting that what we want and think we need and desire is not the most important thing in the world at all, especially when so much of our culture and economy and media are so heavily invested in selling each of us the idea that each of us is number one. When we realize we are not number one, we are a step closer to seeing all living beings as equals.

THE MODESTY OF JOSEPH

There is an old saying that is attributed as an Arab proverb, but that seems to apply to most of humanity throughout its documented existence. It is "I against my brother; I and my brother against my cousins; me, my brother and my cousin against the outsider." In Jacob's family, this saying was put into action with surprising results.

Jacob's son Joseph was just seventeen, and of all the sons that Jacob had by his various wives, Joseph was his most beloved. Joseph had been fathered in Jacob's old age. So frequently around us today we see mature dads delighting in their late-in-life children, appreciating the chance to do fatherhood right. Like those children of older dads, Joseph was Jacob's heart, and he seems to have been a rather ordinary guy, but he had a disturbing gift: he had dreams. They were visions. Even people without grudges can have animosity toward people who have visions. At the least, they might see the person as eccentric, and at worst the person can be damned as a witch, a heretic, or a dangerous individual. Unfortunately for Joseph, the people with whom he shared his dreams had more than a grudge against him. They hated him. Their hatred for him flourished because he was so loved and because the dreams suggested that someday he would have dominion over them all. The haters were his brothers.

Hatred waits for its moments, and one day Joseph left Canaan at Jacob's request to check on his brothers and their flocks of sheep and goats. His task was just to make sure they were all right and report the news back to his father, who understandably had concerns. The countryside could be a dangerous place of wild beasts and bandits, and sons and flocks were wealth. Perhaps Jacob had concerns about whether the sons were acting responsibly. As Joseph tracked down his brothers in Dothan, they saw him coming in the distance and seized upon their chance to kill him. It would be easy enough to pass off the death as accidental. Asiatic lions and cheetahs roamed the ancient lands, and Joseph would have been unlikely to survive an attack.

Only one of the brothers, Reuben, disagreed with the plan to kill Joseph. "Let's not take his life," he said to the others. "Don't shed any blood. Throw him into this cistern here in the wilderness, but don't lay a hand on him."[302] His secret plan was to go back later, get Joseph out of the empty cistern, and bring him home safely to Jacob. The brothers agreed and threw Joseph into the cistern, but Reuben apparently wandered off with the flock after the deed was done. Rescuing Joseph slipped his mind. Meanwhile, a caravan came through that was headed to Egypt, and the remaining brothers hauled Joseph out of the cistern and sold him to the caravan.

Imagine the scene: young Joseph was the son of nomads, presumably strong and in the prime of his life. Yet he was overpowered by his kinsmen, his own brothers, who stripped his cloak off him and threw him into a cistern deep enough that he could not get out by himself. It's possible and even likely that he would have been injured in the fall. Then the brothers hauled

Joseph up—was he angry? Was he even conscious? —and sold him. The Ishmaelites bought him as just another piece of merchandise to be traded, and presumably he was either tied or chained. We can't assume that Joseph just hopped up on a camel and said, "Alrighty then, let's go!"

Now imagine him being sold in Egypt to the captain of the Pharaoh's guard. Joseph was a beloved son. His father had given him a finely-made and ornate cloak, better than any cloak Jacob had given his other sons. However, we have no evidence from the story that Joseph stood before his new owner in a haughty manner and demanded to be returned to his father. He didn't shirk or kvetch or try to escape. He accepted his circumstances and did his job well for years, and everything he did was so successful that Potiphar, his owner, eventually put him in charge of his whole household. Potiphar trusted Joseph utterly. What an opportunity for a sense of inflated ego that could be!

Another opportunity for self-importance also lurked: Potiphar's wife. Joseph was young, strong, and good looking, and Potiphar's wife liked what she saw. She tried to get Joseph in bed with her. Imagine being in your early twenties, full of testosterone and the most important worker in the household, a kind of butler par excellence, with a woman lusting after you. To his credit, though, Joseph turned her down. He didn't want to betray his master's trust and didn't want to betray God, who he believed was protecting him. Here was a young man who had been sold into slavery by his own brothers, who had lost his status and lost his family, yet he saw himself as blessed by God and refused to go against what he saw as God's wishes.

Potiphar's wife was not as upright. One day when she propositioned him and he turned her down, she grabbed his cloak, which came away in her hand as he ran from her. She waited until

her husband came home, then she slandered Joseph. She cried that
Joseph had come into the house to try to rape her but ran away
when she screamed, and then she produced the cloak as evidence.
Joseph was lucky. Potiphar would have been within his rights to kill
him right then. Instead, Potiphar threw him into prison.

It's hard to say what kind of place prison might have been
at that time. It's possible that the prison was a thick-walled and
chambered pit in the ground, which some of the smaller jails
seem to have been. It may have been a cell in the building that
housed the policing forces. Genesis tells us that he was housed in
a dungeon, and having seen ancient dungeons at Carthage—small
dark chambers in the blistering earth—I feel sympathy for him. At
any rate, we can assume that Joseph's prison time was not terribly
pleasant. No matter: despite his discomfort, he was willing to help
his fellow prison mates by using his gift to interpret their dreams.
Nor did he suggest that he was doing anything particularly wise or
magical or special. He told them, "Do not interpretations belong to
God?"[303] He just saw himself as God's mouthpiece.

Eventually, word of his ability to interpret dreams made its way
to Pharaoh, who had been having troubling dreams. Pharaoh called
for Joseph to be brought to him. In advance of being escorted to
Pharaoh he was permitted to wash, shave, and change into clothes
more decent than the rags he would have been wearing by then.
Another person might have seen the opportunity as a chance to puff
himself up and make himself out to be a mystic or shaman, a man
with a power that even the great Pharaoh did not have. However,
Joseph remained humble. Pharaoh told Joseph , "I had a dream,
and no one can interpret it. But I have heard it said of you that
when you hear a dream you can interpret it." In response, Joseph
replied, "I cannot do it...but God will give Pharaoh the answer he
desires."[304] Then he interpreted the dreams and told Pharaoh of the
years of plenty and famine that were to come.

Joseph would have then been about thirty. As compensation for his words and modest demeanor, Pharaoh put him in charge of all of Egypt. It's as if he had been made president of the United States or prime minister of Great Britain—that's how powerful Egypt was and how powerful Joseph became. If ever there was an opportunity for Joseph to have hubris, here it was. Still, Joseph remained upright and temperate. He stored grain throughout the years of plenty, and he never skimmed for himself. When the time of famine came, he used the reserves to sell grain to the people of Egypt and the surrounding lands, who surely would have starved without the stores of food.

One of those surrounding lands was Canaan, and as time went by and Jacob's family began to suffer hunger, Jacob sent his sons to Egypt to buy grain. By that time Joseph was almost 40, and his brothers had not seen him since they had sold him 23 years earlier. When they stood before him, they didn't recognize him. He recognized them, though. Here was his opportunity for vengeance, and a man with his power could easily have had that revenge. Instead, he taught his brothers an important lesson.

Joseph sold the brothers grain, but on the condition that he would hold one of them for ransom until they returned to him with Jacob's youngest son, Benjamin. We can imagine that the brothers were shocked by this; Joseph's actions must have seemed arbitrary and frightening. All those years ago Jacob lost his treasured son Joseph, and now Benjamin was the dearest son of his old age. Eventually, however, the brothers reluctantly returned with Benjamin to purchase more grain and ransom their other brother. Unbeknownst to them, while the brothers were conducting their business, Joseph planted a silver cup in Benjamin's pack of grain. The brothers set off all together to return to Canaan, but Joseph then sent his steward after them. The steward searched the packs, found the silver cup, and denounced Benjamin as a thief, then brought the brothers back to Joseph. Joseph's sentence seems both terrible and just: he says that because of the theft, he will keep Benjamin as a slave. The rest may return to Canaan.

It's a perfect revenge, except that it's a ruse. It was also an effective one. Apparently, the brothers had developed a sense of conscience since selling Joseph. Judah, the ringleader who had plotted to kill Joseph all those years before, now told Joseph (whom he still had not recognized),

> ...if the boy is not with us when I go back to your servant my father, and if my father, whose life is closely bound up with the boy's life, sees that the boy isn't there, he will die. Your servants will bring the gray head of our father down to the grave in sorrow. Your servant guaranteed the boy's safety to my father. I said, 'If I do not bring him back to you, I will bear the blame before you, my father, all my life!' Now then, please let your servant remain here as my lord's slave in place of the boy, and let the boy return with his brothers. How can I go back to my father if the boy is not with me? No! Do not let me see the misery that would come on my father. [305]

When I think about the story thus far, I wonder whether Joseph was enjoying the discomfort of Judah and his other brothers. Did he feel some happiness in their misery? Might he have been serious: did he plan to enslave Benjamin as vengeance?

What happened next puts all those suspicions to rest. Joseph broke down and wept uncontrollably. The whole household heard him. Even Pharaoh heard that Joseph had been weeping. Finally, he revealed himself to his brothers, but not to punish them, and not to lord his circumstances over them. So easily could he have

said, "You wanted me dead, and now I am leaving you to die."
He could have reminded them of the money that they received for
selling him all those years ago, and he could have demanded they
repay it to him many times over. He had that power. Instead, he
told his brothers, who were now terrified because they realized both
Joseph's identity and their predicament, "...do not be distressed and
do not be angry with yourselves for selling me here, because it was
to save lives that God sent me ahead of you."[306] He told them to
go get Jacob and their families and to bring them all to Egypt, and
that he would provide for all of them so that they could survive the
coming additional five years of famine. Jacob and his sons settled
in Goshen, and they prospered. Many years later, Jacob died there,
and Joseph fulfilled his promise to his father to return his body to
Canaan, where he mourned his father in the land of his birth for
a week.

Then, finally, Joseph was presented with a last opportunity for
haughtiness. Even after all the ensuing years, his brothers had not
forgotten how they hated Joseph and plotted against him. They
knew that they took his life away from him. With their father Jacob
gone, they became afraid that Joseph would finally hurt them, so
they sent a message to him begging for his forgiveness.

Like most people, I've been wronged by others. At times, I've
indulged in (or sunk to) elaborate fantasies of what it might be like
to get even. I've watched others do incredibly cruel things, and
the news is full of such stories of people wanting to destroy others
for even imagined slights. However, when Joseph received the
plea from his brothers, he didn't gloat. He didn't take vengeance.
Instead, he wept. They came to him and threw themselves to the
ground at his feet, but instead of crushing them he said, "Don't be
afraid. Am I in the place of God? You intended to harm me, but
God intended it for good to accomplish what is now being done,

the saving of many lives. So then, don't be afraid. I will provide for you and your children."[307] He was kind, and he could be kind only because he was humble.

Joseph married once, so far as we know, and he had two sons. When Jacob on his deathbed gave his blessing to Ephraim, the younger of Joseph's two sons, Joseph hesitated at first, then accepted his father's decision. The 1906 *Jewish Encyclopedia* suggests that Jacob blessed Ephraim because of Ephraim's modesty, and Joseph was a wise enough man to defer to his elder after listening to his father's reasoning. Joseph may have been the most powerful man in Egypt after the Pharaoh, but he did not hold grudges, did not hoard, and he did not set himself above others. Rather, he acted as a wise administrator. His governance enabled the people of Egypt and its environs to survive seven years of famine. When the people ran out of money, he didn't blow them off, call them losers, and leave them to starve. Instead, he took their livestock in return for the food. Then he took the fields of everyone but the priests, enriching not his own coffers but the wealth of Pharaoh himself.

Nor did Joseph leave the people destitute. Rather, he gave the people seed to plant the fields so that they could be tenant farmers, giving a fifth of their produce to Pharaoh. He gave to his brothers and his family the gift of his forbearance and his unselfishness. Then, as he was ready to die, Joseph gave his brothers his final gift, one last vision from God: that God would someday take them and their descendants out of the land of Egypt and give to them a land that he had promised them.[308] Joseph's visions weren't ones of self-aggrandizement. Despite his power, he didn't have the kind of attitude that Kanye West displayed in a BBC Radio 1 interview when he said, "I just told you who I thought I was. A god." For Joseph, Godness and personhood were separate spheres, even if

they were intimately connected. He did not try to be God but to be
the best person he could be, and everyone around him benefitted
from that distinction.

SVETAKETU'S CONCEIT

The late Hindu saint Krishnananda Saraswati once told a story
about humility that he connected to the Chhandogya Upanishad,
which is one of the oldest primary Hindu texts. In the Upanishad,
a young man named Svetaketu, the son of a Brahmin sage, thought
himself very clever and highly educated. Brahmins were the top
caste of Indian society, and it's easy to imagine Svetaketu being
fawned over by those around him who wished to curry favor. One
day he went to the court of the king, and in response to the king's
questions he confidently stated how educated he was. He was so
confident, in fact, that he assured the king that he could answer any
question that the king might ask him.

As I think about that part of the story, I can't help but smile.
My children are guaranteed to stump me on just about any day of
the week. I went to college and have taught for almost 20 years,
but "I don't know" followed by "We should look that up" are
stock answers for me. Sometimes I guess, then shrug and say, "I'm
just making that up." When I think about someone believing she
or he can answer any question someone else might ask, I think of
questions such as "Why does it feel warmer when it snows?" or
"Why didn't our friend Kim want to treat her breast cancer?" and I
think "Good luck with answering that."

Svetaketu didn't have such good luck. The king asked Svetaketu
just five questions. First, he asked, "Do you know where people
go after they depart from this world? When people die, where do
they go?" Then he asked, "Do you know wherefrom people come
when they are reborn into this world?" Third, he asked, "Have you

any idea of the paths along which the soul ascends?" Next came
his fourth question: "Why is it that the yonder world is not filled
with people and overflowing? Always, the world is able to contain
people and it is never flooded with them. What is the reason for
this?" Finally, the king inquired, "Do you know what are the
five oblations that are offered and how the fifth oblation as liquid
becomes a human being?" Not surprisingly, Svetaketu could not
answer any of the questions, and the king upbraided him, asking
him how he could think of himself as so well educated if he could
not answer. Svetaketu was mortified. Suddenly, his confident view
of himself crumbled.

At this point in the story we see the difference between humility
and humiliation. Svetaketu felt humiliated and ran home to his
father, whom he tried to blame for his failure. Krishnananda tells
us that the boy berated his father for not educating him properly.
The father, Uddalaka, was taken aback and asked him what the
questions were, and Svetaketu repeated the questions to him.
In Uddalaka's response we see humility. "If I knew the answers
to these questions, naturally I would have taught them to you. I
myself do not know what these mean...I have never heard of these
things. So, how is it possible for me to give a reply to this query?
Let us both go as students before the king...We have to go as
humble students."

Svetaketu was having none of that, though. He could not face
the person who had exposed his lack of knowledge. The idea of
staying safely in his own family compound, surrounded by all the
people who had praised him for so long, must have seemed much
more reassuring and secure to him.

In contrast, the father went to the king humbly. It's worth
noting that the king was of a lower caste than Uddalaka; he was
a Kshatriya, a member of the same warrior caste to which Arjuna

belonged. Kshatriyas were the second highest caste after Brahmins. It was not for Kshatriyas to teach Brahmins. Rather, Brahmins were supposed to teach Kshatriyas. Therefore, when Uddalaka arrived at the king's residence, the king was ready to give Uddalaka whatever gift of wealth he asked, but Uddalaka didn't want wealth. Instead, Uddalaka told the king the story of his son and the questions, and he humbly asked the king to teach him the answers to the questions.

The king was hesitant. The knowledge was held within his caste, and it had never left his caste. Krishnananda says in the story that the king asked Uddalaka to stay at the palace to prepare. Someone of Uddalaka's status could have stormed out in a huff at such a request, but Uddalaka showed humility. He waited, and he studied, and he prepared until the day when the king was finally ready to share his knowledge with him.

The king's willingness to teach the secrets to Uddalaka also tells us something about the king's humility. The king could have refused. He could have tried to pull a fast one and make something up. He admitted that this knowledge had given kings great power, but he also stated that the time had come to pass on the knowledge. Krishnananda tells us, "Anyhow, the king was ready, he was not reluctant, and he was prepared to share this knowledge with the Brahmin, the elderly man who came as a humble student in the ordinary tradition of obedience and humility. And to him the king spoke the great truth."[309] In the absence of ego, great wisdom was imparted.

The story is about Uddalaka and the knowledge that he came to obtain from the king, but I can't help but think of Svetaketu. He sat at home and closed himself off from such an immense wealth of knowing simply because he was embarrassed. It was easier for him to pretend to be the person that he now knew he *wasn't* rather than to humble himself and to simply accept that he didn't know as much as he thought he did. What shame would there have been in such an admission? None. So often it's easier and more comfortable to BS our way through a situation than to say "I don't know. Can you tell me? Will you teach me?" I confess that as a teacher the hardest lesson for me to learn was that I didn't need to pretend to know things I didn't know. I didn't need to evade questions or give half made-up answers. I could just say, "I don't know. I'll find out for you," or even better yet, "I don't know. I will help *you* find out." Svetaketu could do none of that. A hollow had been carved into him. His ego needed so desperately to cling to the "old" Svetaketu, a person who could never again exist in the same way.

This story teaches us something about the correlation between humility and self-esteem. Humility doesn't mean that a person has low self-esteem. It just means that a person has less self-centeredness. In Krishnananda's story, the humble Uddalaka shows good self-esteem. He confidently goes to the king. He doesn't grovel. He assumes that if he asks, the king will teach him. Nor do I think that Uddalaka would have slunk home if the king *had* said no. Uddalaka was a seeker; because he knew that the knowledge existed in the world, he would have continued to seek it out. The one in the story with the low self-esteem, ironically, was the one with the most ego: Svetaketu. He might have benefitted by taking Lao Zi's words to heart: the Master's "constant practice is humility. He doesn't glitter like a jewel but lets himself be shaped by the Dao, as rugged and common as a stone."[310] The jewel's value is determined by a market. The stone's values are many, especially to those who understand stone.

Western culture has famous examples of someone's carefully polished jewel-like image being shattered. Golfer Tiger Woods was one. After his marital infidelities came to light in an avalanche of sensationalistic press, and lucrative sponsors started to desert him,

Woods struggled to regain his swing. Months went by, and he had won no major championships since the scandal and ensuing divorce from his wife. Still he projected what at least one reporter referred to as "an air of entitlement."[311] Another perhaps even more famous example was cyclist Lance Armstrong, who was stripped of his seven Tour de France titles in October 2012. Even when his former teammates made clear that they were going to testify against him, Armstrong could not or would not admit to his doping. Armstrong had tried unsuccessfully to sue the U.S. Anti-Doping Agency and had successfully sued the British newspaper *The Sunday Times* for libel in 2006 after the paper printed claims that Armstrong had doped while competing. By the end of 2012, the *Times* was preparing to sue Armstrong for over a million and a half dollars now that claims of his doping had been upheld.[312]

The *Dao De Jing* might have offered advice to both Woods and Armstrong: "[The Master] understands that...trying to dominate events goes against the current of the Dao. Because he believes in himself, he doesn't try to convince others. Because he is content with himself, he doesn't need others' approval. Because he accepts himself, the whole world accepts him."[313] It might be tempting to think that Lao Zi's words give the athletes and all of us carte blanche to behave however we'd like, but that would be a wrong interpretation. Lao Zi is telling all of us to know ourselves, to assess ourselves accurately, and to accept our talents and our limits. Throughout the text he encourages us not to force, not to dominate, not to control, and not to be excessive. In other words, he advocates humility. Confucius would have agreed: "With sincerity and truth unite a desire for self-culture. Lay down your life rather than quit the path of virtue," he asserted.[314] Perhaps humility could have prevented the unfortunate choices that both Woods and Armstrong made. At the very least, perhaps it could have helped their image in the aftermath. Like Svetaketu, both Woods and Armstrong were not quite who they appeared to be. Their perceived greatness became a weakness; their true greatness became stunted by lack of humility. Meanwhile, Uddalaka and those in the world like him who have a healthy sense of their own limits have the potential to grow.

JESUS AND SUBMISSION

Humility is a virtue because humility matters, and it's not easy to maintain. Jesus knew how much it matters. As mentioned earlier, he was a star. Proportionally speaking, he could gather as many people around him then as Kim Kardashian can gather in a store today. If Jesus didn't invent flash mobs, he certainly had a corner on them throughout a brief period of his life.

Despite his notoriety, Jesus didn't expect to be carried around town. He didn't expect people to shower him with money and gifts. He didn't even call himself "God." In most translations of the Bible, when Pilate asks Jesus if he is a king, Jesus answers, "You say I am a king" (to be fair, in several translations Jesus' response is that Pilate is correct in saying that he is a king). Despite his ability to perform miracles, he walked to his death, struggling under the weight of the heavy cross from which he would be hung. He created no pyrotechnics and no theater. He practiced what he had preached throughout his life. In the Gospel of Mark, for instance, he tells his disciples, "...whoever wants to become great among you must be your servant, and whoever wants to be first must be slave of all. For even the Son of Man did not come to be served, but to serve, and to give his life as a ransom for many."[315] In the Gospel of Matthew, he teaches the same disciples, "...whoever takes the lowly position of this child is the greatest in the kingdom of heaven."[316] In the Gospel of Luke, Jesus twice asserts that "all those who exalt themselves will be humbled, and those who humble themselves will be exalted."[317] The ultimate humility was accepting his bloody scourging, the taunts, the paralysis of his hands once the nerves were severed in being nailed to the cross, and his slow suffocation and organ failure, all of which he presumably could have thwarted.

Jesus was no pushover, though. His actions in the temple tell us that. His words of frustration to his mother and his followers at various times tell us that he had a very good sense of who he was and what his destiny was. Jesus wanted to act in accordance with the desire of God. In Jesus' view, one of the most important desires of God was that humans should treat each other with love. Love was more important than power. Love was how to approach God. Love meant checking one's pride and ego at the door and meeting people where they were, and Jesus did that. Out of love, Jesus taught even when he understood that people would not understand what he was saying. For anyone who believes that humility is weak and powerless, it's worth noting that this humble man today has more followers around the world and has influenced more lives than the rock stars, athletes, and Kardashians of the world combined.

THE BENEFITS OF HUMILITY

Forget just for a moment about what *you* want to obtain for *yourself.* Instead, consider for a moment whether it is likely that you are going to live in the world completely by yourself. If that's unlikely—and for most of us it *is* unlikely—then think about what kind of society you want to live in. Do you want to live in a society where each is trying to grab what he or she can, backstabbing others along the way (which means that you will be in constant danger of being backstabbed, even as you plot whom you will backstab next), or do you want to live in one in which others are actively trying to help you succeed? Helpfulness is one of the important "so whats" of humility. Researchers Jordan LaBouff and others published the results of three studies in early 2012, asserting that "Humble persons are more helpful than less humble persons," defining humility as "low self-focus and an accurate view of self."[318] By focusing less on ourselves and our endless desires, we open ourselves up to the world of others and their experiences, their joys and pains. We have the opportunity to develop empathy. We can see that there is value in doing for and with others, not just in using others.

Think for a moment about a model of ego and lack of humility: Donald Trump. In his book *Think Big and Kick Ass*, Trump devotes an entire chapter to revenge. He promotes the idea of vengeance in the chapter, presenting it as practically necessary. People are out to get you, he asserts, and you have to "fight back and kick their ass." Revenge, Trump seems to say, is the best medicine. Would you want to be on the receiving end of that kind of revenge, though? In Trump's worldview, Trump prospers. You're either with him, helping him to prosper, or you're against him. There are winners and losers in his view, and the winners are those who measure up to his idea of what they should be, while the losers deserve to lose. However, it's not as if he has never lost. When Trump Airlines went south, he defaulted on his loans, and creditors took over the airline.[319] Trump Entertainment Resorts filed for bankruptcy three times.[320] Trump Mortgage closed after a mere eighteen months in business, in part because of bad leadership hiring decisions.[321] Who paid the price for such hubris? And then, despite such bluster and bravado, Trump became president of the United States, in part because voters were impressed by and appreciated the bluster, as though it would not hurt them.

In contrast to massive ego and its pitfalls, humility translates into business success as well as personal success. Bestselling business author Jim Collins writes that "The most powerfully transformative executives possess a paradoxical mixture of personal humility and professional will." Collins calls such executives "Level 5 leaders" and argues that a research study performed over a five-year period shows that these Level 5 leaders have the capacity to turn business around and to make them great. He uses the example of Darwin Smith, who became CEO of Kimberly-Clark and turned the paper company into the biggest in the world. Smith was far from a weak pushover. According to Collins, he was "fierce" and had an "iron will" that was coupled with his humility. The company wasn't about him; his decisions weren't based on his own ego. Collins notes this trait in all the Level 5 leaders the group studied they would praise the company, and praise their colleagues, but would not focus on their own role. Consistently, they brought their ventures to successes.[322]

Collins' observations dovetail with the 2,500-year-old observations of Lao Zi in the *Dao De Jing*. "Can you love people and lead them without imposing your will?" the philosopher asked.[323] "All streams flow to the sea because it is lower than they are. Humility gives it its power. If you want to govern the people, you must place yourself below them. If you want to lead the people, you must learn how to follow them."[324] Lao Zi seems to advocate here what is known today as servant leadership, one aspect of which is humility. Researchers defined the humility of servant leadership as "the ability to put one's own accomplishments and talents in a proper perspective…daring to admit that one is not infallible and does make mistakes…[and] a proper understanding of one's strong and weak points."[325] Lao Zi further reminds us that moderation is the key, and moderation goes hand in hand with humility: "He who stands on tiptoe doesn't stand firm," he admonishes. "He who tries to shine dims his own light…He who clings to his work will create nothing that endures."[326] In other words, according to Collins and Lao Zi, it's not the Trumps of the world who are destined to do the truly great things that will benefit employees, shareholders, communities, and citizens. Rather, those with a measure of humility will.

Further, humility benefits our dealings with family, friends, and coworkers. Psychological research indicates that if we have the trait of humility, we have better relationships. For example, if we have humility, we are patient. We are less apt to try to control others. We show more empathy and compassion. Researchers have noticed that in economic games and in bargaining games, people with humility cooperated with others; they tried to help. When things go wrong, the humble person is more likely to forgive others.[327] When we have humility, we work harder at making our personal and professional relationships work. We care about the outcome because we care about the other person. Caring about others meshes with compassion. It meshes with generosity. Caring is a form of generosity.

To understand the benefits that humility can have on our relationships is important because at present we live in a culture in which bullying and intolerance seem to be on the rise. The Centers for Disease Control, Yale University, and the British group Charity Beatbullying have all published statistics showing a correlation between bullying and suicide. Thousands of young people commit suicide each year, and 157,000 young people each year in the United States are treated in hospitals as a result of attempts to harm or kill themselves.[328] Bullying is the antithesis of humility. It is rooted in arrogance and indifference and an attempt to feel powerful. Internet trolls and bullies tell bullied and depressed teens that the world would be better off without them and that they should kill themselves, and often enough the teens do exactly that. If we care about the lives and mental health of our youth, we should care deeply about humility, one feature of which is a "suppression of arrogance."[329]

All we have to do to see the abundance of arrogance in the world is to scroll through any online newspaper and read through the comments readers leave. Every day I feel shocked by some of the arrogant vitriol that people express toward people they do not even know. The Internet tempts us all to think we are "experts" in everything. To judge by the comments, many of the commenters see themselves as "experts" in psychology, sociology, police work, forensics, and so on. They find strangers guilty and proclaim that they should be killed, castrated, locked up in dungeons for life, and more. They judge and mock with frightening ease.

It's easy to shrug off such comments and assume that they are from "trolls" and that they have nothing to do with us or our lives. We might convince ourselves such comments are meaningless. It might even be easy to overlook the bullying, although the more compassion we cultivate, the harder the bullying becomes to ignore.

Humility might not seem that big of a deal in the modern world. It might seem old-fashioned. However, humility can improve more than just our workplaces and relationships. It can improve our health. Specifically, a lack of it in the medical profession can have dire consequences.

That's problematic, because the medical profession is not always humble. In his article "A Gentle and Humane Temper: Humility in Medicine," Dr. Jack Coulehan tells readers that as early as 1906, humility was already seen by doctors as a weakness in their profession. The words of Dr. William Osler that year are assumed to have fallen on mostly deaf ears of students at the University of Minnesota: "In these days of aggressive self-assertion, when the stress of competition is so keen and the desire to make the most of

oneself so universal, it may seem a little old-fashioned to preach
the necessity of humility, but I insist . . . that a due humility should
take the place of honor on your list [of virtues]" he said.[330] Dr.
Harvey Chochinov wrote of the hard work required to cultivate
humility and pointed out the importance of cultivating it. In his
view, humility allows patients to feel heard and seen by their
medical caretakers. It encourages providers not to rush toward
decision making. For any patient who thinks that ego in a medical
professional shows knowledge and competence, Chochinov points
out that "Humility, in fact, is a key driver that commits physicians
to the continuous pursuit of knowledge. In other words, too much
arrogance can prevent doctors from knowing as much as they
otherwise could."[331] In short, humility in medical professionals
provides both more satisfaction and better outcomes for patients.

Humility is like a seasoning that enables the flavors of other
virtues, such as effort, generosity, and truth telling, to develop to
their fullest complexity. The Kipsigis ethnic group of Kenya has
a proverb: *menemugei chi met*, which means "One cannot shave
one's own hair."[332] It's an admonition that we are not all-powerful.
We have limits. The Qur'an reminds believers to "Invoke your Lord
with humility"[333] and that the faithful "are those who walk on the
earth with humility and sedateness, and when the foolish address
them, they reply back with mild words of gentleness."[334] There is
a story of the great Sufi poet Rumi displaying great humility to
a priest who had come to see him. As many times as the priest
prostrated himself to Rumi, Rumi repeated the gesture to the
priest. The gesture wasn't empty. Rather, it helped Rumi recognize
what he and others had it common, and that being learned or
accomplished did not make one person better than another.

I have heard that when the Dalai Lama seats himself on his
throne, he takes a moment to remind himself that in the presence

of others, each of us including him is the lowest of all. Reminding himself of that helps him to vanquish ego, His Holiness has said. Of all the virtues that the world's scriptures urge us toward, perhaps humility is the most difficult. Effort, acknowledgement and truth let us see ourselves clearly. Generosity, mindfulness and compassion allow us to place ourselves below others. We can cultivate humility in small steps. We can work to listen more closely and respectfully; we can be less defensive; we can praise others frequently and honestly; we can think about what the needs of others are and how to serve those needs, whether in our families or communities. When we are humble, we are no longer the little gods that we so often like to be, and as a result we have more potential for empathy, kindness, and clear-sightedness.

So What?

Effort. Compassion. Generosity. Acknowledgement. Order.
Truth. Mindfulness. Humility. If we look around ourselves
and listen to others, we might think that these practices are
anachronistic. We might think that such practices are foolish, no
longer suited to the highly competitive world in which we live.
We might try to convince ourselves that they belong to a "less
liberated" time.

Certainly, many people today live in cultures that celebrate
the individual. "What's good for me" can become the driving
force for many of the decisions a person in an individualistic
culture makes, regardless of the wider repercussions. In American
society, for example, the word "morality," which suggests
social obligation, sometimes seems to have become obsolete. It's
worthwhile for a moment to define that word, because morality
can be conceptualized in two different yet potentially related ways.
One way is to refer to the rules of conduct that a group, such as
a culture or society, presents. The other is the definition in which
all reasonable people under certain conditions would agree that
there are certain ways to act. That definition seems to suggest that
there is or should be a code about certain conduct that applies to
all humans.

We can easily understand that some behaviors are culturally
specific. For example, in some cultures people greet each other by
shaking hands. In other cultures, people may greet each other by
kissing cheeks. In yet other cultures, people may greet each other
with no physical touching whatsoever. Other behaviors, though,
would seem to transcend cultures. Reasonable people should be
able to agree, for example, that under normal circumstances it is
immoral for humans to kill or torture other humans. It is immoral

to steal from each other. It is immoral to perpetrate sexual acts on young children. It is immoral to enslave others.

Right now, though, thinking about what is right and wrong seems to have entered a nebulous zone. There is often a sense that anything goes. Cheating is on the rise, and many openly embrace it. They may believe, as one told me, that "winning is the only important thing." In this context, "winning" seems to mean getting what one wants, whether that's a college degree, a job, a sports trophy, a sexual partner, material goods, or other trappings of Western society. People often suggest that there is no universal right or wrong. Rightness or wrongness is up to each individual, they suggest, and as an educator, I've heard that many times. It's as if we have decided as a culture that lack of judgment is a complete virtue. "I wouldn't do X myself," I often hear, "but it's not up to me to say whether someone else should or shouldn't."

Push that thinking, though, and it becomes clear how empty it is as an intellectual exercise. "So," I tell people, "you wouldn't burn down my house, but if you paint your house a color that I don't like, then you wouldn't judge me if I burn down your house, right?" Protests to that idea tend to be immediate and loud. They would be equally loud if a person arrested for DWI were to say, "I've always had a drinking problem. I couldn't help it when I got into my car after drinking six beers. Please forgive me for mowing down and paralyzing your little sister instead of prosecuting me." Suddenly people would have little trouble in passing judgment.

It may be time to question whether "what I want" is really what's best for society. In an op-ed piece for the *New York Times*, David Brooks wrote, "In most times and in most places, the group was seen to be the essential moral unit. A shared religion defined rules and practices. Cultures structured people's imaginations and imposed moral disciplines. Now more people are led to assume that the free-floating individual is the essential moral unit. Morality was once revealed, inherited and shared, but now it's thought of as something that emerges in the privacy of your own heart."[335] The problem is that it doesn't just emerge. It must be cultivated. It doesn't have to be cultivated by belonging to a religion, although that can be one way amongst many to cultivate it. It does, however, need to be cultivated by thought and by the realization that the values are shared for a common reason.

To return to the beginning of this book, we can see a corollary in the world of elephants, which live in very organized societies. Perhaps one of the central concerns of the elephant herd is protection of young elephants. Protecting the young is an element of elephant "morality." The protective behavior is modeled throughout the herd; the behavior is the norm. It would be absurd to think that some elephants would act to protect the young, but that other elephants would not; in elephant herds, there is not such concept as "Protecting calves is right for that elephant, but not for me. I don't have a calf right now, so it really isn't my concern. I don't care if the other elephants don't like my attitude." Rather, elephants protect calves because protecting calves is right. Protecting calves is an outgrowth of elephants' social nature, and doing it helps to ensure the continuation of their society. In fact, many of the females in an elephant herd are related.

Granted, humans are not elephants, but there are benefits for humans to adopt similar approaches. In a world that is seeing shocking violence and intolerance in many places and over many issues, it may be socially beneficial to decide that some actions are universally beneficial and are "shoulds" that apply to us and others. If the concepts of rightness and wrongness seem obsolete, and if the trend is to think that religion is the root of all evil, then the predictable response to the ideas in this book is to dismiss them. On reflection, however, there are compelling reasons not to dismiss all the concepts presented here.

First, atheism is not a reason to dismiss them. As discussed earlier, the idea of the Infinite does not necessarily mean the idea of a creator God. One does not need to believe in a deity to believe that aspects such as truth or generosity are behaviors that are generally beneficial to humankind. Evidence exists that they are beneficial: trust based on truth enables our relationships, our health care, our successful investment, and more. Generosity enables us to care for the vulnerable members of our society, even in our own families. Generosity prompts us to care for aging parents, for example. Generosity gives people the benefit of the doubt. Rather than believing in God, one can choose to believe in a universal morality.

Second, the subjectivity of religious experience is not a reason to dismiss them. The behaviors outlined in the book – truth telling, effort, forgiveness, compassion – aren't rooted in just one religion, and they all go far beyond religion. A person doesn't need to believe in a particular religion to be compassionate to others. A person doesn't need to believe in a particular religion to forgive transgressions or to make effort to do or say the right thing. These values and behaviors are based not on "the word of God" but on evidence. They are consistent across moral systems.

Third, the idea that these values and behaviors come from faith-based systems is not a reason to dismiss them. For one, faith does not play an equal role in religions. Some religions are based in faith, while others are based in analysis and logic. Faith simply refers to a sense of certitude, and it is not necessarily incompatible with evidence and logic. One doesn't have to believe in God to have faith; disbelief in God is faith, too. Faith is part of the secular world. If I am a lawyer, for example, and I interview twenty eyewitnesses who corroborate my client's version of events, it is reasonable for me to have the opinion that my client is telling the truth. Another might call that having "faith" in my client's version of events. I cannot have perfect knowledge, because I cannot be inside my client's head. I am not omniscient. Therefore, I believe in what the evidence indicates. To trust in verifiable evidence is a cornerstone of the widely accepted scientific method.

Fourth, the idea that religious texts are simply hearsay, as Thomas Paine posited in *Age of Reason*, is not a reason to dismiss them. If we are not obliged to believe hearsay simply because the information is not told directly to us, as Paine argues, then we have no basis for a legal system; we would not be obliged to believe the testimony of witnesses to whom defendants or plaintiffs entrusted information. That various religions may have used their own texts to attack the ideas of other religions is not our problem. That long and sorry history is a given and doesn't concern us, because our focus is where they agree, not where they disagree.

For that matter, even Paine asserted that "religious duties consist in doing justice, loving mercy, and endeavoring to make our fellow-creatures happy." For those who find the word "religious" problematic, replacing it with "social" or "moral" might be more palatable. In Buddhism's *Precious Garland Sutra*, the great philosopher Nagarjuna put it even more specifically. "Those who realize what benefit self and others and always perform these are wise," he wrote. His next words are similar to the ideas in the Ten Commandments: "Not killing, not stealing, forsaking the mates of others, refraining completely from false, divisive, harsh and senseless speech, thoroughly forsaking covetousness, harmful intent, and the views of Nihilists, these are the ten gleaming paths of action; their opposites are dark. Not drinking intoxicants, a good livelihood, non-harming, respectful giving, honoring the

honorable, and love—practice in brief is that."[336] There is right
and wrong, Nagarjuna tells us. There is good and not-good, and
we should not be afraid to acknowledge them and to assert which
is which. Believing in the idea of good does not make us weak
or idiotic. It makes us noble. It makes us fully human, capable of
deciphering right from wrong. To give, to love, to be honest, to
strive. Such actions have both honor and power.

The power is transformative. For example, in 2016,
approximately 815 million people went hungry. Because of
malnourishment, approximately 155 million children are stunted.[337]
Those numbers are staggering, and they are reducible through
generosity and compassion. It is easy, in times of economic
contraction, to think, "I can't afford to do for others." For some
who may be suffering with unemployment and loss of a home and
who may be supplementing their own diets with food banks and
food stamps, that thinking may well be true. However, others
have seen just a contraction in their wealth. That contraction may
be expressed through less consumer spending, fewer vacations,
and the like. Those with means, even with contracted means, can
still create real change for those who may be living in poverty in
the world. Might that effort create material discomfort for the
giver? Yes, and that is where effort is necessary. To make such an
effort, the giver must believe that there is a compelling reason and
that the giving serves a greater good. If any of us can experience
suffering—and we all do because we are human—then why would
we not do what we can to help ease the suffering of others? There is
something profoundly cruel and nihilistic about thinking, "Because
I suffer sometimes, you should suffer, too. I don't care about
your suffering." Transformation comes when we can say, "Some
suffering is curable, and I can help to cure your suffering. Perhaps
the cure is temporary, or perhaps the cure is permanent, but I can

help to lift you up off that bottom rung of Maslow's pyramid."
That is true morality.

What we can do: we can start by questioning our own
prejudices and inactions. Why do we have suspicions against
others? Why do we judge? What keeps us from acting more
beneficially in our homes and in the world? Do we suffer from
addictions? What is the root of our unhappiness?

Then we can act. Perhaps we can volunteer to help support
peace and justice. Perhaps we can join a grass roots organization.
Perhaps we can open communication in our homes and have hard
but necessary conversations to clear the air. Perhaps we can mend
or at least apologize for our part in broken friendships or work
relationships. Perhaps we can commit to being merciful in thought
and action to strangers.

We all have our arguments against such courses of action.
My mother, for instance, was a firm believer that members of our
family should be told what they wanted to know, not necessarily
the truth. Sometimes she tried to make us lie to our grandparents
or each other. I could argue that her disregard for the truth was
well-intentioned because she said that she wanted to spare people
immediate pain. In hindsight, though, most of us would have
preferred the immediate short-term pain to the web of lies that
sometimes developed and almost always eventually exposed. Worse
was the climate of distrust that all the lies created. Her lack of care
for the truth has caused me suffering that I will carry throughout
the rest of my life.

The question is whether we are sure that what we see is all
there is and that our own selves are all that matter. To touch the
elephant, from the title of the book, means to radically shift our
thinking to consider what we don't know and don't see and to think
about how we fit into that previously unimagined picture. Until we

can do that, we will be stuck in our conditioned reality, living our lives on cruise control as though we have forgotten that we even have a brake and accelerator, peering at life through the small view of a periscope and thinking that we are viewing a complete horizon as well as the entire vastness of the ocean.

In the smallest day-to-day situations, we can make unwise decisions based on what we don't perceive. I was reminded of this as I contemplated surgery for my daughter's geriatric dog. The dog had a fatty tumor, which I discovered when she fell while running up the stairs, landing headfirst on the porch. Within days of the discovery, she was limping profoundly. I took her to our regular vet, who suggested surgery. I scheduled the surgery date, the idea of doing the surgery worried me. Would it just make her suffer more? At the last minute, I scheduled her for a second opinion. The doctor examined her carefully, listened to the story, and then suggested that when she fell on her head, she probably had injured her neck.

I wanted to believe that, so I brought the dog home and waited for her to get better. Meanwhile, the tumor kept growing. The limping grew worse. Her energy declined. She was obviously uncomfortable. I kept waiting for the neck injury to resolve.

Finally, several months later, I took her for surgery as a last-ditch effort. The doctors successfully removed a tumor the size of a baseball. Within two weeks the dog was racing around again, and she continued to race around until she died over a year later. The point is that I didn't see the whole picture and whole dog. First, I saw the tumor, which frightened me. Then I imagined a neck injury and had faith in it because the tumor frightened me. In the end, I had to be willing to see the whole picture, to face my fears, and to trust that decisive action was the right action despite the risks.

If I was so conditioned to avoid doing what was right for the dog because of my own fears, imagine then how conditioned someone may be who believes in an authoritative God, or someone who believes in a cruel God, or someone who has a lot of energy and is invested in believing that religion is just all rubbish. The tendency may be to reject certain ideals simply because they come from religion. It may prove difficult if not impossible to see past one's own anxieties, anger, smugness, and so on, to ask the very important question, "Why do all of the world's religions stress *these* particular ideas? What is the value of *these* behaviors? Why are they important? Is there something more than just ourselves for which to strive, and if there is, what might that be?"

It's not my intent in this book to try to convince anyone to go out and join a religion. It's not my intent to try to convince anyone to believe in God. Faith or the lack of it is a personal matter. What is more than a personal matter is how we choose to live and how we choose to treat each other. Geologists and Eastern religions alike agree: actions have consequences. So do the lack of actions. What people choose to consume and to discard and to value, for example, will affect the lives of those they will never meet, thousands of miles away. We may not stop to think, perhaps, that when we throw away our electronic devices they may end up in an African country where workers will scavenge metals from the equipment, all the while breathing in toxic fumes from an unregulated recycling process. To touch the elephant means to see that big picture and then to see even the bigger picture. It means to see ourselves as agents of change, creators of action both good and bad, and to consciously and mindfully try to do good through understanding the interconnectedness of beings. It means caring about more than our own immediate gratification.

Does that mean we are part of the elephant? Yes. Through such kinds of right action, we are more than just part of the big picture. We are part of the Infinite.

I'm reminded of the parable that Rudyard Kipling tells in the story *Kim*. In it, an ancient lama tells the story of an elephant who escaped captivity. However, he could not remove a leg-iron fastened on him that caused him agony. Other elephants tried to help remove it, but they couldn't, and the elephant continued to suffer.

One day, however, he came upon a newly-born elephant calf that was orphaned when its mother died giving birth. The elephant immediately thought to help the calf. He stood over it, protecting it, and convinced an elephant cow to give milk to the infant. For the next thirty-five years, the elephant protected, befriended and guided the growing and then young adult calf. For all that time, he suffered bitterly from the constricting leg-iron that buried itself further and further into his leg.

Kipling writes, "Then one day the young elephant saw the half-buried iron, and turning to the elder said: "What is this?" "It is even my sorrow," said he who had befriended him. Then that other put out his trunk and in the twinkling of an eyelash abolished the ring, saying: "The appointed time has come." So the virtuous elephant who had waited temperately and done kind acts was relieved, at the appointed time, by the very calf whom he had turned aside to cherish...for the Elephant was Ananda, and the Calf that broke the ring was none other than The Lord Himself."[338]

We can break the rings that fetter ourselves and that fetter others. For all the historic squabbling amongst the world's religions, they can give us the tools to break those irons, all the more ironic as the religions continue to create and to struggle to break their own entrapments. We have the potential to see our precious human existence for what it is, an opportunity to transcend our baser "animal nature" and to fully integrate ourselves in the sphere of the Infinite and the sacred, not just through our hopes and dreams, but through our actions and arduous work. Those who believe in the Judeo-Christian God can fulfill the promise that we are made in God's image. Those who believe in no God can simply work marvels of all sizes. "Our faith is contraried in diverse manners by our own blindness," Dame Julian of Norwich wrote in her *Revelations of Divine Love*, and our faith or lack of it need not be particularly religious. It may be simply our lack of faith or opinion that there is any compelling reason to do what is right. Indeed, we may even lack faith or opinion that there is anything inherently right to do. To touch the elephant means to step out of our blindness into full self-actualization. It means to step from the mundane into the sublime, beyond the double rainbow, and beyond ourselves into a world of infinite possibilities and the potential for infinite good, carried on the back of magnificent wisdom.

Epilogue: Rebuilding the World

"What can I do?"

Like so many people, like so many readers, I ponder this question every day. In the summer of 2018, immigrants in detention wrote a desperate letter to Americans, begging for help in reuniting their families. How do I help them? What can I do? In Holocaust class, students and I talk about the laws that allowed millions to be marked for murder and ponder what our response would be to laws that would target vulnerable populations in our own country: what would we do? I think about the scenes I've witnessed in everyday life, a person screaming at and threatening a child, a person being rough with an animal, that I have turned away from, frozen in confusion about what to do.

What can we do? What should we do?

Acknowledging that the world's religions share values that can help us live together happily, peaceably, healthily, is a start, but not enough. We must act.

This isn't a self-help book. I cannot tell you, "Do this, and here's how. By doing it, life will magically become awesome." Life will still be a struggle. There's no magic pill and no magic book that will suddenly and easily make life, as Mary Poppins might say, supercalifragilisticexpialidocious.

Instead, I will offer ten questions, three stories, and some suggestions. They are a starting point. They can be related to the Jewish idea of *tikkun olam*: that the world is broken, and that it is our responsibility to fix it. I can only urge you to accept that responsibility and to find what you can do. We are limited only by our imaginations. We do not have to sit by helplessly, feeling emotionally numb to the daily news, awash in hopeless thinking or, worse, ennui. We can be transformers in our homes, our families, and our communities.

TEN QUESTIONS

1. If you were to think in a different way about the effort that you could make to improve your life, the lives of others, or to develop true wisdom, what might you think?
2. Whom do you see as less important than yourself, and what causes that belief?
3. What do you think are the obstacles to compassion in your life and in the world?
4. If you are not as generous as you could be, what stifles your generosity? What fears and resentments keep you from being more generous?
5. What rules do you believe you are meant to live by? Why do you believe you must follow those rules?
6. What keeps you from a sense of peace and happiness, and what is just one thing you could change for the better by acknowledging something or someone other than yourself?
7. Why do you trust what you "know? In what ways do you resist the truth, and why do you resist it?
8. What are three things you could say or do to bring more honesty into your life?
9. What methods do you regularly use to distract yourself throughout the day, and what techniques can you incorporate into your life to become more mindful?
10. Why don't you think others measure up to you, and how might practicing more humility in your life benefit you and those around you?

THREE EXAMPLES

One: Mindfulness, Generosity, Forgiveness

After the Wild Boars soccer team and their coach were rescued from the Thang Luang Nam Non cave in Thailand, they were taken to hospital, where they remained for over a week. During that time, details of their survival came to light. Their coach, Ekapol Chantawong, was credited with helping the boys survive. He gave them his own food so that they would have nourishment, but perhaps most importantly, he guided them in meditation. His guidance helped them regulate their breathing and helped them to keep themselves calm and still. Calmness and stillness meant that they expended less energy and used less oxygen than they might have otherwise.

The parents of the boys rallied around Chantawong. The parents of one of the boys sent him a letter stating, "thank you for taking care of the boys and for helping them stay safe in the dark."[339] Additionally, Thailand is considering given the coach and three of the boys, all four of whom are refugees, citizenship. [340]

Two: Effort and Truth

On June 30, 2018, tens of thousands of people across the United States assembled and marched in the "Families Belong Together" protest against the separation of immigrant parents and children. In Washington D.C., where approximately 30,000 people gathered, one stood out: a twelve-year-old girl named Leah. She stepped up to the microphone and told her story of her fear of being separated from her mother, her constant anxiety that she might come home to find that ICE had taken her mother away, of her inability to be a twelve-year-old with normal twelve-year-old concerns.

"This is evil," she said of family separations. "It needs to stop. It makes me sad to know that children can't be with their parents. I don't understand why they're being so mean to us children. Don't they know how much we love our family? Don't they have a family too? Why don't they care about us children?"

"I live with the constant fear of losing my mom to deportation," she continued. "My mom is strong, beautiful, and brave. She is also a person who taught me how to speak up when I see things that aren't fair."[341] She wept as she spoke; her desolation was palpable. Her nerves must have been stretched in front of all those people. Through her tears, through her anguish and clear suffering, her strength shone and went viral.

Three: Compassion and Humility

When *Reader's Digest* solicited stories from readers about how compassion touched their lives, the magazine compiled two dozen anecdotes. One, from Stacey Lee, told Lee's story of wanting to buy a dress in a second-hand shop for her granddaughter. Lee didn't have money to pay for the dress and asked the shopkeeper if the dress could be held until she had the funds, but a stranger overheard the conversation and insisted on buying the dress for her, over Lee's protests.

The woman who bought the dress related that she had been homeless once, and that she had survived thanks to the generosity and compassion of strangers. Now her life had improved, and she was committed to helping others.[342] She was able to have true empathy for Lee and to act, not out of pity, but out of recognition for the struggles each of us may face at any time in our lives.

SUGGESTIONS

Not one of the above examples is going to thwart nuclear war. None is going to avert a terrorist attack. None is going to stop violent crime.

However, each helps rebuild the world in a more compassionate, more community-oriented, more "thou" focused rather than "me" focused way. Each is, to paraphrase Neil Armstrong, "one small step" for a person, yet "one giant leap" for society in imagining harmony and happiness.

As you ask, "What can I do?" ponder the questions. Your own answer to the question might be as simple as writing a letter to a politician. It might be to write a letter of forgiveness to someone who has wronged you. It might be to write a letter of apology to someone you have wronged. Perhaps you will decide to donate time or money to benefiting the life of another. Perhaps you will donate a kidney or a piece of your liver to someone who will die without the organs. Perhaps instead of despising a homeless person, you'll buy the person lunch. Perhaps you will acknowledge that your prejudices are harming others and limiting you. Perhaps you will try to get to know someone of a different ethnicity or social class. Perhaps you will acknowledge your anger and go to therapy to learn to deal with it. Perhaps you will let go of a grudge. Perhaps you will take a class at a community college and further your education. Perhaps you will listen deeply to your own inner voice or to someone with whom you interact. Perhaps because of listening you will heal a relationship with yourself or others. Perhaps you will run for government, or join a board, or fix a bike for a kid or adult who needs one.

Perhaps, if you despise religion, you may even find a grudging respect for the wisdom of the world's cultures that sees the worst in our species, and calls us to struggle against our baseness and strive instead for the best we can be. Hatreds, war, violence, and aggression are cancers that devour our societies and devour us. We have the power to cure ourselves. Doing so kindles the spark of the Divine, however we imagine that, in each of us.

NOTES

1   Haberman, Clyde. "This Is Not a Drill: The Threat of Nuclear
     Annihilation." *The New York Times.* 13 May 2018. https://www.nytimes.
     com/2018/05/13/us/nuclear-threat-retro-report.html

2   Durkheim, Emile. *The Elementary Forms of the Religious Life.* London:
     The Free Press, 1915. https://archive.org/details/elementaryformso00durk

3   Krug, Etienne G. et al. "World Report on Violence and Health." *World
     Health Organization.* 2002. https://www.who.int/violence_injury_
     prevention/violence/world_report/en/introduction.pdf

4   "N.J. High School Player Sues Coach for Telling Him to Slide." *Coach and
     A.D.* 3 May 2018.

5   McPherson, Angie. "Visit the Ten Happiest Countries in the World."
     National Geographic Travel. 12 Aug. 2016.

6   "Archeologists Dig Up 'Oldest' Human Sacrifice." *Sudan Tribune*, February
     16, 2008. http://www.sudantribune.com/spip.php?article25984

7   Centers for Disease Control and Prevention, "Assault or Homicide,"
     National Center for Health Statistics, http://www.cdc.gov/nchs/fastats/
     homicide.htm.

8   "Rohingya crisis: U.N. rights chief 'cannot rule out genocide." *BBC.* 5
     December 2017. https://www.bbc.com/news/world-asia-42234469

9   Burton, Tara. "Study Theology, Even if You Don't Believe In God." *The
     Atlantic.* 30 October 2013.

10   "Most Important Problem." *Gallup*, April 2017. http://www.gallup.com/
     poll/1675/most-important-problem.aspx

11   "Wealth: having it all and wanting more." *Oxfam*, January, 2015. https://
     www.oxfam.org/en/research/wealth-having-it-all-and-wanting-more

12   Cohen, Patricia. "Fueled by Recession, U.S. Wealth Gap Is Highest in
     Decades, Study Finds." *New York Times*, December 17, 2014. http://www.
     nytimes.com/2014/12/18/business/economy/us-wealth-gap-widest-in-at-
     least-30-years-pew-study-says.html?_r=0

13   Hjelmgaard, Kim. "10 Greatest Threats Facing the World in 2014."
     USA Today, January 16, 2014. http://www.usatoday.com/story/news/
     world/2014/01/16/wef-biggest-risks-facing-world-2014/4505691

14   Volkow, Nora, M.D. "America's Addiction to Opioids: Heroin and
     Prescription Drug Abuse." *National Institute on Drug Abuse*, May 14,
     2014. http://www.drugabuse.gov/about-nida/legislative-activities/testimony-
     to-congress/2014/americas-addiction-to-opioids-heroin-prescription-drug-
     abuse

15 "Inside a Killer Drug Epidemic: A Look at America's Opioid Crisis." *The New York Times*, January 6, 2017. https://www.nytimes.com/2017/01/06/us/opioid-crisis-epidemic.html?_r=0

16 Curtin, Sally C. et al. "Increase in Suicide in the United States, 1999-2014" *Centers for Disease Control and Prevention* NCHS data brief no. 241, April 2016.

17 Izadi, Elahe. "Nearly a Third of U.S. Women Have Experienced Domestic Violence." *Washington Post*, September 8, 2014. http://www.washingtonpost.com/news/post-nation/wp/2014/09/08/nearly-a-third-of-u-s-women-have-experienced-domestic-violence

18 Werner, Kennett. "White supremacists committed most extremist killings in 2017, ADL says." 18 January 2018. *NBC News*. https://www.nbcnews.com/news/us-news/white-supremacists-committed-most-extremist-killings-2017-adl-says-n838896

19 Konnikova, Maria. "How Facebook Makes Us Unhappy." *The New Yorker*, September 10, 2013. http://www.newyorker.com/tech/elements/how-facebook-makes-us-unhappy

20 Buckels, Erin E, Paul D. Trapnell, and Delroy L. Paulhus. "Trolls Just Want to Have Fun." *Personality and Individual Differences* 67 (2014), 97-102.

21 Gen. 6:9.

22 Gen. 6:19.

23 Gen. 22:2.

24 Deut. 28:9.

25 Num. 13:32.

26 Ibid.

27 Ibid.

28 Vargas, Jose Antonio. "My Life as an Undocumented Immigrant." *New York Times*, June 22, 2011. http://www.nytimes.com/2011/06/26/magazine/my-life-as-an-undocumented-immigrant.html

29 The Upanishads, II, 23:1-2.

30 "For Those Who Make the Effort Realize God." *Forum for Hindu Awakening Inc*, 2009. http://www.forumforhinduawakening.org/understanding/stories/god-realization

31 *The Bhagavad Gita* 7.

32 *The Bhagavad Gita* 3.

33 *The Bhagavad Gita* 7.

34   Ibid.

35   Ibbotson, Sophie. "Jainism and the Legendary Delhi Bird Hospital."
      Wildlife Extra, https://timesofindia.indiatimes.com/city/gurgaon/Treated-
      and-set-free/articleshow/11866804.cms

36   Uttaradhyayana Sutra, 20:52.

37   Uttaradhyayana Sutra 27:30.

38   Huggler, Justin. "A Deadly Belief is Reborn: Beyond Life, Beyond Death."
      The Independent, August 4, 2005. http://www.independent.co.uk/news/
      world/asia/a-deadly-belief-is-reborn-beyond-life-beyond-death-303493.html

39   *Qur'an* 17:9.

40   *Qur'an* 17:19.

41   "Make the Right Effort." *HaqIslam*, January 8, 2010. http://haqislam.org/
      make-the-right-effort

42   Catalani, Ronault (Polo). "Moving Into Our Future." *Asian Reporter,* June
      20, 2011, 7.

43   "Wall Street in Crisis: A Perfect Storm Brewing." Labaton Sucharow's U.S.
      Financial Services Industry Survey. July 2013.

44   Wilson, Mark, Nickolas C. Smith, and Paul S. Holmes. "The Role of Effort
      in Influencing the Effect of Anxiety on Performance: Testing the Conflicting
      Predictions of Processing Efficiency Theory and the Conscious Processing
      Hypothesis." *British Journal Of Psychology* 98, no. 3 (2007): 411-428.

45   Heckert, Teresa M. et al. "Relations Among Student Effort, Perceived
      Class Difficulty Appropriateness, and Student Evaluations of Teaching: Is It
      Possible to "Buy" Better Evaluations Through Lenient Grading?" *College
      Student Journal* 40, no. 3 (2006): 588-596.

46   Singh, Simon. *Fermat's Enigma: The Epic Quest to Solve the World's
      Greatest Mathematical Problem*. NY: Anchor, 1998.

47   Von Drehle, David with Aryn Baker. "The Ebola Fighters: The Ones Who
      Answered the Call." *Time,* December 10, 2014. http://time.com/time-
      person-of-the-year-ebola-fighters/

48   "Ebola Virus Disease." Fact sheet N103. *World Health Organization*,
      September, 2014. http://www.who.int/mediacentre/factsheets/fs103/en/

49   Mayo Clinic Staff. "Exercise: 7 Benefits of Regular Physical Activity." *Mayo
      Clinic*, February 5, 2014. http://www.mayoclinic.org/healthy-living/fitness/
      in-depth/exercise/art-20048389

50   Mark 5:26.

51   Sutton, Chris. "Hysterectomy: A Historical Perspective." *Balliere's Clinical Obstetrics and Gynaecology*, Vol. 11, Issue 1, March, 1997. 1-22, https://www.sciencedirect.com/science/article/pii/S0950355297800478

52   Abbasi, Jennifer. "Fertile Gals Look and Sound More Attractive: Study." *Live Science*. December 12, 2012.

53   Mark 5:28.

54   Mark 5:27.

55   Mark 5:34.

56   John 8:5.

57   John 8:7.

58   Chumley, Cheryl. "Syrian Woman Accused of Adultery is Stoned to Death by Her Father." *The Washington Times*, October 23, 2014. http://www.washingtontimes.com/news/2014/oct/23/syrian-woman-accused-of-adultery-is-stoned-to-deat

59   USGS Earthquake Hazards Program. http://earthquake.usgs.gov

60   "God Signed Name in Tsunami, Claim Clerics." *Sydney Morning Herald*, January 10, 2005. http://www.smh.com.au/news/Asia-Tsunami/God-signed-name-in-tsunami-claim-clerics/2005/01/10/1105206024347.html

61   Haught, Nancy. "Oregon Islamic Academy Helps Out in Japan." *The Oregonian*, June 8, 2011. http://www.oregonlive.com/living/index.ssf/2011/06/religion_notebook_oregon_islam.html

62   *Qur'an* 24:22.

63   Beach, Alistair. "Coptic Christians Under Siege as Mob Attacks Cairo Cathedral." *The Independent*, April 8, 2013. http://www.independent.co.uk/news/world/africa/coptic-christians-under-siege-as-mob-attacks-cairo-cathedral-8563600.html

64   Muhaiyaddeen, M.R. Bawa. *The Islam and World Peace*, Part One. *Fellowship Press*, 2010. http://www.bmf.org/iswp/peace.html

65   *The Analects of Confucius* 15:23.

66   Lev. 19:18.

67   *The Dao De Jing* 7.

68   *The Bhagavad Gita* 5:18-19.

69   *The Mahabharata*, Book 13: Anusasana Parva, Part II, Sect. CXIII.

70   Streeter, Kurt. "Embracing the Love of Amma, the 'Hugging Saint.'" *Los Angeles Times*, June 18, 2010.

71 Noceda, Kristofer. "Embracing the World with Love." *The Oakland Tribune*, June 4, 2010. https://www.culteducation.com/group/814-amma/1661-embracing-the-world-with-loves.html

72 "About Amma: How She Began." *Amma.org* http://amma.org/about/how-she-began

73 Buchanan, Emily and Bhasker Solanki. "Gujarat's Astonishing Rise from Rubble of 2001 Quake." *BBC News*, January 29, 2011. http://www.bbc.com/news/world-south-asia-12309791

74 Velyanswami, Satguru Bodhinatha. "Waves of Distress." *Hinduism Today*, April/May/June 2005. http://www.hinduismtoday.com/modules/smartsection/item.php?com_mode=flat&com_order=1&itemid=1400

75 Udanavarga chapter. 5, verse 18.

76 Varma, C.B. "The Story of a Tigeress." *The Illustrated Jataka and Other Stories of the Buddha.* https://www.ancient-buddhist-texts.net/English-Texts/Garland-of-Birth-Stories/01-The-Story-of-the-Tigress.htm

77 *The Dhammapada* 14:183.

78 *The Dhammapada* 10:133.

79 Nhat Hanh, Thich. "You are the Flame at the Tip of the Candle." Letters from Thay, *Plum Village*, June 23, 2011. https://www.facebook.com/thichnhathanh/posts/171733896222749

80 H.H. The Fourteenth Dalai Lama of Tibet, Tenzin Gyatso. "Compassion and the Individual." *The Office of His Holiness the Dalai Lama.* http://www.dalailama.com/messages/compassion

81 Ibid.

82 Ibid.

83 Yangsi Rinpoche, *Practicing the Path*. Somerville, MA: Wisdom, 2003, 301.

84 Yangsi Rinpoche, *Practicing*, 302.

85 H.H. The Fourteenth Dalai Lama of Tibet, Tenzin Gyatso, *The Compassionate Life*. Somerville, MA: Wisdom, 2001, 23 and 31.

86 Mutoigo, Ida Kaastra. "My Journey to Banda Aceh." *CRCNA*, June 28, 2008, 7.

87 Ibid.

88 Hahn, Elisa. "Woman Saves Best Friend by Giving Her a Kidney." *King 5 News*, April 7, 2010. https://www.king5.com

89   Adams, Char. "Police Officer Saves Baby Girl Through Emergency Liver
      Transplant: 'We'll Forever Be Connected.'" *People*. 2 Jan. 2018. http://
      people.com/human-interest/police-officer-saves-baby-girl-liver-transplant

90   Spiegel, David. "Compassion is the Best Medicine." *New York Times*, June
      12, 1994. http://www.nytimes.com/1994/06/12/opinion/compassion-is-the-
      best-medicine.html

91   Hale-Spencer, Melissa. "Stories of Compassion and Collaboration are Told
      as Three Faiths Share Their Holy Days, Albany, NY." *Altamont Enterprise*,
      September 13, 2007, 14.

92   Ibid.

93   Martin, Sami K. "Patricia LeFranc, Acid Attack Victim: I'm a Monster."
      Christian Post Europe, April 3, 2012. http://www.christianpost.com/news/
      patrica-lefranc-acid-attack-victim-breaks-her-silence-im-a-monster-72581

94   Feldman, Megan. "The Heart of Darkness." *Spirit*, Southwest Airlines,
      November , 2012, 84-92.

95   Khamisa, Azim, "If Laughter is Best Medicine, I Need A Refill." *Azim
      Khamisa.com*, January, 2012. http://www.azimkhamisa.com/newsletter

96   "Azim Khamisa and Ples Felix (USA)." *The Forgiveness Project*. https://tkf.
      org

97   Gandhi, Mohandas. Interview, *Young India*, April 2, 1931. Reprinted in
      Collected Works of Mahatma Gandhi Online. Vol. 51. Sect 346, 302.
      http://www.gandhiserve.org/cwmg/VOL031.PDF

98   Niebuhr, Reinhold. *The Irony of American History*. Chicago: University of
      Chicago Press, 2008, 63.

99   Williams, Dan. "Hamas's Gaza Jubilation Proves Israel Is At
      Risk: Netanyahu." *Reuters*, December 9, 2012. http://www.
      reuters.com/article/2012/12/09/us-palestinians-hamas-netanyahu-
      idUSBRE8B806520121209

100   "No More Taking Sides." *On Being*, American Public Media, Transcript
      4939, November 29, 2012. https://onbeing.org/programs/robi-damelin-ali-
      abu-awwad-no-more-taking-sides

101   Luke 23:34.

102   McFadden, Robert D. and Angela Macropolis. "Wal-Mart Employee
      Trampled to Death." *New York Times*, November 28, 2008. http://www.
      nytimes.com/2008/11/29/business/29walmart.html

103   *Qur'an* 2:261-277.

104   Jami at-Tirmidhi 1961.

105 *Qur'an* 2: 264 and 2: 270.

106 "The World Bank In Yemen." *The World Bank.* March, 2017. http://www.worldbank.org/en/country/yemen/overview

107 Cambanis, Thanassis and Rebecca Collard. "How ISIS Runs a City," *Time.* 26 Feb. 2015. http://time.com/3720063/isis-government-raqqa-mosul/

108 Khalidi, Rashid."The Arab Spring." *The Nation*, March 21, 2011. http://www.thenation.com/article/158991/arab-spring

109 Bloomfield, Adrian. "Iran Man Pardoned from Acid in Eye Punishment at Last Second." *The Telegraph,* July 30, 2011. http://www.telegraph.co.uk/news/worldnews/middleeast/iran/8673778/Iran-man-pardoned-from-acid-in-eye-punishment-at-last-second.html

110 Deut. 24:12-13.

111 Deut. 24:14-15.

112 Deut. 24:19-21.

113 Deut. 24:22.

114 Gen. 4:3-4.

115 Lev. 1:14.

116 Gen. 4:13-14.

117 Gen. 4:15.

118 Lev. 25:8-16.

119 Hilkhot Matanot Aniyim 10:7-14.

120 Blau, Reuven and Mike Jaccarino. "Huge Crowd Attends Brooklyn Funeral of Murdered Schoolboy Leiby Kletsky." *NY Daily News*, July 13, 2011. http://www.nydailynews.com/new-york/huge-crowd-attends-brooklyn-funeral-murdered-schoolboy-leiby-kletzky-article-1.161742

121 Matthew 19:21

122 Luke 12:13-21.

123 Luke 7:36-50.

124 Ascher, Barbara Lazear. "On Compassion." http://barbaralazearascher.com/images/essays/compassion/oncompassion.pdf

125 Varma. "Silava Elephant." *The Illustrated Jataka.*

126 *The Dhammapada,* 8:108.

127 Mehta, Rohit. *The Call of the Upanishads.* Delhi: Motilal Banarsidass, 1970, 190.

128 Pierce, Charles P. "Sweet Charity: The Benefits of Giving Back." *O Magazine*, March, 2008. http://www.oprah.com/omagazine/The-Benefits-of-Giving-to-Charity

129 Jansen, Vincent and Minus van Baalen. "Altruism through Beard Chromodynamics." *Nature* (2006): 663-666.

130 Stelloh, Tim. "Yankees Fan Generosity is Returned, with $50,000 to Ease His Debt. *New York Times*, July 13, 2011. http://www.nytimes.com/2011/07/14/nyregion/sporting-goods-vendors-to-ease-yankees-fans-debts.html

131 Schwartz, Paula. "Linda Mussman, Claudia Bruce." *The New York Times*, July 22, 2011. http://www.nytimes.com/2011/07/24/fashion/weddings/linda-mussmann-claudia-bruce-weddings.html

132 Frank, Adam. "Life Gives Sight to a Chaotic Universe." *NPR*. 13.7: Cosmos & Culture, September 10, 2013. http://www.npr.org/blogs/13.7/2013/09/10/220988227/life-gives-sight-to-a-chaotic-universe

133 Stiles, Lori. "Early Human Hunters Had Fewer Meat-sharing Rituals." *University of Arizona*, August 18, 2009. https://uanews.arizona.edu/story/early-human-hunters-had-fewer-meat-sharing-rituals

134 Lange, Karen. "Tales from the Bog." *National Geographic*, September, 2007. https://wps.prenhall.com/wps/media/objects/12330/12626747/myanthropologylibrary/PDF/A_NG_23_Lange_522.pdf

135 Perry, Alex. "Killing for Kali." *Time*, July 22, 2002. http://content.time.com/time/magazine/article/0,9171,322673,00.html

136 Gen. 9:9.

137 Gen. 17:2-4.

138 Gen. 17:6-14.

139 Lev 14:2-26.

140 Deut. 24:1.

141 Lev. 18.

142 Lev. 20:14 and 25:46.

143 Exod. 20:2-3.

144 Deut. 6:5-13.

145 Deut. 6:13 and 28:9.

146 Lev. 19:16-18.

147   Harrington, Daniel. *Wisdom Texts from Qumran*. Oxford:Taylor & Francis, 2002, 73.

148   Exod. 20:13.

149   "Lectio Divina." *Mount Melleray Abbey*, July, 2011. http://www. mountmellerayabbey.org/index.php/about/page/lectio-divina

150   Psalm 102:1-8.

151   Norris, Kathleen. *The Cloister Walk*. NY: Penguin, 1996, 22.

152   Matthew 4:8; Luke 4:5-7.

153   Matthew 5:17.

154   Mark 1:40-45.

155   Rumi, Jalal al-Din. *The Essential Rumi*. Trans. Coleman Barks. NY: Harper One, 2004, 60.

156   Hafiz, *The Gift*, "Tired of Speaking Sweetly." Trans. Daniel Ladinsky. NY: Penguin, 1999, 187.

157   *Qur'an* 33:41-42.

158   *Qur'an* 50:16.

159   *Qur'an* 3:103.

160   *Qur'an* 3:131-132.

161   *The Analects of Confucius* 8.

162   *The Analects of Confucius* 13:3.

163   *Dao De Jing* 2.

164   *Dao De Jing* 8.

165   *Dao De Jing* 23.

166   *Dao De Jing* 16.

167   Vohs, K. D. , J. P. Redden, and R. Rahinel. "Physical Order Produces Healthy Choices, Generosity, and Conventionality, Whereas Disorder Produces Creativity." Psychological Science (2013). http://pss.sagepub.com/content/early/2013/08/01/0956797613480186

168   Gardner, Rod, Richard Fitzgerald, and Ilana Mushin. "The Underlying Orderliness in Turn-Taking: Examples from Australian Talk." *Australian Journal of Communication* 36, (3) (2009): 65-89.

169   "Imaging Method Reveals Remarkable "Architecture' of the Brain." *AAAS*, EurekaAlert, December 16, 1997. http://www.eurekalert.org/pub releases/1997-12/WI-IMRR-161297.php

170 *Adi Granth*, Japji Sahib 2:4.

171 Beck, Guy L. Ed. *Sacred Sound: Experiencing Music in World Religions*. Waterloo: Wilfrid Laurier University Press, 2006, 145.

172 *Adi Granth*, Japji Sahib 7: 31-32.

173 *Adi Granth*, Guru Arjan Dev, "Sukhmani," 262.

174 Elliott, Steve. "Sikh Soldiers Allowed to Serve, Retain Their Articles of Faith." *U.S. Army*, March 25, 2010. http://www.army.mil/article/36339/sikh-soldiers-allowed-to-serve-retain-their-articles-of-faith

175 Ibid.

176 Exod. 20:6; Deut. 5:10.

177 Job 1:21.

178 Job 2:10.

179 Job 5:8.

180 Job 9:4.

181 Job 23:5.

182 Job 28:28.

183 Job 40:9.

184 Job 42:2.

185 Job 42:3-5.

186 Hosea 1:8.

187 Hosea 2:20-21.

188 Amos 3:2.

189 Amos 6:21-24.

190 Micah 3:4.

191 Micah 5:5.

192 Micah 8:8.

193 Zechariah 9:14-15.

194 Zechariah 3:18-19.

195 *Dao De Jing* 25.

196 *Dao De Jing* 39.

197 *Dao De Jing* 21.

198   *Dao De Jing* 16.

199   Julian of Norwich. *Revelations of Divine Love,* ed. Grace Warrack. London: Methuen and Co., 1901, Chapter V, 27.

200   Ibid. 29.

201   Ibid. Chapter X, 47.

202   Ibid. 46.

203   *Dao De Jing* 70.

204   *Mahabharata*, Udyoga Parva, Sect. VII.

205   *The Bhagavad Gita* 18:55-65.

206   Psalms 91:2.

207   Psalms 118:8.

208   McVicker, Steve. "Billie Bob's (Mis) Fortune." *Houston Press*, February 10, 2000. http://www.houstonpress.com/2000-02-10/news/billie-bob-s-mis-fortune

209   Paul 4:7.

210   *Qur'an* 5:16.

211   Loeffert, Martha."The Power of Prayer." *American Jails,* 28, no. 2 (2014): 40-44.

212   "An Update on Thay's Health: 13 December." Plum Village, *Communaute Bouddhique Zen Village des Pruniers*, December 13, 2014. http://plumvillage.org/news/an-update-on-thays-health-13-december

213   "The Twelve Steps of Alcoholics Anonymous." *Alcoholics Anonymous General Service Office.* http://www.aa.org/assets/en_US/smf-121_en.pdf

214   Vanderburgh, Reid, M.A, personal interview, January 12, 2015.

215   Fiorentine, Robert. "After Drug Treatment: Are 12 Step Programs Effective in Maintaining Abstinence?" *The American Journal of Drug and Alcohol Abuse,* Vol 25, No. 1 (1999): 93-116.

216   Cronin, Blaise. "Collaboration in Art and in Science: Approaches to Attribution, Authorship, and Acknowledgment." *Information & Culture* 47, no. 1 (2012): 18-37.

217   Hussain, Feryad. "'Heart-talk:' Considering the Role of the Heart in Therapy as Evidenced in the Quran and Medical Research" *Journal Of Religion & Health* 52, no. 4 (2013): 1203-1210.

218   Wu, Cheng En. *Monkey,* trans. Arthur Waley. NY: Grove Press, 1943, 75.

219 Wu, *Monkey*, 74.

220 Wu, *Monkey*, 75.

221 Wu, *Monkey*, 76.

222 Mundaka Upanishad Chapter III Verse 6.

223 Taittiriya Upanishad Chapter I, section 11, Verse 1.

224 Maha Narayana Upanishad Verse 78.

225 *The Bhagavad Gita* 10:14.

226 *The Bhagavad Gita* 10:4.

227 *The Bhagavad Gita* 10:41.

228 Swami Venkatesananda, *Enlightened Living: A New Interpretive Translation of the Yoga Sutra of Maharishi Patanjali* (Chiltern Yoga Trust: South Africa, 2008), http://www.swamivenkatesananda.org/SiteFiles/books/Enlightened%20Living%20by%20Swami%20Venkatesananda.pdf

229 Yoga Sutra II.3.

230 Yoga Sutra I.42.

231 Yoga Sutra I.43.

232 *The Bhagavad Gita* 18:72.

233 *The Bhagavad Gita* 18:73.

234 *The Dhammapada* 6.

235 Ibid.

236 Ibid.

237 Gen. 26:1-10.

238 Gen. 27:1-29.

239 Psalms 33:4.

240 Deut. 32:4.

241 Allen, Douglas., ed. *The Philosophy of Mahatma Gandhi for the 21st Century.* NY:Lexington Books, 2008, 165.

242 Matt. 26:38.

243 Matt. 26:58-67.

244 Matt. 26:70.

245 Matt. 26:71.

246 Matt. 26:73-75.

247   Matt. 26:31-35.

248   John 4:24.

249   John 6:35-36.

250   John 6:60-64.

251   For information on Dharmakirti and conceptual illusion, the author refers to John D. Dunne's *Foundations of Dharmakirti's Philosophy.* MA: Wisdom Publications, 2004, 85-88.

252   John 1:17.

253   John 3:21.

254   John 8:32.

255   John 8:45.

256   John 14:6.

257   John 18:37-38.

258   July 24, 2011.

259   Shahidi, J. "Not Telling the Truth: Circumstances Leading to Concealment of Diagnosis and Prognosis from Cancer Patients." *European Journal Of Cancer Care* 19, no. 5 (2010): 589-593.

260   Guibert, Susan. "Study: Telling Fewer Lies Linked to Better Health and Relationships." *Notre Dame News,* August 4, 2012. http://news.nd.edu/news/32424-study-telling-fewer-lies-linked-to-better-health-relationships

261   Sommer, Jeff. "The Benefits of Telling the Ugly Truth." *New York Times,* May 1, 2011, BU4.

262   Harris, Sam. *Lying.* Cleveland: Four Elephants Press, 2013.

263   Rumi, *The Essential Rumi*, 109.

264   Eccles. 3.

265   Eccles. 3:13.

266   Eccles. 9:17-18.

267   Prov. 4:23

268   1 Kings 3:9.

269   1 Kings 3:13.

270   Num. 20:8.

271   Moore, Thomas. *Care of the Soul.* NY: Harper Perennial, 1992, 204.

272   Isaiah 5:12-13.

273 Shantideva, *Bodhicaryavatara* Ch V:1-3.

274 *The Dhammapada* 23.

275 iii. Sampajanna Pabba.

276 Vedananupassana.

277 Dunne, Dr. John. "Mindfulness: Authority, Translation and Practice." Kathmandu University Center for Buddhist Studies at Rangjung Yeshe Institute, 6th Annual Symposium on Buddhist Studies: "Buddhism Translated: Language, Transmission and Transformation," December 13, 2008.

278 Ashliman, D.L., ed. The Tortoise That Refused to Leave Home. " *The Jataka Tales.* http://www.pitt.edu/~dash/jataka.html.

279 Emerson, Ralph Waldo. *Nature,* Chapter. 1. http://www.emersoncentral.com/nature1.htm

280 *The Bhagavad Gita* 2:70-72.

281 *The Bhagavad Gita* 6:6-21.

282 *Dao De Jing* 16.

283 Ibid.

284 *Dao De Jing* 10.

285 *Dao De Jing* 76.

286 *Dao De Jing* 56.

287 John 15:1-12.

288 Romans 7:19-23.

289 Romans 12:3-8.

290 Romans 13:11-12.

291 Hafiz, "It Felt Love."

292 *Qur'an* 3:200.

293 Smalley, Susan et al. "Mindfulness and Attention Deficit Hyperactivity Disorder." *Journal of Clinical Psychology* 65.10 (2009): 1087-1098.

294 Zylowska, Lidia et al. "Mindfulness Meditation Training in Adults and Adolescents with ADHD: A Feasibility Study." *Journal of Attention Disorders* 11(6) (2008): 737-746.

295 Brewer, Judson et al. "Mindfulness-based Treatments for Co-occurring Depression and Substance Use Disorders: What Can We Learn from the Brain?" *Addiction* 105.10 (2010): 1698-1706.

296   Hartmann, Mechthild et al. "Sustained Effects of a Mindfulness-Based
      Stress-Reduction Intervention in Type 2 Diabetic Patients." *Diabetes Care,*
      May 2012; 35(5): 945–947.

297   Taylor, Jim and Gregory Scott Wilson. *Applying Sport Psychology: Four
      Perspectives.* IL: Human Kinetics, 2005, 58.

298   Huffington, Ariana. "Mindfulness, Meditation, Wellness, and Their
      Connection to Corporate America's Bottom Line." *Huffington Post,* March
      13, 2013. http://www.huffingtonpost.com/arianna-huffington/corporate-
      wellness_b_2903222.html

299   Ghorbani, Nima, P. Watson, and Bart Weathington. "Mindfulness in Iran
      and the United States: Cross-Cultural Structural Complexity and Parallel
      Relationships with Psychological Adjustment." *Current Psychology* 28.4
      (2009): 211-224.

300   Somaiya, Ravi and Alan Cowell. "Politicians and Protestors Assail
      British Police." *New York Times,* August 12, 2011. http://www.nytimes.
      com/2011/08/12/world/europe/12police.html

301   Burns, John, Ravi Somaiya, and Alan Cowell. "Cameron, in Speech,
      Pledges Swift Reaction to Rioters." *New York Times,* August 11,2011.
      http://www.nytimes.com/2011/08/12/world/europe/12britain.html

302   Gen.37:21-22.

303   Gen. 40:8.

304   Gen.41:15-16.

305   Gen. 44:30-34.

306   Gen. 45:5.

307   Gen. 50:19-21.

308   Gen. 49-50.

309   Saraswati, Swami Krishnananda. The Chhandogya Upanishad. "Chapter
      One: Vaishvanara-vidya. The Panchagi Vidya." *The Divine Life Society.*
      http://www.swami-krishnananda.org/chhand/Chhandogya_Upanishad.pdf

310   *Dao De Jing 39.*

311   Crouse, Karen. "Humbled, but Still Short of Humility." *New York Times,*
      March 2, 2012, B10.

312   "Lance Armstrong Sued for More Than $1.5M by U.K. Newspaper Over
      Libel Case." *CBS News,* December 24, 2012. http://www.cbsnews.com/
      news/lance-armstrong-sued-for-more-than-15m-by-uk-newspaper-over-
      libel-case/

313 *Dao De Jing* 30.

314 *The Sayings of Confucius.* trans. Lionel Giles. Senate, 1998, 61.

315 Mark 10:43-45.

316 Matt. 18:4.

317 Luke 14:11 and 18:14.

318 LaBouff, Jordan et al. "Humble Persons Are More Helpful Than Less Humble Persons: Evidence from Three Studies.," *Journal of Positive Psychology,* Vol. 7, Issue 1 (2012): 16-29.

319 Webley, Kayla. "Trump Airlines." *Time,* April 29, 2011. https://time.com/4343030/donald-trump-failures

320 Suddath, Claire. "The Bankruptcies." *Time,* April 29, 2011. https://time.com/4343030/donald-trump-failures

321 Gandel, Stephen. "Trump Mortgage." *Time,* April 29, 2011. https://time.com/4343030/donald-trump-failures

322 Collins, Jim. "Level Five Leadership: The Triumph of Humility and Fierce Resolve." *Harvard Business Review,* July, 2005. https://hbr.org/2005/07/level-5-leadership-the-triumph-of-humility-and-fierce-resolve

323 *Dao De Jing* 10.

324 *Dao De Jing* 66.

325 van Dierendonck, Dirk and Inge Nuijten. "The Servant Leadership Survey: Development and Validation of a Multidimensional Measure." *Journal of Business and Psychology*: Springer. 26(3)(2011): 249–267. http://www.ncbi.nlm.nih.gov/pmc/articles/PMC3152712/ In this quote, van Dierendonck and Nuijten also refer to the research of K.A. Patterson (2003) and Morris, Brotheridge, and Urbanksi (2005).

326 *Dao De Jing* 24.

327 Peters, Annette, Wade Rowat, and Megan Johnson. "Associations between Dispositional Humility and Social Relationship Quality." *Psychology.* 2.3(2011): 155-161. http://www.scirp.org/journal/PaperDownload.aspx?paperID=5521

328 CDC. "Youth Suicide." *Suicide Prevention,* August, 2012. https://www.cdc.gov/violenceprevention/suicide/index.html

329 Coulehan, Jack. "A Gentle and Humane Temper: Humility in Medicine." *Perspectives in Biology and Medicine,* 54.2 (2011): 206-16. http://www.ncbi.nlm.nih.gov/pubmed/21532134

330 Ibid.

331   Chochinov, Harvey Max,M.D., PhD., "Humility and the Practice of
      Medicine: Tasting Humble Pie." *Canadian Medical Association.Journal*
      182, no. 11 (2010): 1217-8. http://www.ncbi.nlm.nih.gov/pmc/articles/
      PMC2917943

332   Bangura, Abdul Karim. *Kipsigis*. NY: Rosen, 1994, 13.

333   *Qur'an* 7:55.

334   *Qur'an* 25:63.

335   Brooks, David. "If It Feels Right..." *New York Times*, September 12, 2011.
      http://www.nytimes.com/2011/09/13/opinion/if-it-feels-right.html?_r=0

336   *Precious Garland Ratnavali of Nagarjuna*, trans .Vidyakaraprabha and Bel-
      dzek and corrected by Kanakavarman and Batsap Nyimadrak.

337   "World hunger again on the rise, driven by conflict and climate change, new
      UN report says." World Health Organization, 15 Sept. 2017. http://www.
      who.int/mediacentre/news/releases/2017/world-hunger-report/en/

338   Kipling, Rudyard. *Kim*. NY: Barnes and Noble, 2004, intro. by Jeffrey
      Meyers, 162.

339   Taylor, Kristin Clark. "Thai soccer coach meditated with boys to keep
      them calm in the cave. We can all learn from them." *The Washington
      Post*. 11 July 2018. https://www.washingtonpost.com/news/inspired-life/
      wp/2018/07/11/thai-soccer-coach-meditated-with-boys-to-calm-them-in-
      the-cave-we-can-all-learn-from-them

340   Beech, Hannah. "Stateless and Poor, Some Boys in Thai Cave Had Already
      Beaten Long Odds." *The New York Times*. 10 July 2018. https://www.
      nytimes.com/2018/07/10/world/asia/thailand-cave-soccer-stateless.html

341   Arneson, Krystin. "Families Belong Together March: Watch Incredible
      Speeches by Diane Guerrero, Kerry Washington, America Ferrera, and
      More." 1 July 2018. *Glamour.com*

342   "24 Stories About the Touching Kindness of Strangers That'll Make You
      Tear Up." *Reader's Digest*.com https://www.rd.com/true-stories/inspiring/
      kindness-strangers/